Marketing the Professional Services Firm

Marketing the Professional Services Firm

Applying the Principles and the Science of Marketing to the Professions

Laurie Young

John Wiley & Sons, Ltd

Other Wiley Editorial Offices

John Wiley & Sons Inc., 111 River Street, Hoboken, NJ 07030, USA

Jossey-Bass, 989 Market Street, San Francisco, CA 94103-1741, USA

Wiley-VCH Verlag GmbH, Boschstr. 12, D-69469 Weinheim, Germany

John Wiley & Sons Australia Ltd, 42 McDougall Street, Milton, Queensland 4064, Australia

John Wiley & Sons (Asia) Pte Ltd, 2 Clementi Loop #02-01, Jin Xing Distripark, Singapore 129809

John Wiley & Sons Canada Ltd, 22 Worcester Road, Etobicoke, Ontario, Canada M9W 1L1

Wiley also publishes its books in a variety of electronic formats. Some content that appears
in print may not be available in electronic books.

Library of Congress Cataloging-in-Publication Data

Young, Laurie.
  Marketing the professional services firm : applying the principles and the science of marketing to
the professions / Laurie Young.
     p.   cm.
  Includes bibliographical references and index.
  ISBN 13 978-0-470-01173-7 (cloth : alk. paper)
  ISBN 10 0-470-01173-4 (cloth : alk. paper)
  1. Service industries—Marketing.   2. Professional corporations—Marketing.   I. Title.
  HD9981.5.Y68   2005
  658.8—dc22

                                                                          2005010793

British Library Cataloguing in Publication Data

A catalogue record for this book is available from the British Library

ISBN 13 978-0-470-01173-7 (HB)
ISBN 10 0-470-01173-4 (HB)

Typeset in 11/15 pt Goudy by SNP Best-set Typesetter Ltd., Hong Kong
Printed and bound in Great Britain by TJ International Ltd, Padstow, Cornwall, UK
This book is printed on acid-free paper responsibly manufactured from sustainable forestry
in which at least two trees are planted for each one used for paper production.

To Paul, Chris and Mark, who make me more proud every day

Contents

Foreword

This is the third marketing book that I've written and has been, by far, the hardest. The previous two were on technical subjects (strategic management of customer care and the design of new services), but this aims to bridge a large gap. The gap is between the immediate needs of a huge and diverse industry, the professional services sector of modern economies, and the evolving competence of the marketing profession in service businesses.

I now have quite extensive experience of professional services. I have been a marketing director in an IT services business trying to launch professional services, a global marketing partner in a leading firm and have advised various professional service firms (from single partner practices to some of the world's largest businesses). I have also founded, built and sold one of these businesses. Yet I also have long experience of service marketing and remain fascinated by the development and application of the subject. It is frustrating, therefore, to see so many consummate and successful professionals missing out on the value of modern service marketing practice because of ignorance, prejudice or poor experience.

Until recently the phrase 'professional services marketing' was, largely, an oxymoron. For many these words were as unwelcome together as 'good' and 'morning' after a hard night out. Some professionals regard marketing as a sales-driven or advertising-focused activity which is completely at odds with excellent client service and good technical execution. When they do discuss business needs with marketing specialists, many find the experience and language to be more suited to consumer products than high end expertise.

As a result, many of the people who carry a marketing title in professional services firms are not career marketers. From the administrator who arranges client events to the outgoing partner doing their development stint in marketing management, there are a good number of people who are trying to interpret marketing jargon and practice for the benefit of their firm.

Nevertheless, the industry does engage in a wide range of marketing activities and those activities are increasing due to unprecedented changes to law, ownership, competition and regulation. Leaders of professional services firms take decisions about the direction of their firm based on market insight and changing competitive landscapes. These strategic marketing issues range from brand development, sector penetration, and client service to new market entry and client relationship management. Client service and support staff also engage in marketing projects and decisions. They might run client hospitality events, design a new service or create a thought leadership piece. In a very real sense, everyone in a professional services firm is likely to get involved in marketing to some extent.

Yet, as with other specialisms, marketing involves a wide range of concepts, techniques and processes which, properly used, make it cost-effective and successful. Anyone can use common sense and business experience to build their own house, to conduct their own legal defence or to manage their finances. However, they are likely to do it better if they use well-worn approaches and rely on the advice of a professional.

So it is with marketing. Expertise added to common sense and business knowledge can make the firm more successful. Many professional services firms now face changes to their market which will affect the returns and success of everyone within their business. They will need to think about how they grow their business and how they manage the process of client development. At the same time, the marketing community now has a range of concepts, techniques and processes which are reliable and relevant to service businesses. I hope that this book will help to make them accessible to the industry.

Laurie Young

Acknowledgements

Writing this book has been like running a long race. It took planning, effort and endurance, especially for the very long last lap. I could not have finished it without the help of several people.

My thanks go particularly to my head 'coach' Laura Mazur of Writers 4 Management. She has been encouraging and goading in equal measure at appropriate times. She teased out and refined the case studies and helped me with the very detailed task of pinning down references to published work. The Wiley team, particularly Francesca Warren and Jo Golesworthy, have also provided invaluable support and help.

A number of people provided case studies. Many thanks to the following: Kevin Bishop of IBM Business Consulting Services, Rae Sedel of Russell Reynolds, Mike Stevenson of Michael Page, Gillian Kahn of Berwin Leighton Paisner, Simon Hardaker of QinetiQ, Mark Allatt of Deloitte, Alan Brooks of Clarkson Hyde, Jan Lindemann of Interbrand, David Munn of ITSMA, David Wallace of Shepherd + Wedderburn, David Haigh of Brand Finance, Paul Fifield of the Fifield Practice, Walter McKone, Joel Kurtzman and Keith Arundale of PricewaterhouseCoopers.

Finally, I want to pay tribute to the specialists and academics whose work I point to in the text. I know very few, having met some fleetingly at conferences over the years, but I admire their work. I want to particularly acknowledge the thorough and careful work of Phillip Kotler, Christian Gronroos, Leonard Berry and Valarie Zeithaml. On many occasions I have used their concepts and tools in day-to-day marketing work and found them to work for the benefit of the shareholders who employed me. That is the highest compliment I can pay them and I hope this text contributes a little to the further use of their body of work.

About the Author

Laurie Young is a specialist in the marketing of services and customer care. His career includes senior positions with PricewaterhouseCoopers, BT and Unisys. In the 1990s he founded, built and sold his own professional service firm, focussing on service marketing. Over the years he has advised a number of firms, from small, single partner, practices to large, multinational organisations on the contribution of services marketing to shareholder value.

Also by Laurie Young: *Competitive Customer Care* with Merlin Stone and *Making Profits From New Service Development*.

Introduction: setting the scene

Overview

The professional services industry is one of the largest and most diverse sectors of modern economies. The common attribute that all firms within it share, whether they are business-to-business or consumer-oriented businesses, is that professional skills form the basis of what they offer to clients and the qualifications needed are generally a barrier to entry for aspiring newcomers. How each firm approaches its market and the processes it develops, however, differ according to its skill set, its size, the ownership structure and the type of projects it takes on. This introduction to the industry details each of these and their relevance to the firm. It also examines the role that professional services marketing should increasingly play in what is, in many instances, a maturing market. This is a challenge for firms where the concept of marketing is still underdeveloped, and for marketers who have been trained in more traditional product marketing.

Profile of the professional services industry

The professional services industry is a vast and varied sector of modern economies which is estimated to be worth up to $700 billion worldwide

(Scott, 1998). Subsectors within it are also large. For instance, US legal services have been estimated to reach $156 billion by 2005, whereas the UK legal services sector is said to be worth £6 billion and growing at 20% per annum.

The industry encompasses a wide range of businesses, from accountancy partnerships, executive search firms, education, training and coaching providers, legal and architectural specialists, through to consultancies in various specialisms, marketing agencies and the growing services arms of publicly listed companies. It includes an array of medical practitioners such as doctors, dentists, optometrists/opticians, pharmacists, psychotherapists, osteopaths and physiotherapists. There are also a variety of retail professionals such as hairdressers, veterinarians and realtors/estate agents, which range from single shops to large chains.

The industry comprises any business for which professional skill is the basis of their offer to clients and qualifications provide a barrier to entry against new suppliers. It can be categorised by skill set, size, ownership and type of project. Each affects the approach that leaders of the business take to their market and the processes they adopt to grow their revenues.

Skill set

The most obvious defining characteristic of a professional services firm is the skill set it offers to its clients. The training and experience involved in becoming a professional, in any of the wide range of services, is the basis of the offer to clients. The expertise is what clients seek and pay for.

However, there are different returns within each area of expertise and different market forces. For example, professionals can charge and earn more if they acquire deeper knowledge or join leading firms in their own sector. An accountant will earn different returns as an individual practitioner than as a partner in a major firm. They would also earn differently as a generalist or a forensic expert or as a due diligence specialist in a merger and acquisitions deal. A strategy consultant will earn differently as a single practitioner, as part of a merchant bank or as a consultant in a niche firm.

The way they market themselves during their career also affects their route and their earnings, while the marketing of the businesses they are part of, which can be different in different corners of their markets, affects their returns as well. In one they might benefit from the brand, in another they might focus on personal reputation, and in yet another they might offer packaged services. Exploiting the principles of marketing in the development of a professional's career and the marketing of the firms they are part of, whether intuitive or formal, therefore affects their success.

There are also differential earnings between the sectors of the industry. The returns of a merchant banker or corporate lawyer are radically different from those of a human resources (HR) consultant or hairdresser. In addition, each sector of the industry has characteristics, networks and approaches which are established within it, so that marketing approach, strategy and technique have to vary according to the skills offered by the firm. A change of skill must, therefore, change the way the firm acts in its market. For instance, when different professionals merge their skills to form a multidisciplinary practice, the new entity can falter while it finds a new market momentum across the different sectors it now serves. Similarly, when firms build their skills into packaged services or software, their market approach must change radically.

Size

The size of a professional services firm gives it characteristics which affect its business growth. There are several major inflection points in this growth which should be taken into account in marketing strategy and programmes. They are:

- **Single practitioners:** smaller firms based around a single fee earner.
- **Boutiques:** based around two or more fee earners, which often become rooted in a particular geographic location or a certain set of skills. Properly focused, these firms can often return good earnings to their owners by becoming niche suppliers.
- **International networks:** these are professional services firms which operate internationally with local offices in many countries. They can be a unitary firm with one profit pool, an association of either smaller firms or independent partners, or an integrated federation of locally formed firms.
- **Publicly listed firms** or professional services businesses within such firms.

The sole practitioner

The first inflection point is when a sole practitioner sets up a business based around a particular skill. This might be an accountant setting up their own practice, a hairdresser or pharmacist establishing a shop or a redundant middle manager becoming a consultant in a particular speciality. Many internationally famous firms started this way.

For the business-to-business practitioner, such as an accountant, the limit to growth at this point is the number of days or hours that can be sold. For a retail service aimed at consumers, like an optometrist/optician, the growth limit will be based upon the number of appointments that can be handled in a day, plus the extra margin from the sale of physical products like glasses and contact lenses. The common concerns of these fledgling businesses are: gaining clients, building a pipeline of business and cash flow. These must be managed while maintaining the quality of work that motivated the fee earner to get into the field of practice in the first place.

Marketing and business development is therefore as important to these small firms as it is to any larger business containing a sophisticated marketing department. The fee earner, although alone and cash constrained, needs to have a marketing strategy. They need to enhance reputation, gain recognition and manage client service. Those who have thrived have found ways to handle this demanding mix of needs.

As revenues grow, the proprietor begins to consider one of the major issues of all professional services businesses: the nature and amount of 'support'. Support is an ill-defined term for functions of the business which are non-fee earning. Larger firms may have a director or partner responsible for 'support' or 'operations'. However, they share with these fledgling businesses the prime consideration of engaging support: whether the cost enables the fee earner to earn more for the firm, increasing both revenue and margin. Poorly done, the firm ends up increasing the former but not the latter.

Support can be varied. It can be directly employed or subcontracted. For instance, sole practitioners might employ a secretary as demand increases. This frees them from basic administrative tasks in order to carry out more client work. Similarly, a consumer-based retail professional might employ a receptionist. In the early days of growth, mimicking the desire of larger firms to keep down non-fee earning overheads, this task is often done by friends, part-timers or family members.

Many of these sole practitioners will stay at this level of fees quite happily, with the cap on the amount that can be earned compensated by relatively good margins. If they want to grow, however, the next inflection point comes when the sole practitioner begins to hire junior professionals to execute work. Business-to-business practitioners might hire recently qualified professionals to work on projects, while retail professionals, on the other hand, will usually look for growth by extending the brand franchise. A hairdresser or pharmacist, for instance, might acquire or join forces with a counterpart in a different location to broaden the reach of the business or they may try to create a unique franchise by mentoring junior professionals to do work 'their way'.

Again, the success of these growth strategies depends on the ability of these newly hired people to 'leverage' the fee earner by releasing their time to bring in more work. However, without the right marketing and business growth strategy, sole practitioners can become trapped by their own success. Growth in demand can cause them to take on more support to administer the business and more professional staff to execute it.

Yet, if they do not have some form of competitive differentiation that allows higher fees or the generation of a healthy pipeline, margins will not increase and may, particularly in times of recession, decrease. They then become trapped by a need to generate income to feed the machine they have created. As years go by, the stress caused by generating work that increases revenue but not margin causes some to get out of the business altogether. Others will try to recruit employees who will also bring in revenues. Yet others will move on to the next inflection point: partnership with other fee earners.

Brand Finance moves to the next stage

Brand Finance is a niche consultancy with offices in a number of countries around the world, including the UK, US, Canada, Brazil, Spain, Holland, Singapore, Malaysia, Hong Kong and Australia. The chairman is the respected American marketing academic/expert, Don Schultz.

The firm, an unquoted plc, offers services in brand valuation, brand due diligence, value-based marketing and brand licensing. Founded in

London in 1996 by David Haigh, it illustrates how to grow professional services beyond the single practitioner inflection point.

Taking a clear stance

When he set the firm up, Haigh already had a high profile in the area of brand valuation, stemming both from his previous jobs, in accountancy and marketing, and from his numerous publications and conference presentations. Rather than use his own name for the firm, he chose 'Brand Finance' so that it wouldn't be anchored to just one person as it grew. He also wanted the firm to have a clear positioning statement ('bridging the gap between marketing and finance' is the firm's trademarked strapline) from the start.

One of the key elements of the firm's marketing was his decision to brand proprietary processes and product descriptions. These include: a brand risk analysis methodology, a demand drivers analysis (to identify the percentage of intangible earnings attributable to brands), and a structured process for evaluating brand strength.

By 2000 the firm had grown to 30 people, although at that stage Haigh himself was still the only principal 'rainmaker'. In addition, he had begun to expand overseas by establishing offices in other countries. By the middle of 2001, however, with the demise of the dot.com boom, business had begun to slow. With declining revenue and a fixed cost base, a new strategy was needed.

First, the staff in the head office were reduced by about half, to lower fixed costs. At the same time, a new model of ownership was introduced to the subsidiaries in other countries. A 49% stake was offered to local management who were closer to the demands of the particular markets. This had the effect of creating entrepreneurial energy in the young network.

Spreading its wings

By 2004 the business employed an equal number of direct employees and freelancers, with 20 full-time staff and about the same on a consultancy basis. It was showing healthy annual growth from two main lines of work. The first was technical valuation for tax, legal and accountancy specialists. The other was the work done for marketing specialists as a basis for commercial and marketing decisions, including brand architecture, brand modelling, brand portfolio reviews and return on investment.

The firm's strategy is now to achieve sustainable growth from two main sources: finding the right people to keep the business pipeline full and nurturing the international network. The firm has begun to broaden further its 'rainmaker' group substantially with key appointments in the US, UK, India, Singapore and Australia.

Partnership with other fee earners

The next inflection point is when the business grows to the point where the single practitioner will no longer be able to cope with being the only fee earner. Colleagues who can actively generate new business are needed. By finding others who can generate revenue, the firm can earn greater returns and margin. Options include: joining forces with other practitioners to form a partnership; merging with, or selling out to, another firm; or recruiting potential fee earners. It is notoriously difficult to negotiate this inflection point successfully and it is the graveyard of many ambitious and talented professional services firms, for several reasons.

First, recruitment of fee earners is not as straightforward a route as it sounds. Finding the right people can be very difficult, because people capable of generating large fees (see Chapter 8 on 'rainmakers') tend to be very driven individuals, with large social networks. They are unlikely to be found at affordable rates in existing firms. They are also not likely to be attracted by a reward package which consists of a simple salary plus bonus. If professionals are talented enough to be both technically excellent and able to build a pipeline of business, they will be ambitious for more than a salaried role in a small firm.

The other route to growth, forming a partnership, also has its drawbacks. Partnerships can be quite risky because the fee earners need to work very closely together and are interdependent. However, the working relationship can deteriorate due, for example, to different approaches to work or different fee earning capabilities. In addition, the partners' assets are vulnerable in adverse circumstances, adding strains to the professional relationship because partnerships can be so hard to dissolve.

Nevertheless, banding together with other fee earners, by whatever route is chosen, is the way sole practitioners can break through this inflection point in business growth. Potential partners may operate in a similar field and help maintain the focus of the growing firm. Alternatively, they might be sought because they have supplementary business skills (for example, a surveyor and an architect might work together) creating a multidisciplinary practice to reduce risks by supplementing revenue streams. Once there are four to five rainmakers, these small boutiques can grow their fees substantially.

Clarkson Hyde develops its brand to expand into new services

Clarkson Hyde began life as a small, UK-based accountancy practice but has embraced more skills in a bid to grow the business into a multi-disciplinary professional services firm. It is a good example of a geographically based boutique broadening its skill base to even out cash flow while building the brand to differentiate itself in its market.

The firm is rooted in a particular geographic area of the UK, the southeast, which includes London. It has a number of clients in other parts of the country, while it services international work through a network of associate firms. The majority of clients are manufacturing and service organisations which are focused on growth and/or adding value to their business and which fall mainly into the £1 million ($1.9 million) to £20 million ($37 million) bracket, although it also works with a number of significantly larger companies.

Becoming multidisciplinary

It was founded as an accountancy practice in 1923 by two partners, John Clarkson and Frank Hyde. It was bought by current senior partner Malcolm Coomber in 1979 and in the last few years has been actively pursuing growth by expanding beyond its core accountancy offer. As of 2004, the Hyde group consisted of eight partners, four directors and 30 staff. It comprised a number of different services based on a mix of partnership and limited companies in its business.

For instance, Hyde Law was set up in October 2003 by a senior legal practitioner. He had worked with large law firms but was keen to set up his own commercial law practice in association with an organisation which could offer both resources and a client base. Other businesses have been established as limited companies: Hyde Consulting, which has built up a strong track record over the past few years in corporate finance; Hyde Marketing, which offers marketing and business development consultancy; and Paradigm Hyde Films, specialists in film finance. CH International, an international network of like-minded associate firms in 23 countries, has also been developed.

Changing to a market approach

By January 2004 the company was aware that it needed a new approach to marketing if it was to get the best income for its different businesses. The head of Hyde Marketing, Alan Brooks, with a background in professional services marketing, also took the role of the firm's marketing director. His brief was to use the principles of strategic marketing and business development to help achieve the firm's growth objectives across the various disciplines.

This process has included a number of key elements:

- Increase the flow of potential business for the new services.
- Develop and implement a clear differentiating strategy for the Hyde brand.
- Establish business development processes to maximise sales opportunities from both existing clients and 'introducers' (such as banks and brokers), who are a potential source of new business.
- Maximise the partners' time by filtering leads.
- Establish a series of regular and ad hoc marketing activities to raise the firm's profile and generate 'warm' leads.
- Launch and integrate the marketing of new services as they are added to the mix.

One of the first steps was to gain an understanding of the brand's positioning and how to exploit its strengths. In a firm of that size this is obviously intimately related to the senior practitioners themselves. He found a fair degree of unanimity around the firm about its perceived values, which he incorporated into a formal brand framework which underpins all the marketing communications and relationships with clients, prospects and introducers.

Living the values

Those values include: an emphasis on the quality of work; being easily accessible (the firm avoids using voicemail, for example); and being unpretentious. It particularly values a small number of key introducer relationships (rather than being 'all things to all people'). A commercial approach to client issues is reinforced by recruiting senior staff with experience in commerce as well as the professions.

The marketing activities which flow from this include:

- A reputation-building programme.
- Networking based upon a clear account/relationship management programme.
- A constant flow of contact with clients, prospects and introducers to maintain visibility – using regular events, direct mail, email shots and newsletters.
- A monthly email to all staff to update them on the firm's progress.
- Monthly marketing and sales reports to partners and managers which show the impact the marketing activity has had on business development.

This more structured approach has saved the time of the professionals across the network and enables marketing activities which would not otherwise happen.

International networks

The next inflection point is when the boutique becomes part of a bigger network. Some firms achieve this by selling out to one of the large global networks. This might be one of the big marketing services group, a publicly quoted firm, one of the large accounting practices or a consulting firm. The smaller firm might be integrated into the parent firm, or it may be kept intact because it is perceived to have a certain value either through brand reputation, client access or specialist skill. The acquiring firm may have sought the boutique because of any of these attributes.

The acquiring firm will normally be able to increase both revenue and margin through the acquisition. Revenue might be enhanced by giving the boutique access to its major clients and marketing programmes, while margins might be improved because the newly acquired firm will benefit from the stripping out of administration and support costs through gaining access to firm-wide central services. For the partners of the boutique, there is normally a capital sum available over a three- to five-year earn-out period, and the staff gain enhanced career opportunities in a wider group.

Growth strategies for the larger firms themselves vary according to their size and structure. An integrated international firm that has one profit pool is likely to emphasise natural growth through development of fee earners or sector penetration. A decentralised network, or federation of practices, on the other hand, is more likely to grow by acquisition, gaining access into new geographic territories, skill areas or industrial sectors.

Growing retail professional services

Retail professional services have a unique dynamic to their business which means they need to be grown in a particular way. They tend to provide low margin, high volume services which are supplemented by relevant product sales. They are characterised by the 'footfall per square metre' of the retail industry, i.e. the number of clients coming through the store. Growth considerations must therefore take into account consumer needs and choice, store location and design, increase in footfall, sales promotion and product merchandising.

Owners can take a 'premium' approach, earning high margins (e.g. hairdressers such as Nicky Clarke or John Frieda), or a least-cost approach, creating a chain of stores which employs young professionals while their earnings are low to keep costs down. There have been a number of notable successes in this field, where integrated chains have been created to take advantage of the inefficiencies of a market dominated by single practitioners, as the case studies on Walgreens, Specsavers and Coldwell Banker in Chapter 1 show.

Marketing for these firms is about the site of shops and effective merchandising as much as the client service and reputation management typical of the rest of the professional services industry.

Ownership

The ownership structure is also a defining characteristic of professional services firms because it affects the firm's culture and decision-making process. Sole partnerships are, by their very nature, dominated by a single owner, usually the principal who started it. That person will probably have built up a personal reputation and be strongly motivated by the business concept. So the culture of the firm will revolve around the character, moods and the style of that individual.

As the number of partners increases, a management structure will evolve. For instance, one partner may be elected as 'managing partner' and, if growth continues, may have to give up client work in order to dedicate their time to management issues. Partners generally do not like being managed and, as the partners being managed are also the owners of the firm who vote the managing partner into position, the leadership must work by consensus. Decisions and initiatives which are not supported by a majority will eventually lead to management change. From time to time, leaders do need to take a clear and urgent decision which partners will live with. If, however, a sequence of dictatorial decisions appears to be leading the firm in a direction which threatens partner take, leadership will be changed by the partnership.

Partnerships can be wonderfully collegiate, liberating and flexible for the partners. Once consensus is reached, the whole firm can act with a speed that large corporate firms find hard to emulate. However, reaching a consensus in the first place can be difficult and so decision-making can be slow in routine areas of business that do not demand immediate or senior attention. In fact, there is often very little clear decision-making. Initiatives in a partnership are often created by a wide consultation or 'buy-in' process which creates a momentum for an idea. Providing no one strongly disagrees with the initiative, it will become, more or less, common practice within the firm.

Partnerships also tend to be hesitant about making investment decisions because partners tend to look for annual profit share. Many are suspicious of longer-term investment projects, not distinguishing between current and capital budgets. In the long run, then, a partnership that competes against a corporate firm which is investing in systems and processes is likely to find itself at a competitive disadvantage.

In addition, there is usually a very clear demarcation between the partners, client service professionals and the support staff, unlike a publicly quoted company where everyone is an employee. This can cause a two-tier status which, unless properly managed, can be resented by staff, affecting motivation and client service. (The equivalent division in corporate firms is between those who have stock options and those who do not. However, as stock options can be more ubiquitous than partnerships, this causes less division within client service teams.)

As a result of this culture, marketing can also be relatively fluid in a partnership. First, client service staff may themselves undertake a wide range of marketing activities, from arranging seminars to producing published reports. Second, any specialist marketing resources will be constrained by the firm's caution at investing in non-fee earning 'support'. The specialist function is rarely given exclusive responsibility for the approach to the market, and often there is no formal link between marketing specialists across the network.

This type of ownership is in sharp contrast to firms that are accountable to shareholders. There is a common perception that the professional services industry is characterised by a partnership-dominated culture. While this is the case among many accounting and law firms, an increasing number of the world's biggest professional services firms are owned by publicly traded companies (such as IBM Global Services, or WPP). Yet others are publicly traded firms in their own right, such as search consultants Heidrich & Struggles, recruitment firm Michael Page (see case study in Chapter 7), and merchant bank Goldman Sachs. These firms have a different leadership style which affects their culture and approach to market.

In a publicly quoted business shareholders delegate day-to-day management to a senior executive team. They, in turn, delegate their authority, through approved methods of governance, to various specialists in the business such as operations, IT, marketing and human resources, who have the authority and budget to make decisions pertinent to their areas of responsibility.

IBM Business Consulting Services: building a new professional services company

IBM Business Consulting Services is the world's largest consulting services organisation and part of IBM Global Services, the world's largest business and technology services provider. It was formed in mid-2002 by combining IBM's existing Business Innovation Services division with the $3.9 billion acquisition of PwC Consulting, the biggest in IBM's history. By the end of 2004 there were 60 000 consultants and staff in more than 160 countries in the $13 billion-a-year business. (see Chapter 11 for an analysis of how the firm ensures quality of service).

A new competitive positioning

This has placed IBM in a new competitive space by blending the depth of business insight and client knowledge of the former PwC Consulting professionals with existing services and technology expertise of IBM's Business Innovation consultants. The company-wide positioning of 'new answers, real business outcomes' reflects IBM's determination to be recognised for its ability to deliver measurable business results for clients as well as for the technology solutions underpinning them.

The driving force behind creating Business Consulting Services was IBM's desire to maintain its lead in the rapidly changing IT space and combine it with a parallel lead in the professional services market, according to Kevin Bishop, Business Consulting Services strategy and marketing leader for Europe, the Middle East and Africa. While the industry has profited from the flow of technological innovation for the last 10–15 years, the environment is increasingly shifting to one where clients are demanding that their suppliers have a comprehensive understanding of their business in order to deliver strategic business benefits. The creation of IBM Business Consulting Services was thus seen as an integral part of IBM's total value proposition in its overall move from a technology-oriented company to a full service company.

A key part of this is what the company calls Business Performance Transformation Services (BPTS). This moves well beyond handling a company's data warehouse and sees IBM exploiting its own internal strengths to improve, redesign and sometimes run significant parts of a client's operations, allowing them to focus on their core activities. For example, IBM now manages most of the human resources for Procter & Gamble, Sprint's call centres and the after-sales support for Philips Consumer Electronics. By using the same asset base across different companies, unit costs are driven down for multiple clients. The formation of IBM Business Consulting Services is, therefore, at the heart of IBM's ability to deliver these complex engagements.

Combining different cultures

Any combination of cultures is difficult and in moving private professionals into a publicly quoted company this is particularly felt around the demands and obligations of regular fiscal reporting, notes Bishop.

Closely allied to that is the need for predictability of outcome. In sharp contrast to a partnership, companies need to manage expectations carefully, since stock market behaviours often seem to reward meeting or exceeding expectations rather than good performance as such.

This learning experience has not been purely one way. IBM was also keen to learn from the consultants steeped in the professional services environment. For instance, in a product business much of the profit in a project is determined on making the sale since quality and price are largely determined in the software development lab or factory. However, in this new environment, a 'sale' is just the start of an engagement. It is the *delivery* of the outcome that matters, especially if contractual terms are framed around the delivery of specified business benefits.

This means forming much closer relationships with clients than even IBM, an acknowledged leader in key account management for many years, has been used to. So the company is looking to the Business Consulting Services consultants to act as agents of change within IBM. They should identify changes the company needs to make and help introduce the expertise that a professional services culture can bring (in terms of pinpointing benefit opportunities in clients, coaching, support and delivery excellence).

IBM has found the majority of former PwC Consulting partners have embraced the move as it has given them expanded opportunities to engage with clients and, more importantly, to feel the satisfaction of seeing their ideas turned into actual business outcomes across a wider range of a clients' needs than they may have had previously. Other groups such as human resources and marketing have also welcomed becoming part of IBM because of the breadth of career opportunities, strength of organisational structure and enhanced prestige.

The role of marketing

The marketing department operates through a matrix structure with the most important axis being an industry specialism. The other axis is about understanding the challenges being faced by functions such as human resources, finance or logistics. As Bishop has noted, research into the attributes most valued by clients of a professional services firm include: 'knows my industry' and 'has real business process expertise'.

One particular focus of the marketing process is therefore gaining a detailed appreciation of the 'hot' issues in the market and guiding where the company should be targeting its efforts – a key client requirement in the professional services environment. Portfolio management is a widely used technique within the marketing group for this. Grids of market attractiveness are analysed against market capability and set within the framework of a rich mathematical database – this then allows a clear 'choice of the attractive places to play'.

Alongside some of the more traditional activities (such as running events and promotions), marketing also supports new service design and development by helping to identify those engagements that could become the basis of new business stream by being 'mass customised' for new clients, such as the business transformation deals with Philips or Sprint. This complements the new service design and development work done out in the field by consultants with their clients.

Maintaining professional excellence

Another key differentiator is that of 'high calibre people'. There are two main functions that play a role in continuing professional development. While they are not a formalised part of the marketing department, marketing plays a key role in getting everything aligned around the right subject matter, the right message, and the right timing.

> The first is learning and knowledge, which is considered so central to the company that there are professional knowledge managers who oversee the collection and transfer of knowledge by codifying it and entering it into internal reference databases. Marketing then takes subsets of this knowledge and builds wider communications plans around them. The other is internal communications, which creates both 'push' communications such as newsletters, and 'pull' communications, particularly with intranets, so that people can get the information they need when they need it, whether they are in the firm or out at client sites.

At the most basic level, the need of publicly traded firms to report results to the financial markets means that leaders must be more disciplined about forecasting and reporting revenues than those operating in a private partnership. These public companies tend to use more systematic marketing, sales and account management processes. They are also able to employ first class professionals to lead projects without partner-level profit sharing. Their reward is based partly on share options, whose value increases according to the views of the capital markets on performance criteria such as future earnings. Quoted firms, therefore, frequently have a cost advantage, which affects their pricing and allows them to penetrate markets, previously dominated by partnerships, with a different price and quality offer.

This difference in ownership structure therefore leads to a difference in the approach to marketing and sales. Marketing in corporate firms tends to be functional. Specialists are usually given a clear role in a hierarchically structured department with a clear mandate, budget, tasks and processes. No one else in the company is expected to initiate marketing programmes.

Sales and account management can also be different. For example, corporate firms seem to find it easier to deploy consistent and ubiquitous standards of service internationally than partnerships because of their more centralised structure. Partnerships, on the other hand, have to mobilise a complex network of relationships to achieve the same end.

Type of project

Professional services firms can also be categorised according to the type of project work they engage in. David Maister, in his definitive work on the subject (Maister, 1993), describes three main kinds of client work firms undertake:

- 'Brains'. This is where the firm sells its services on the basis of the highly professional and technical skills of its staff, dealing with unique and particularly complex situations. The key elements involved are creativity, innovation, and the development of new approaches, concepts and techniques. These types of firms will be top-heavy with highly skilled and highly paid professionals.
- 'Grey hair' projects, on the other hand, while needing a certain amount of customisation and intellectual flair, are addressing areas in which the firm has already had experience and can sell its knowledge, experience and judgement. More junior staff can be employed to do some of the tasks.
- Finally, 'Procedure' projects involve well-recognised and familiar types of problems. However, because the client believes an outside firm will be more efficient, or lacks the staff capabilities to do the work itself, it will bring in a professional firm with demonstrable experience. There will be a far higher proportion of junior staff for this type of project than for the previous two.

The dominance of the type of work affects the marketing approach of the firm. A 'Brains' dominated firm will tend to communicate the individual skills of its gurus and focus upon 'thought leadership'. A procedural firm, on the other hand, will put its focus on efficient proposal management, profit through contracting, scalable service propositions and generic campaigns. It is more likely to stress a range of different services that are available.

Another way of categorising the work is by 'annuity' or 'project'. Annuity contracts, such as a financial audit or regular benchmarking projects, give reliable cash flow and, often, a steady client relationship. Annuity work, however, tends to have lower margins than high quality project work. The dominance of this type of work affects the marketing approach of the firm. Annuity providers will try to raise their margins and use the contract to win other work, whereas a firm dominated by project work will experience erratic cash flow and will tend to focus on building a healthy pipeline of business. One viable strategy for a firm of this sort might be to create new offers which are annuity based. For example, a research company may try to create a membership-based omnibus programme to which clients regularly subscribe.

ITSMA: creating an annuity model

The Boston-based Information Technology Services Marketing Association (ITSMA) offers advice on service marketing to firms in the IT, telecom and professional services sector. It has operations in the US, Europe, Japan and India. Current members in the US include leading businesses such as IBM, Microsoft, Cisco, Hewlett-Packard, Nokia, SAP, Accenture and BearingPoint.

The business model is an annuity-based one, offering its corporate members a range of benefits in return for annual membership fees. These include:

- Continuous insight into marketing and sales trends, benchmarks, best practices and new ideas through research reports, briefings, information services and a research library.
- Advice and guidance on key marketing and sales challenges.
- Special member pricing for events and multi-client research studies.
- Customised research, consulting, training and events.
- Being part of a community which can share ideas and further state-of-the-art knowledge and understanding.

ITSMA was founded in 1994 by Richard Munn, whose career comprised extensive experience in market research, latterly as president of the IT specialists Dataquest. In 1992, he began to consider doing something to address what he felt was the underserved but growing group of professional service marketers in the IT industry.

He could see the potential for building a workable business model based on a community of like-minded professionals with their similar needs and concerns. It would be one that would develop and advance the profession by sharing best practice, publishing thought leadership research and providing advice. A key component of ITSMA's success was creating a company different from and complementary to the traditional IT market research and analyst firms.

Having worked in leading research companies, Munn was aware of the risk to stability and cash flow arising from a project-based business. He therefore created ITSMA as an annuity business, inspired by other member-based organisations. Munn refined the concept further by offering benefits that would breed affinity and loyalty among the membership and thus be sustainable over time. He set up a board of advisors from senior representatives of leading member firms. By the end of the first year, ITSMA had 40 corporate members, and by the time it celebrated its 10th birthday in 2004, it had over 120.

A changing market

The professional services industry has been in existence for several centuries. Lawyers, designers, accountants and architects have been operating for many hundreds of years. However, the volume and diversity of this market has grown markedly over the past half century. This growth has also seen the advent of new types of services, or the reinvention of older ones. For example, executive search and direct marketing agencies are, primarily, an invention of the latter half of the twentieth century. On the other hand, executive training is, in some cases, now being replaced by a new service called 'executive coaching'.

Although there are always new concepts and growth areas in professional services, much of the industry is showing signs of maturing. This has been for a number of reasons, probably the most profound of which is the education of modern buyers. In the past, clients tended to look to the learned professions for help and assistance in an unquestioning way. The huge barriers created by years of training made the public dependent and unquestioning.

That attitude has now changed. Not only are people much more willing to question and challenge the views of professionals, but business buyers are more informed, often subjecting firms to competitive pitches. They will ask for explanations, sometimes ask for a second opinion and even demand service in the form of excellent 'bedside manner' in addition to technical advice.

On top of that, there has been an unprecedented onslaught on the stature of the professions through changes in regulation. A prime example of this is the well-publicised regulatory rigours imposed on the accountancy profession after the Enron debacle.

Like other industries before it, the professional services sector is faced with new market dynamics which mean that it cannot take natural demand for granted and this has implications for the way the businesses are run. The huge growth in professional services over the last 50 years means that many firms are currently geared towards structuring resources in response to largely unstimulated demand. When demand falls off, their response tends to be to cut resources rather than stimulate the market. This strategy, however, is not viable in a mature market. As the sector is indeed maturing in developed countries, firms need to become more sophisticated in the way they go to market, learning to become more market oriented rather than supplier driven (Kotler *et al.*, 2000).

The fundamental drivers of revenue growth

There is a natural momentum to the revenue growth of a professional services firm and at its centre is the reputation that flows from doing excellent work. Clients approaching a professional services firm for the first time are unsure. They have few means of assessing the quality of the work they will receive because it is not tangible or manufactured in advance. They can only judge by certain clues such as referrals from people they trust, the nature of the employees they meet or the impression created by the firm's offices, website or brochures.

In addition, clients must surrender themselves to the supplier's process, increasing their discomfort. Research shows that the surrender of personal control to the supplier in this way invokes emotions of discomfort and distress (Bateson and Hoffman, 1999). As a result, once a project is successfully completed, the client feels a sense of relief and will talk about the service to others. Positive (and negative) stories then begin to proliferate about the firm, creating a reputation. If that reputation is positive it will generate repeat business from the same client or referrals to different clients.

The two main drivers of future revenue growth are therefore the quality of work and the quality of client service. This creates a strong reputation, which eventually turns into a brand, and this, in turn, draws in more work, as illustrated in Figure I.1. This 'demand-pull' has two very powerful benefits for professional services firms. First, it keeps the cost of sales low because the firm does not have to go out and get work. Second, it enables firms to keep prices high because, if clients come to them, practitioners can focus on

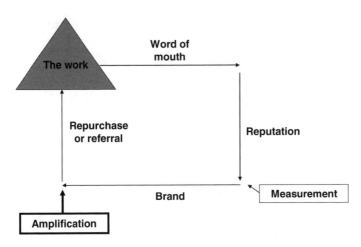

Figure I.1 *The role of reputation in generating work.*

diagnosing the need. Pricing becomes a consequence, not a focus, of discussion. Reputation enhancement is thus the essence of how professional services grow and flourish, creating demand-pull, while keeping cost of sales low and prices high.

It follows, then, that marketing activity should be aimed at enhancing the firm's reputation. This can be achieved by individuals in the firm making themselves more visible by finding ways to illustrate their expertise. For example, they might write articles, be interviewed by relevant media representatives and speak at high profile conferences.

The issue for the industry is whether structured marketing techniques, as introduced by other industries, can enhance the natural momentum of the firm in order to increase revenue and margin still further. The growing experience of firms, marketing specialists and academics who study this area is that it is possible for various marketing activities to be built into the normal business of the firm, as illustrated in Table I.1. Properly done, this will increase revenues and control or reduce cost of sale.

To be successful, however, the leadership needs to find ways to engage with the marketing profession, making its techniques, processes and approach relevant to the firm's needs. For the corporate firms, particularly those with a product heritage, this may involve investigating and institutionalising the techniques of service (rather than product) marketing. For partnerships, it may mean adopting a more systematic approach to marketing and introducing new skills.

Table I.1 *Linking marketing to the firm's growth.*

What grows a professional service business?	Why?	How 'marketing' can contribute
• Good work through good people	• Clients talk • Reputation grows • Reputation creates demand	• Amplify 'word of mouth' • Turn reputation into a brand • Create 'demand-pull' • Objective quality measurement
• Networking	• Relationships help sales	• Structured relationship management • Create events
• Speeches on public platforms	• Visibility helps sales and reputation	• PR – media appearances • Conferences • Thought leadership • Editorial/articles
• Good strategy	• Focuses resources on opportunities	• Identification • Prioritisation and targeting • Coordinated approach

Unfortunately, the history of marketing as a specialism, with its bias towards consumer products, tends to deter professional services practitioners from using it as fully as they could. Yet there are relevant, practical techniques which can improve the health of the business for those willing to explore them.

A brief history of marketing

Marketing encompasses a range of techniques that grow revenue. It is defined and explored in depth in Chapter 7. The term is used to cover a wide range of activities (from account management and sales through to press management and advertising) and a broad supply industry (involving research, brand, design and consulting firms). As with other specialisms, business leaders can succeed with its techniques using instinct, business experience and common sense.

However, at a time when the professional services sector faces unprecedented issues concerning the way it deals with its clients and markets, the industry should take advantage of the well-established tools, techniques, processes and perspectives marketing has to offer. Leaders readily engage a range of specialists (such as lawyers, human resources managers and accountants) to improve business performance. It is thus sensible to engage specialists in service marketing to help focus the firm's approach to its market.

Unfortunately, the history of marketing has, until relatively recently, made such relevant marketing expertise difficult for the leaders of professional services firms to access. They do not see it as applicable to their businesses when marketing specialists seek to contribute their skills. After all, the marketing function came to the fore in the consumer goods sector and much of its approach and theory is still based upon the experience of these businesses. In the mid-twentieth century, as markets matured and became more saturated, consumer goods companies needed to move their stock more effectively. This led them to institutionalise the discipline of marketing, with a focus on advertising and branded goods aimed at clear segments of buyers. Companies like Procter & Gamble, Unilever and Mars flourished by becoming marketing led and creating branded value propositions. The theories of marketing, developed by academics at this time, were thus largely based on the experience of the consumer goods industry.

However, over the next few decades marketing became more significant in other industries, such as the car industry in the early 1970s and the computer industry during the early 1990s, as they, in turn, matured. Then, in the second half of the twentieth century, the combination of two powerful forces saw marketing increasingly being applied to service businesses.

First, new sectors of the economy were opened to market forces. Companies in the leisure, utilities and financial services sectors all had to rethink the way they go to market, as competition increased and buyers became more sophisticated and demanding. For example, the privatised utilities found themselves having to compete for the first time, while European banks saw their steady market disrupted by new legislation. As a result they have had to invest in marketing techniques and create new sales and marketing functions.

Second, there has been a progressive shift in most developed economies from manufacturing to service dominance, to the point where services are estimated to account for almost two-thirds of most Western countries' gross national product. This demanded the attention of marketing academics. The differences between product and service marketing were first explored in earnest by various academics in the early 1980s. There are now schools of academics in the US, Asia and Europe which have

Table I.2 *Relevant service marketing theory.*

The differences between product and service marketing

Academics suggest several differences between product and service marketing. All have direct applicability to how professional services firms grow.

- **Intangibility.** Services are intangible and consist of an action or a deed. Services can't be seen felt, tasted or touched.
- **Inseparability.** The buyer finds it difficult to distinguish between the service and the person delivering the service. The employee is intimately involved in the service itself and becomes part of the service's value in the buyer's mind.
- **Simultaneous consumption.** A service is performed, manufactured, as it is bought. It can't be made in advance.
- **Perishability.** Services are perishable. They can't be stored, saved, returned or easily changed. There will therefore be problems with meeting periods of high demand and in managing to optimal scale of resource.
- **Heterogeneity or variability.** Service delivery is hard to standardise, and since services are the performance of a series of actions, no two services are ever exactly alike. Also, buyer demands are different so they relate to service providers in different ways.
- **Ownership.** The ownership of a service does not pass to the buyer in the way it does with products. Buyers may rent the brains of consultants, trainers and advertisers but they do not buy the human being involved. This can cause issues with perceived value which service suppliers must take special efforts to overcome.
- **Process.** Services have a process through which the client must move. This creates emotions in the buyers which do not occur when buying products and can alter the strategic framework of service markets.

sponsored research into service marketing, sometimes in cooperation with industry.

The body of knowledge about how generic service businesses are marketed has therefore grown. Much of it is relevant to professional services firms. In short, the scientific process has been applied to services marketing such that marketing specialists and leaders of professional services firms can now reach for a number of techniques and processes with confidence.

The recognised differences between consumer goods marketing and service marketing illustrate this. They are summarised in Table I.2. Each requires the business to take different marketing actions than a consumer goods company, and all are directly relevant to professional services firms. For instance, the phenomenon of 'inseparability' means that professional services, unlike manufacturing companies, must put great emphasis on internal marketing, motivating their staff to communicate the firm's values to clients. As client service staff are constantly engaged with clients, often generating new work themselves, the role of marketing in a professional services firm is as much about facilitating market-oriented behaviour at the client interface as it is about running a specialist function.

It can best be compared to a sports coach. A professional coach helps an athlete improve performance by suggesting the appropriate techniques based on expertise and experience. The coach often cannot perform to the athlete's standard but can make a big difference to their performance. Similarly, service marketing specialists can coach professionals in a range of marketing and business development skills which will grow their business effectively.

Another example is Professor Leonard Berry's model of service marketing in Figure I.2 (Berry and Parasuraman, 1991), which is contrasted to product marketing. In product marketing, the first step is pre-production research, followed by manufacturing and then post-production push, such as advertising, to induce trial. The use of the product by the buyer then reinforces the brand's positioning. However, with the marketing of services, while there is some pre-production research to configure the service, it is the experience of the service by the customer that creates 'word of mouth'. This, in turn, affects the brand reputation either positively or negatively.

This exactly matches the experience of professional services firms where word of mouth, resulting from the work, influences repeat purchase and referrals. If a business is facing bancruptcy, and an insolvency practitioner is able to turn it around rather than winding it up, or if a lawyer wins a difficult case, or if a hairdresser does a wonderful job for an important night out, the client feels a sense of emotional relief from the good service. This leads to enhanced reputation, and hence repeat business and/or referrals from positive word-of-mouth recommendations. Client dissatisfaction, on the other hand, will have a detrimental effect, particularly since people have a tendency to talk negatively more often than positively about their buying experiences.

Enter the marketer

As a result of these considerations many leading professional services firms have begun to recruit professional marketers. (In the past, their marketing has been handled either part-time by client service staff or by talented administrators.) The problem is that 'classically trained' marketers are to be

Nature and roles of goods marketing

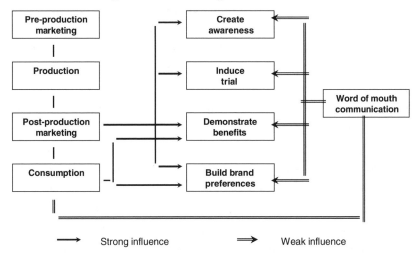

Nature and roles of service marketing

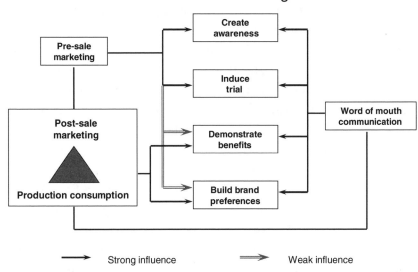

Figure I.2 *Relevant service marketing theory – Leonard Berry's diagram.*
Source: Berry and Parasuraman (1991). Reprinted with the permission of The Free Press, a Division of Simon & Schuster Adult Publishing Group, from MARKETING SERVICE: Competing Through Quality by Leonard L. Berry and A. Parasuraman. Copyright © 1991 by The Free Press. All rights reserved.

found largely in leading consumer goods companies. Their training and experience is very different from the culture and needs of a professional services firm. Even the best consumer marketers, hired to 'bring some marketing' to professional services firms, struggle for two main reasons.

First, while the need for marketing in professional services firms is becoming increasingly apparent, consumer goods marketing techniques are largely inappropriate. So, when faced with the demand for a new way of marketing, product marketers often find they lack knowledge. On the other hand, most leaders in a professional services firm, faced with someone with 'classical marketing training', will more often than not feel that their business is too different for these marketing techniques to apply, even if they treat the marketer with respect.

Second, marketing is underdeveloped in many professional services firms. In partnerships it is viewed as 'support' and does not lead the approach of the business to market, as it does in successful consumer goods companies. This can make things very hard for marketers who have moved to the sector from more marketing-oriented companies. They have been used to operating within a well-established marketing infrastructure, which doesn't exist in a professional services firm. So they are faced with the challenge of explaining just what marketing is to the majority of colleagues who won't understand or value its purpose.

Bemused by a lack of practice, process and authority, they often find marketing is treated as a peripheral function or reduced to the erratic use of some of its components. Many become enmeshed in internal politics and a struggle for resources which limits their ability to achieve. The usual result is that the marketers have to rein back the expectations of what they can achieve and do the one or two strategically important things which the firm allows them to do and which it is prepared to fund.

If a marketer is to be successful in a professional services firm, they should have a comprehensive knowledge of relevant service marketing techniques. In addition, they need partner level sponsorship to encourage dialogue and effective integration with the firm's processes. This sponsorship will help marketers to negotiate the political landscape, to create infrastructure and to adjust their language and style to suit the firm's culture. Just as important, it can nudge leaders to open the organisation to new approaches. Finally, the marketer needs excellent communications skills. They will then be able to contribute to the firm's performance in a changing market.

Shepherd+ Wedderburn: introducing structured marketing into a law firm

Shepherd+ Wedderburn is a Scottish-based law firm with offices in Edinburgh, Glasgow, Aberdeen and London. Founded in 1922, it provides a full range of legal services to corporate, commercial, public sector and private clients of a range of sizes throughout the UK. In 2004 there were 50 partners and 450 staff in total, with turnover of around £30 million ($54 million).

In 2000 the firm was facing a number of challenges. First, the market was changing and the firm's market position was under attack. For example, competitors were modernising their management processes as well as successfully using marketing to heighten their profile in the market. Second, clients were increasingly asking law firms to pitch for business, rather than, as in the past, relying on personal networks. The firm was also keen to expand business beyond Scotland.

The new chief executive decided to hire a marketing director who could help the firm refine its strategic vision and develop a more marketing-led approach to the business. With an MBA from London Business School and having worked in companies like Sony and the Royal Bank of Scotland before joining Shepherd+ Wedderburn as marketing director, David Wallace was eminently qualified. However, he soon found that working in marketing in a partnership was very different. Many partners were very sceptical about the value that marketing could bring, whereas others did not even have a view. He thus set out to consult and reach consensus on common approach.

He carried out research among the partners and staff to get a clearer idea of where the firm stood, asking them basic questions such as where the firm was now, where it should be going and who the competitors were. He also commissioned external research among clients. Those findings, such as the fact that clients felt the firm's partners rarely discussed other services it could offer, and that they were keen on developing closer relationships, helped him begin to design a marketing strategy to address these issues.

For example, he encouraged partners to make simple changes such as developing an agenda before client meetings, which they circulated to the client ahead of time to make sure all points were covered. They also sent a note after the meeting outlining what had been agreed. The aim was to move beyond the typical relationship, where a lawyer waits to be instructed, and instead turn it into more of a business partnership. Another approach he used to heighten the understanding of marketing was to bring in a few of the partners to each major marketing project he undertook, including the hiring of any external agencies.

Marketing has since become much more involved in strategic issues such as exploring potential markets, from initial research through to market development and promotional activities. In addition, in 2002, the firm embarked on a major rebranding project. The aim was to emphasise key brand values that capitalised not only on the firm's perceived qualities but which could also be aspirational for the staff. They included 'trust' as the core value, which was accompanied by 'authoritative', 'engaging', 'open-minded', 'innovative', 'incisive' and 'assured'. The goal was to help the firm cultivate a more youthful, dynamic image.

That same year the firm won the Scottish Marketing Awards' Grand Prix, which not only raised the firm's profile but began to make an impact on recruitment of law graduates. Since then marketing has overseen activities such as launching a client magazine, a series of legal e-bulletins, an annual charity partner programme, and a host of online campaigns. In 2004 David Wallace won the top award for marketing director of the year at the UK Legal Marketing Awards ceremony for 'challenging the status quo to achieve real business results'.

However, the main success has been the rise in fees from new instructions, the changed perception of the firm and, over time, more support from the partners for the approach. The key lessons have been that, to embed a more marketing-oriented culture, support from the lead partner is critical, and that marketing specialists have to make their case step by step to gain influence in an initially alien environment.

Summary

This introduction to the professional services sector has shown what a wide array of skills, sizes, types of ownership and projects characterises the sector. The leaders of each firm, from the sole practitioner to the international network, should use these as the framework within which to define their approach to their markets. This must be done in the realisation that the fundamental drivers of future revenue growth are the quality of work and the quality of client service, leading to enhanced reputation. Marketing has a key role to play here. It is imperative that leaders carefully analyse how the principles of service marketing, rather than the more traditional precepts of product marketing, should be adapted to increase revenues and margins successfully.

PART I
Strategic Issues

There are a number of important strategic issues that all firms, whatever their size or shape, need to take into account in the pursuit of growth. The first is the overall approach to strategy: developing the strategy which is right for the firm. Successful strategy doesn't work in a vacuum, however. It needs to be based on extensive analysis of the firm's market. It encompasses client segmentation, brand and competitive strategies and capabilities and, where appropriate, internationalisation and cultural differences. All have a mandatory component and this section examines these issues in depth.

1

Growth strategies

Overview

Strategy sets the direction in which a firm wants to go. The leadership of every firm has to develop a strategy rooted in the realities of the market and communicate it throughout the firm. It can be explicit, formal, intuitive or informal, but, without it, the business could be fatally damaged. Strategy is neither short term nor tactical. It calls for the formulation of a perspective on the market and the firm's position within it, taking into account its size, skills and market environment. This chapter examines a range of possible marketing strategies applicable to different firms, from a sole practitioner through to a boutique up to large international firms.

The value of strategy

Good strategy is a framework of ideas, developed by the leadership, which sets a course that the leadership wants for the firm by creating a common purpose. It involves making decisions about direction, communicating those decisions and allocating the resources to go in that direction. A firm's strategy should become a touchstone for all decisions throughout the organisation.

In fact, all strategic devices and tools, such as mission statements and visions, are aimed at achieving this common understanding. Properly communicated, members of the firm will use it as a reference point when making decisions. Without it, decisions throughout the firm are based on the judgement of local people with a local perspective and information which, while valid, may conflict with the perspective of the total firm. Chaos and lack of results can then follow. It contrasts to tactics, which are short term, action oriented and accomplish limited goals.

All firms, even when no strategy is explicitly developed or communicated, must take a direction. However, if that direction is a rudderless drift, or if it flies in the face of market realities, or if it is not communicated throughout the firm, the health of the business is likely to be damaged. The leadership of the firm has, therefore, a duty of care to create clear, market-conscious, achievable strategic direction.

It is well known that many strategy techniques came originally from the military, where they evolved over a long period of time to help improve decision-making, resource allocation and success. Military history has shown that success in the heat of battle is more likely if there has been prior thought given to likely scenarios. For instance, the Chinese general, Sun Tzu, said in 500 BC (Sun-Tzu et al., 1996): 'In warfare first lay plans which will ensure victory and then lead your army to battle; if you will not begin with stratagem but rely on brute strength alone, victory will no longer be assured.'

A little forward planning, using methods that have been successful elsewhere, reduces risk and increases the likelihood of success. Stunning military successes as diverse as the Roman campaigns against ill-disciplined tribes, Napoleon's conquest of Europe and General Norman Schwarzkopf's 'Operation Desert Storm' in Kuwait, have demonstrated the power of experience and forethought.

If good strategy is effective in military endeavour it is likely to be effective in business. Over time business leaders have adopted and shaped many of the military's strategic techniques in order to improve their chances of success and developed many of their own. If, after thousands of years of bloody combat, mankind has learned that good strategy is more effective than rushing at the other side with sticks, business leaders should surely acknowledge that good business leadership is a little more than 'gut feel' or decisions made on the hoof.

Strategy as a management discipline appears to have been through several evolutionary phases. In the 1970s, for example, it consisted of new management tools (such as the Boston matrix or scenario planning), focusing largely on the corporate strategy of large corporations. By the 1980s strategy was often overseen by large, central strategic planning functions in multinationals running complex strategic models. This was reinforced by the apparent success of Japanese firms and their famed focus upon long-term planning.

By contrast, in the 1990s, the combination of recession, the collapse of the Asian model and a tougher competitive environment, with the perception that business must be more short term, created much more of a feverish, short-term focus. This culminated in some of the excesses of the dot.com boom, when the lack of a proper business model was no barrier to raising large amounts of capital. Since the burst of the dot.com bubble and the associated recession, strategy has become more short term and need driven. In fact, many of the strategy houses report that strategy projects have become a distress purchase, responding to hostile bids or the need for turnaround. The appetite for large, long-term strategic planning and analysis appears to have diminished in many sectors. Strategy, in the sense of longer-term detailed strategic plans, is less valued.

The professional services industry can learn from this experience. Whatever the size and shape of the firm, leaders need to take time to think of the future health of their business and how they go to market. They need to focus on the strategic imperatives relevant at any one time and allocate resources appropriately to chart the next steps of the firm. This should be done in a style and manner geared to the culture of the firm and the judgement of the leadership. It can be elaborate, documented or intuitive. But it should be done.

Marketing specialists would argue that within business strategy are issues related specifically to the market which require marketing tools, judgement and experience. For instance, Nirmalya Kumar of the London Business School (Kumar, 2004) argues that numerous decisions taken by chief executives are, in fact, marketing decisions which influence the direction of the firm. Leaders should therefore aim to adopt market-oriented strategy and planning.

At the very least, leaders should take a perspective on the market and their firm's position within it. Yet this is not as straightforward as it appears.

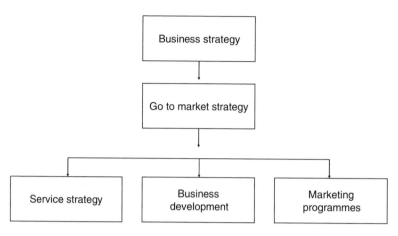

Figure 1.1 *The interrelationship of different types of strategy.*

For example, they may wish to base their decisions on client research. However, the clients that are researched, the techniques used to gain insight and the interpretation of results will all affect the quality of the decisions based on this approach. A wrong research approach could reduce the quality of strategic decisions and damage the firm.

This also applies to issues like competitive strategy, opportunity analysis, brand strategy, segmentation of markets and channel strategy. These elements of marketing strategy need to be developed and integrated with the business strategy and are rounded out if experienced specialists are engaged in their formulation. This interrelationship of strategic perspectives is illustrated in Figure 1.1.

Approaches to determining strategy

The development of strategy can be either 'procedural' (where a number of prescribed steps are followed to arrive at a particular point), 'functional' (where it is someone's job to draw up a well-presented and detailed strategic document), or 'extant' (consisting of a pattern of decisions by a business leader which are largely intuitive and often seen in retrospect).

All of these approaches to strategy are seen in the professional services industry. A procedural approach is often present, for example, in large corporate firms with a technology heritage, whereas extant strategy is often seen in smaller, one-partner firms. All have their strengths and weaknesses and none is an ideal approach.

(i) The procedural approach. Recommended by many business schools and followed by many companies, this approach follows a logical process to determine strategy. It comprises a calendar of interrelated planning activities, often driven by a company's need to report results to financial analysts and shareholders.

This approach will often distinguish between different time horizons influenced by the firm's market and investment horizon. There may be a set of 'one-year' operational plans focusing upon short-term goals, in addition to medium-term (three- to five-year) plans where investment is needed. The strategic framework needs to embrace them all. It will often distinguish between corporate planning, strategic market planning and business unit planning (Table 1.1). For instance, IBM has a well-crafted, detailed

Table 1.1 *The difference between corporate business plans and strategic market plans.*

A well-crafted corporate plan might contain:
- Business vision
- Business mission
- Corporate objectives
- Strategic intent
- Target returns
- Business unit targets
- Broad inorganic growth plans
- Organic growth plans
- Potential disinvestments
- Intended market positions
- Corporate brand strategy
- Asset utilisation

A strategic market plan might contain:
- Market objectives
- Target segments
- Positioning intentions
- Sales and revenue goals
- Target share in key markets
- Portfolio strategy: new services, relaunches, withdrawals and associated activities.
- Competitive strategies
- New market entry
- Major strategic programmes and initiatives
- Quality plans and subsequent quality measures
- Exit plans
- Internal and external communication objectives

planning process to which the service business (one of the largest in the world, incorporating several professional services business units) must comply.

(ii) The functional approach. In this approach a function exists which has responsibility for the creation and management of strategy. This may be held by a director of strategy who works closely with the chief executive and may also include an executive responsible for marketing strategy. Such a role will often also include responsibility for research, competitive intelligence, internal reporting and market analysis. Strategic planning is the focus of the role. The unit is expected to manage the planning timetable, execute ad hoc strategic studies and share their analytical perspective in appropriate debates. Some large professional services firms have executives in this role.

(iii) Extant strategy. Determined only by a retrospective view of direction, extant strategy is the direction deduced from decision-taking of, normally, one dominant business leader. The pattern of past decisions reveals the direction of the firm. Staff in such firms can feel that they have no strategy to follow because there aren't well-crafted written documents or clear planning schedules. Nevertheless, experience shows that firms led in this way can be dramatically successful, achieving their strategic intent, particularly if the leader makes the direction clear to the people in the firm.

Marketing strategies for the professional services firm

For the single practitioner

There are several different possible marketing strategies open to the single practitioner. Each depends upon their aspirations and their resultant business strategies.

For instance, their first marketing task is to focus on the launch of the business. This, however modest or grand, is a 'market penetration strategy', penetrating the target market in order to establish the business. A fast, volume penetration might include a memorable start to achieve impact and limited price penetration such as a discount or free trial in the first few months of trading. The single practitioner might also work in association with a network of other independent practitioners (a distribution strategy), in order to feed each other work.

On the other hand, a practitioner wanting to concentrate on low volume, high value projects may aim for a longer-term, soft launch to build up demand and reputation. Both need to be clear about their own offer and the clients they intend to serve. This needs to be precise and clearly thought through. Vague ideas of esoteric management concepts, or a lack of knowledge of who buys the type of service, will put their livelihood at risk.

Tactics associated with the volume approach are likely to include a visible launch. This might comprise an announcement to all possible contacts, followed by an invitation to a 'launch' party. Such an event, perhaps associated with interviews with local press and the trade association, will rest in the memory of the audience and will yield referrals as the latent business reputation grows.

Exponents of a low volume, high value approach, however, must be prepared for a longer haul. They must take the time to build a reputation by speaking at conferences, publishing articles and networking. They must focus on quality of image, quality of execution and quality of client care. Some offer a 'no question, money back' guarantee to clients if dissatisfied. Also, if their target conversion rate is one in three bids, they must be prepared to spend the early months of the business losing more than they win. Bravery and generosity to clients in these early days are important attributes of the high value practitioner.

The marketing strategy of the single practitioner is next focused on initial growth. This again is a market penetration strategy. The practitioner needs to consider marketing objectives such as: target annual revenue, achievable day rate, primary project offer, client penetration, partners to work with and intended visibility. They should also set up, preferably independent, mechanisms to understand how satisfied clients are with the work, their propensity to buy again and the likelihood of them referring the business to others in need. (In the early days this mechanism could be a colleague, relative or friend but it needs to be independent, because people are often reluctant to be honest.) Records should be kept of this feedback so that trends can be examined as the business grows.

Revenue is a derivative of the time the practitioner intends to sell (say 150 days a year) and the day rate achievable (a judgement based on industry average and personal standing). This becomes the pricing strategy of the firm. The target market might be firms or individuals in a geographic area or those interested in either a particular skill or sector expertise. Many small firms grow by obtaining work from one major client, others by a volume of small projects. The practitioner needs to decide where they wish to focus.

Growth may also come from referrals from other firms. The practitioner must therefore decide who in their circle of contacts they wish to cooperate with. Other single practitioners are often willing to refer potential work as a service to their clients when they are seeking a particular skill. The new entrant needs to handle these with care, executing work well and, over time, making referrals back. They must also make no attempt to steal the client. Negative reputation arising from such poor behaviour soon circulates in a pool of small independent providers, damaging the business.

An early decision is how to enhance reputation. The practitioner might join relevant professional associations for networking, they may try to gain press coverage, and they might contribute articles to relevant publications. While the drive for this comes from the practitioners themselves, they should consider using specialists. For instance, a public relations (PR) provider will find it relatively easy to gain placements for articles in relevant magazines (plus writing skills if needed) and speaking spots on conference platforms. They will also find it easier to sell the single practitioner to these communications channels than the practitioner themselves. The practitioner must decide the level of investment in such a resource and the period over which they wish the return to grow.

The 'guru' strategy

Those single practitioners wishing to focus upon margin rather than volume growth should consider a 'guru strategy'. The aim is to build a personal reputation, even fame, which will generate strong demand for an individual's expertise. This is primarily a pricing strategy. The practitioner must generate sufficient demand to create a strong pipeline of high value work. They must never compromise on their day rate. Successfully and carefully done, this strategy yields high returns.

Suppose the industry average day rate of single practitioners in the field is, say, $3000. An allocation of 50 marketing (and administration) days to achieve 150 sold days will achieve annual revenue of $450000. A successful guru strategy will achieve a day rate which is much higher than industry average. If, for example, the sole practitioner invests in reputation enhancement programmes costing $50 000 a year plus extra administrative support of $50 000 (to allow sold time to remain at 150 days), day rate may be doubled in three years. Revenue of $900 000 less $100 000 enhanced costs yields a healthy payback. Some single practitioners are, at the time of writing, achieving day rates of $10 000 or even $20 000 depending on market and reputation.

The guru strategy is critically dependent on the creation of demand. The potential guru must have first-rate technical knowledge, good communication abilities and excellent consultancy skills. They must combine this with a marketing strategy which focuses on reputation enhancement. If the guru is lucky enough to match their technical expertise to a current wave or fad in management thinking, then a personal fortune is made. Associated with these growth strategies is a deliberate intent to keep costs low by having minimal employees; i.e. not to build an organisation.

Profiting from a guru strategy

The hairdresser: Vidal Sassoon

Vidal Sassoon has become synonymous with the concept of the celebrity hairdresser. Although he might not have strictly been the first (that accolade belongs to his mentor, Raymond 'Teasy-Weasy' Bessone); he was the first to develop a precision and modern approach to cutting hair, with styles such as the 'Bob', which still influences hairdressers today.

His hair styles epitomised the 'Swinging London' scene of the 1960s and early 1970s. Even more interestingly, he was the first hairdresser to be able to claim the status of a brand in his own right. Along with the set-up of salons in key cities around the world, he also oversaw a wide range of hair products still on the shelves today. Today the Sassoon educational facilities in North America and Europe train over 15 000 people a year in his methods.

In October 2004, he settled a suit with the brand owner Procter & Gamble over what he alleged was lack of resources being put into the product line.

The strategist: Dr Paul Fifield

In a crowded marketplace single practitioners have to use the one weapon available to them to succeed: their reputation for good work and hence their personal brand. Dr Paul Fifield, a marketing strategist practising in the UK, came to that realisation early in his career. In the last decade or so he has pursued a 'guru' strategy, based not only on presentations and a series of well-received books on marketing strategy, but word of mouth from satisfied clients and recommendations from all the students he has taught over the years.

His decision to focus on marketing strategy, as opposed to tactics, began early in his career with his first degree. He followed that with an MBA and then a PhD on marketing strategy and segmentation in Western Europe from Cranfield School of Management. During this time he gained management experience by working in marketing positions in a number of companies.

In 1985, he and three other Cranfield MBAs decided to band together to form the Winchester Consulting Group, offering strategy consultancy and highly tailored management development for senior managers. This was to prove an uncomfortable but important lesson in the potential perils of partnership, since it was dissolved five years later, leaving him with substantial debts to pay off.

It also taught him the value of independence. The Fifield 'brand' had already gained credibility both from his many years working as a course director and senior examiner of the postgraduate diploma at the UK's Chartered Institute of Marketing, the world's largest professional body of marketers. But what really helped gain momentum was the publication of the first edition of his seminal book, *Marketing Strategy* (Butterworth-Heinemann, 1992) (Figure 1.2). He has also written books on strategic marketing management and international marketing strategy. In addition, he continues to give lectures and presentations.

Fifield has taken care to make sure the Fifield Practice operates within the well-defined niche of marketing strategy, or helping companies align themselves to the markets they want to serve. As he says, 'To be a successful brand in a niche you have to be clear about exactly what you do.'

Figure 1.2 One of Dr Fifield's books.
Reprinted from Marketing Strategy, Second Edition, Paul Fifield, Copyright (1998), with permission from Elsevier.

The osteopath: Walter McKone

Walter McKone is a UK osteopath based in London who has enthusiastically embraced the 'guru' strategy. The result has been that over the last 20 years he has built up a thriving practice, attracting patients not only from the UK but also from as far afield as Australia and Africa.

He has grown his business mostly from word of mouth from satisfied clients. Even more importantly, however, he has actively promoted himself as a brand through lectures, presentations, articles and books. For example, he is a senior tutor of paediatrics at the British School of Osteopathy in London, from which he graduated in 1984, while his books include *Osteopathic Athletic Health Care* (Nelson Thomas, 1997) and *Osteopathic Medicine: Philosophy, Principles & Practice* (Blackwell Science, 2001) (Figure 1.3). His latest book examines the decline of osteopathy from a medicine to a physical therapy.

Over time he has used these platforms to develop and deliver a far more inclusive and pragmatic approach to the discipline, arguing that

Figure 1.3 *Cover image courtesy of Blackwell Publishing.*

osteopathy has to be seen as more than manipulation and a 'one-end' product. Instead, osteopathy should return to its roots based on the philosophy of the scientist and poet Johann Wolfgang von Goethe and first put into practice by its founder, Andrew Taylor Still, a surgeon during the American Civil War.

He has continued to develop himself professionally in a number of ways. For example, having decided that he needed more experience with treatment for trauma that demanded a quick outcome, he became involved with American football. He started working with teams in the UK in the mid-1980s as the sport became more popular, and then in the US, with teams like the Dallas Cowboys, Chicago Bears and finally as a full-time osteopath with the London Monarchs.

He has also run workshops for companies in areas such as motivational speaking, stress management and how to exploit the imagination, while weekly slots as a radio presenter help him gain a wider audience. As he says, 'My kind of branding has to be personal. And when your brand is a human rather than a product you are only limited by your own imagination.'

Exit strategies for the single practitioner

Marketing has a hand to play in the exit strategies of sole practitioners and can, in fact, make a sizeable difference to the practitioner's personal take on closure of the business. Apart from simply closing the business, one of the exit strategies is to recruit a successor. Through contacts, networking or advertising, a qualified candidate with the right skills can be found. The best approach is a progressive handover taking, say, three years. Marketing plays a part in building a pipeline of work for the new partner, handing over existing clients and managing expectations.

Marketing really comes into its own, however, if the chosen exit route is a sale of the business. Ideally, a professional who intends to sell should consider this at the very start of the business. Strategies put in place at the beginning will maximise returns when it comes time to sell. For instance, larger firms will normally be interested in a smaller firm for brand, reputation, intellectual capital, staff or unique client relationships. At the start, the practitioner should consider a number of these, then minor, issues, such as the name of their firm. (An entity called after the names of the owners is harder to sell as a small going concern because it is too associated with the founder and harder to build into an independent business once the founder has moved on.)

In addition, as the firm grows, any systems, articles or processes should be captured, perhaps in the shape of published books or training courses. This registers them clearly as the firm's intellectual property. Similarly, large clients should, if possible, be asked to sign 'frame agreements', or contracts committing them to volumes of work. All will help create value in the firm and all are effective marketing devices.

At least two years before the target sale time, the practitioner should invest money in a PR specialist to build publicity for the firm. This might be articles in management publications or industry association journals. This is a slightly different target audience and set of objectives to normal, business building, reputation enhancement. In the target sale year a prospectus, the marketing document, should be written. This is the basis of approach to target acquirers. It must contain an analysis of the firm in its market and its unique characteristics. It should also forecast revenue scenarios for different types of business partners.

Finally, marketing has a role to play in the handover once the (painful and demanding) negotiations are under way. Staff will need to be included at the right time and a programme of communication to clients instituted. If the nature of the sale is an 'earn-out' then marketing normally has to be aimed at the acquirer's account teams and key accounts to attract work from them. Staff must also build a programme of visits to the large managed accounts in order to maximise the value of being in a more substantial entity and to hit profit targets. If acquired by a much bigger firm, the practitioner must communicate to existing business unit leaders and firms in the network.

Health warning

A professional, setting up a firm with the intention of selling, needs to take a hard look at what this involves over the long term and what is needed to be successful. First, they need to build a business and take it through, probably, two full economic cycles. While doing this they need to build in capabilities which will distinguish it from competitors, as described above. Then, preferably at the start of a new economic cycle, they need to attract and close a deal with a buyer. There will then be a three- to five-year earn-out where the capital they earn is affected by the performance and profit of the firm, now part of a larger group.

Many rugged independents and entrepreneurial professionals find survival in these circumstances to be particularly hard. The need to fit in with the group's strategies, investment constraints and budgets can severely test the patience of the previously independent business owner. The full process is therefore likely to be a 15- to 20-year journey with a relatively modest capital return. It is not for the faint-hearted and has been the graveyard of many ambitious professionals' dreams.

Marketing strategies for the retail professional service

Marketing strategy for the retail professional begins before they start the business. Having trained in their area of professional expertise, they need to think like a business person from the start.

Are they to start by buying a small running business which has an established clientele? If so, do they understand the health of that business? How can they ensure it is a good buy? Are the financials reliable? If it is a successful business, will they be able to maintain the success? Why is the current owner selling? (If it is to move to new premises nearby, they are likely to take clients with them.) If the business is run down, how can they market it to increase its potential? What will they offer to grow revenues and attract new clients? And will the business sustain the extra costs of taking the actions to make such improvements? They ought to think through all these issues, creating a realistic business and marketing plan.

If they are not buying an existing business, they need to think about the site of their new shop, competitors in the area, the clients it can attract and how they will launch the business. They must design the layout of the premises to attract clients and display stock to gain extra revenue from product sales. They need to think about how will they launch and market the business, and how they will recoup the initial set-up costs in the years ahead. If they are going to a bank for a loan, normally they will have to capture all this in a business plan.

Once the business is established, one strategy to grow the retail professional service firm is through a version of the 'guru strategy' for single practitioners. This involves gaining (normally through free trials) celebrity or high profile clients. Once an elite clientele is attracted, high prices and high quality must be maintained. Over time, publicity and PR through consumer magazine coverage and high profile industry competition wins reinforce the stance. As the strategy develops, ranges of branded products can be released and a 'school' for young professionals will expand the franchise.

Another marketing strategy open to the retail professional is to build a retail network. In many retail professional service sectors there are inefficiencies built into the market. For instance, a plethora of small, one-person businesses is not an efficient way to serve a large market. Each has to negotiate directly with suppliers and separately provide all the functions of a business. At the same time, there is no common brand, so no great impact in the minds of potential clients. Competitive advantage can be gained by creating a network or retail chain, which can bring efficiencies that can be passed on to buyers. At its most simple, specialisation of functions such as merchandising, recruitment and buying allow chains to make savings that single owners cannot.

On the other hand, there are other potential savings from building a chain through the deployment of professionals. A business of, say, 10 shops which employs 10 young professionals on salary to undertake work is able to distribute profit differently than 10 individual businesses where each professional determines their own take. The efficiencies of the chain are also likely to generate more profits. In fact, these efficiencies can change the nature of the value proposition.

In the UK, for example, the value proposition of opticians for many years was based around the skill of eye testing. People went for a test and then had to wait days for glasses to be made. Retail chains now exist that make glasses on the spot and offer designer choice. The value proposition is now about easily accessible facial appearance, not the optician's skill as such. The marketing strategy of these chains is to build a brand and to develop effective sales and merchandising skills.

Other methods of building chains and maximising brand impact are through a partnership structure, with agreed common standards or franchising. This offers professionals business ownership and profit within a tightly defined market approach.

Creating retail chains from professional services

Pharmacy: Walgreens grows through service quality

Walgreens is a successful national retail pharmacy in the US. It was founded in 1901 by a pharmacist, Charles R. Walgreen, who opened his first shop in the competitive market of Chicago with the aim of transforming what he saw as the old-fashioned approach to running a drugstore. His focus on innovation, including the style of service and the introduction of a wide range of merchandise, helped him to open 20 stores by 1920.

His expansion was rooted in his ability to hire managers who could build on his vision of quality and service. By 1984, Walgreens had 1000 stores across the country, which rose to just over 4500 by August 2004. The current goal is to have 7000 by 2010 by opening new stores rather than through acquisition. Sales in fiscal 2004 were almost $38 billion, the 30th consecutive year of record sales and profits.

Optician: Specsavers profits from partnerships

Specsavers Opticians is a UK-based chain of optical retailers with more than 600 stores in the UK, the Republic of Ireland, the Netherlands and Sweden. It was founded in 1984 by Doug and Mary Perkins, who met while studying for their optometrist qualifications at Cardiff University in Wales. They set up a small chain of opticians in the UK's West Country, and then retired. However, when the UK government deregulated professionals in the mid-1980s, freeing them to advertise their products and services for the first time, the Perkinses decided to re-enter the market.

They opened their first Specsavers store on the British offshore island of Guernsey, with the emphasis on affordable eyecare. The brand's subsequent expansion has been through joint or shared ventures with appropriate practitioners, who have responsibility for the day-to-day running of the business. The parent company provides support services, expertise, experience and information. This includes business planning and development, recruitment, training, purchasing, marketing and IT.

Its sales in 2003 were £545 million ($983 million), with over 16 million registered customers in its main UK market. Along with opening more locations in its existing markets, it is also planning further expansion in continental Europe and has begun to diversify into the hearing aid market.

Real estate: Coldwell Banker expands through franchise

Coldwell Banker is one of the leading full-service realtors in the US. It has more than 3600 independently owned and operated residential and commercial real estate offices with over 114 000 sales associates globally in areas such as Europe, Asia, Central America and the Caribbean.

Its focus on service has been the core of its business philosophy since its inception. Its founder, Colbert Coldwell, set up his agency in reaction against the profiteering being made from vulnerable sellers following the huge earthquake in San Francisco in 1906. He joined forces with Benjamin Arthur Banker in 1914.

They built the firm up over the years by franchise, finding the right professionals to extend the brand in new markets. Now, as well as holding a leading position in residential real estate, it has niche positions in other markets, including resorts, new homes and luxury properties. It is also one of the largest telephone/Web-based lenders in the US, while Coldwell Banker Commercial is one of the leading commercial franchise operations.

Marketing strategies for the specialist boutique

A boutique is a niche player in the market. Their ability to earn above average earnings is based on some form of differentiation, which simply means that they are different to competitors so that clients have a clear choice. They cannot afford to become the same as other suppliers or fees will drop to industry average levels. Their difference might come from technical expertise, mix of skills, geographic knowledge, sector knowledge or, more rarely, style of client service. Sometimes the difference is little more than perception in the clients' minds caused by reputation or fame.

The marketing strategy must be to preserve at all costs their point of differentiation. They must understand the clients' values and perceptions, and then work to build on them. They must invest in internal communication and training in the area of differentiation. They must also communicate to the market in general about their point of differentiation. Interbrand, for example, is a marketing consultancy which specialises in brand issues. The case study in Chapter 10 details its respected and well-known annual study on the best global brands, a superb example of thought leadership, which reinforces its point of differentiation.

International marketing strategies for the professional service firm

No firm, of whatever size, can ignore the international dimension of business. They may simply have clients with international operations or their growth might take them into other countries. This involves resourcing and penetration strategies into other parts of the world and the setting of international brand strategies (explored in Chapter 6).

Marketing strategies for the large firm

Large corporate entities that own professional services businesses tend to include their professional services arm in their strategy development process. As they generally have a functional approach to business, it is likely that these firms create a marketing strategy or strategic framework as part of their generic strategy process. They may wish to extend their service offers, move into new markets (whether geographic or sector oriented) and they may wish to extend their brand franchise. Each should be detailed and resourced in strategic plans.

Partnerships, or those which have recently become public companies, are likely to have a strategy debate during the planning cycle of their business which refers to the market. It is sensible to make this intuitive and sometimes erratic reference to the market more explicit. Devices to gain as objective as possible a view of the market will reduce risk of failure and the engagement of experienced specialists in the strategy debate are likely to round out decisions.

There is also an argument, particularly if the leader of the firm's marketing function is a professional marketer with leadership status, and not just a partner seconded as a part-time rotation, for an explicit marketing strategy to be developed and communicated. Such an approach will prioritise resource allocation, communicate priorities to partners and give direction to marketing specialists throughout the firm. It will give structure to their day-to-day work and decision-making.

Summary

Leaders of firms who ignore the critical role that strategy should play are gambling with the very survival of their business. A failure to think through the direction in which they should be headed, and the routes to get there, can be fatal. As this chapter has described, there are a number of approaches to determining strategy which professional services firms can use. It can be elaborate, documented or intuitive. The method chosen will vary according to the type of firm, its aspirations and its resources. But however it is developed, business strategy must be rooted in well-researched market realities in the context of the competitive environment.

2

Gaining market perspective

Overview

Leaders of firms should develop a process which enables them to take stock of their target market on a regular basis. This process should include a regular assessment of their business, the market environment and their competitive position. This chapter outlines a number of tools and techniques which can help firms gain an objective market perspective, such as a market research study and a full market audit. It also looks at techniques to turn that knowledge into a basis for making decisions about exploiting new opportunities or withdrawing from declining areas of business.

Why market understanding is essential

Whether the professional services firm consists of a single practitioner or is a large sophisticated international organisation, whether it is highly rational and procedural in devising its business plans, or whether it is largely intuitive, the leaders of the firm need to understand their market in order to make sound decisions which safeguard the future health of their business.

There is a vulnerability here that arises from what is generally the greatest strength of professional services firms: closeness to the client. As professionals are in close contact with their clients, dealing with confidential and important issues, it is natural for them to assume that they know the market in which they operate. However, one company or one client does not reflect the trends and forces at work across a market as a whole. Poor decision-making or erratic leadership, as people change priorities in the light of the latest client encounter, can result from such a myopic perspective. So it is essential that, from time to time, the leaders step back and take stock of their market.

It is also sensible to have a business process which collects market data in order to provide as objective a view as possible of the changing business environment. If circumstances are changing, existing assumptions about what succeeds are dangerous. It is rational to get a perspective on any changes in the market and to take a view of the implications.

There are straightforward methods to collect such an external view and garner market-based insights. Some take an economic view of a market and some a behavioural approach. Each has yielded valuable insights for business leaders. This chapter discusses how the professional service firm can sharpen its perspective of its market using these tools, detailed further in Part III. These will aid leaders in gaining a relatively objective view of their position in the market.

A reprise of relevant concepts

A clear view of market definition: what business is the firm in?

The first and most fundamental issue that leaders need to think about is how they define the market they are operating in. This may sound simplistic, but there are numerous examples of businesses failing, or being destroyed, because their owners have not defined their target market properly. It is important because there is an assumption built into the fabric of a business that gives a direction to its activities. If this assumption is not aligned to the market, the business will, ultimately, fail.

The classic study of how easily this can happen was undertaken by Theodore Levitt (Levitt, 1960, 2004). In his analysis he referred to the US railway industry. The railway companies were the computer companies of their age. When they first appeared they were handling a stunning new technology that would revolutionise life in the nineteenth century as much as computer power has done in the twentieth. This was the first time in human history that mankind could go faster than a galloping horse. The industry created new towns, new jobs and new concepts (among others, the idea of holidays).

By the 1870s there were hundreds of thousands of miles of track in the US alone, some crossing the entire country. The railway companies then earned huge profits. So anyone approaching the chief executive of one of these companies, in, say, 1910, and predicting that there were major new threats to the business that could see them virtually bankrupt by the 1930s/1940s, would be dismissed as speaking complete nonsense. And yet, thanks to the development of the car and the aeroplane, that is exactly what happened. The railway companies struggled because they defined their businesses as 'trains' rather than 'transportation'. Had they focused their businesses on the 'transportation market' they would have invested in these new technologies and moved their businesses in new directions.

How does this apply to professional services firms? An example is the executive search industry which, since its inception, has defined itself as specialising only in top-level search. This means that practitioners have looked for top talent who are already in jobs, using their databases or personal contacts. This outlook has set the culture and style of the firms in the industry. They have therefore tended to disdain candidates who are 'write-ins' or are between jobs. They have also tended to focus on getting company assignments, sometimes thoughtlessly treating candidates as an expendable resource, even though they might be a buyer on a future occasion.

This approach yielded high margins when their industry was young and the headhunter held a mystique which opened doors. But, recently, they have been buffeted by a number of powerful forces: recession, new regulation, upstart boutiques and the irritating introduction of professional buyers (human resources directors). Worse, mature clients are no longer buying on the basis of the brand of key firms and the mystery of the headhunter's contacts is being questioned. As a result they are being asked to account for their practitioners' industry expertise and undertake demeaning 'beauty parades'.

What market are they in? If the leaders define their market as 'high end executive search' they are limiting themselves to a model of business which operates in a small potential fee pool. Another option could be to define the market as executive 'recruitment'. This would involve them in recruitment advertising and interviewing (called 'selection') across all levels of management. This might allow them to track and advise talented executives in an industry sector as their career progresses.

Another option would be to define the market as 'top talent management', which would demand a more hands-on approach with a company's existing executives, offering 'top executive team benchmarking', 'internal development', and advice on organisational structure. They would then be able to conduct assignments in the light of both internal and external candidates. In fact, many suppliers in this industry have moved in one or other of these directions.

Leaders of professional services firms must thus define for their firm the market on which they focus. This must be done in clear, client-centric terms. It must then be communicated to partners, senior executives, staff, clients and target clients.

Insights from the phases in the growth of a market

The phenomenon of market maturity occurs when there are multiple suppliers and multiple buyers. An economic concept first observed in the 1950s, it is depicted in Figure 2.1, which uses total industry sales over time as the axes of the graph. The concept suggests that a market evolves through several key stages: introduction, growth, maturity and decline. Firms have different success criteria and cost challenges in these different phases of market development. In response, they should adopt different strategies.

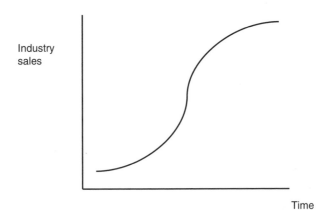

Figure 2.1 *The phenomenon of industry maturity.*

The tool is described in detail in Part III with the associated strategy recommendations.

Suppliers in a market can find themselves buffeted by the forces at play in each phase of development. However, if leaders understand what phase their market is in, they can set strategic direction for their firm in the light of that insight. For instance, at the time of writing, executive coaching is at the introductory phase. Suppliers should therefore educate the market in the concept and grow their business by inducing trials. In this phase, too, costs are likely to be high and firms can be unprofitable. Far from trying to exploit 'first mover advantage', firms in other industries have waited for upstarts in new corners of their markets to burn investment before buying them out.

Some professional services firms are still in the growth phase of their market. There is strong natural demand for their service and, in many cases, work just 'walks through the door'. In this phase the firm has to concentrate on servicing demand. Leaders will focus on obtaining and deploying skilled resource. They must ensure that there are efficient processes to capture and meet demand. It is also possible to concentrate on internal needs, ignoring competitor moves because there is sufficient demand for all.

On the other hand, many professional services (such as financial audit, advertising and many aspects of law) now operate in mature markets. Classic signs of maturity include:

- Informed, demanding clients.
- Most buyers have a good knowledge of the offer, which means firms have to concentrate more on getting value from existing buyers rather than enjoying easy growth from new customers.
- Price pressure and slowing growth.
- Rationalisation and consolidation in the market.
- The rise of niche suppliers.
- New laws and regulations.

Firms in such market conditions need to change their approach. Leading firms are particularly vulnerable. They will have succeeded on the basis of servicing huge demand during the growth phase of the market. If they do not respond quickly to the changed conditions, their costs will remain static while their revenues drop dramatically. Niche firms, on the other hand, are in a very strong position. As the whole market fragments, their appeal to one segment of buyers allows them to dominate various parts of the market. When these forces played out in the computer industry, the once-mighty IBM nearly went bankrupt while the upstart Microsoft cantered through to market dominance. Similar dramas will play out in the professional services industry.

Leaders of professional services firms must undertake analysis of their market and take a view of where the market in which they operate, however they define it, has reached in its maturity. From this they can deduce strategy options which can form part of the ultimate business and marketing strategies.

Understanding competitive position

Leaders are frequently imprecise about the competitive positions of their firm. They will muddle the aspiration of being market leader with 'best' or 'premium'. They will lack an external perspective on their position and will frequently base such judgements on anecdotes rather than hard data. But competitive position matters. It matters because it is based on client perceptions of value, and it matters because, by holding a clear position, a firm can maximise its margins. Just as importantly, a clear position communicates to the recruitment market, attracting high calibre staff, thus enhancing quality and margins.

Figure 2.2 illustrates a perceptual map of a service market, which is explained in detail in Part III. The horizontal axis represents 'perceived price', and the vertical 'perceived quality'. Perceived price and perceived quality are components of clients' perceptions of value, and the map should be properly constructed through research or dialogue with clients. The map shows the value preferences of different clients. Some want a 'no-frills', least-cost service whereas others want a highly engineered service.

For example, someone who shops at Harrod's food hall in London will think they get value for their money because the quality of product is thought to be worth the higher prices. Contrast that to someone who shops at a local market because they are more interested in lower prices. Yet both perceive that they get value for money. The firm has to understand their *clients'* perception of value, rather than make assumptions about what clients want.

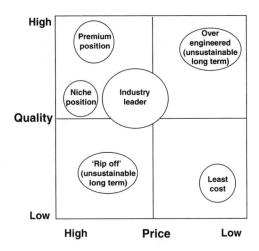

Figure 2.2 *Competitive positioning – the perceptual map.*
Source: Lambin (2000), adapted by Young (2005)

Each company, either by design or default, takes its own position in the market. It might be as 'market leader', with dominant share and the ability to influence the rules of engagement. Such leaders set price expectations and service standards for the whole market. Or it might be as a 'follower' which is smaller than the market leader and able to earn a profitable existence by providing a healthy alternative either in terms of price or the features of the service involved. Other competitive positions include 'least cost', 'premium' or 'niche' provider.

The two unsustainable positions are in the top right and bottom left corners. Low costs and high quality mean that the service is overengineered and can't continue in the long term. The combination of high prices and low quality in the lower left quadrant is often caused by a distortion in the market such as a monopoly or where lack of transparency means buyers can't make clear comparisons. Nor is the map static. It is dangerous, for example, for the market leader to assume its position is inviolable, since niche providers can progressively capture segments of the market and mount a challenge for leadership.

The perceptual map can be used in several ways. First, it can be used as a catalyst to debate strategic positioning in the market and the firm's resultant business and marketing strategy. For instance, a firm may find through acquisition that it has become the volume market leader of its industry. However, to maintain that position, it must adopt the behaviour of a market leader, taking a stance on price, quality and leading industry issues. Alternatively, a firm might find that it can maximise margins by remaining a niche provider. In this case it needs to determine exactly how it is different from the market leader, communicating that to employees, introducers of work and clients.

Second, the perceptual map can be used to set competitive strategy. For instance, a 'follower', which finds itself number two in a market with a vulnerable market leader, might decide to challenge for leadership. The map can be used to determine the number of clients they should target and what the value proposition should be. It can also be used to anticipate the likely reaction of other competitors.

Third, the perceptual map can be used to set the service strategy which is appropriate for the firm's strategic position. Often a business aims for the 'best quality' or the 'highest performance' whatever its market position. It is not uncommon for a profitable niche supplier to have a client service plan aimed at promoting the 'best' service in the industry or 'delighting' all customers. This is a stance which is likely to be as damaging as it is inappropriate. It is as costly as it is ridiculous to seek to 'delight' all clients and to offer the same bland service as all other suppliers. The service strategy must match the competitive position or strategic intent of the firm.

Finally, creating perceptual maps based on both clients' perceptions of value and the firm's own view of where it sits can help with internal communications. It highlights the gaps between what the firm believes and what the client actually thinks. This enables the firm to create internal communications and education programmes to bridge the gap.

The changing market for insolvency services in the UK

The UK market for insolvency services illustrates how useful value maps can be in alerting firms to potential dangers. In the early 1990s the market was divided between the big firms and boutiques dedicated to insolvency practices at the higher end and individual practitioners who dealt with the lower end of the market (about 40%) (Figure 2.3).

The big firms had become accustomed to being given insolvency business from the leading banks, which dealt with problems in companies to which they had lent money. These banks tended to use a virtual rotation

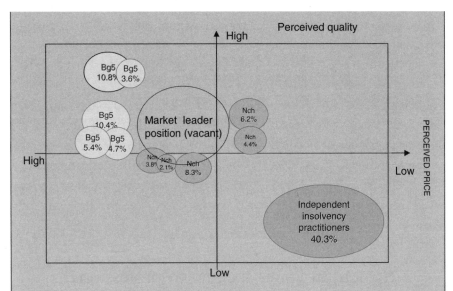

Figure 2.3 *Perceptual map, UK insolvency, 1990s.*

system, choosing partners from an approved list of firms to lead assignments. Larger insolvencies went to the bigger firms (either because of perceived complexity or international reach), whereas boutiques tended to be awarded smaller, more price-sensitive jobs.

But the market was changing. First, many of the banks had changed their strategy and had a 'cleaner' lending portfolio than previously. Second, there was a growing emphasis on turnaround, requiring different management skills. Third, there were new lenders entering the market, both foreign banks and asset-based lenders who were not so tied to traditional suppliers. In addition, a new insolvency law was mooted which would change the responsibility for choosing an insolvency firm, swinging the influence on the buying decision away from the large, highly centralised banks towards their smaller, often regionally based clients.

All these factors would disrupt this tidy market and change behaviour. The barrier between the big firms and the individual practitioners would begin to disappear. This, in turn, would mean that they could no longer be complacent about business and would have to find ways to market to this new audience. The perceptual map, if constructed using client data, would give insight into market conditions and help to chart a course through the changes.

For instance, at least two of the then 'Big Five' firms claimed to be market leader, but analysis showed they were not. Based on the perceptual map above, once the semi-monopolistic distortion was removed from the market, a new market leader would emerge, threatening the position of the bigger firms. It could move into this position by increasing its volume through finding a new value proposition. Alternatively, one of the niche providers could take a more dominant position because they were nearer to market pricing expectations and more in tune with the new buyers emerging in the market.

Structural issues specific to professional services markets

There are a number of issues which affect the structure of professional services markets that need to be considered in addition to the more generally recognised market factors. These yield unique insights into the dynamics of professional services markets and can facilitate competitive advantage.

Asymmetry of information

Professional services markets are structured around asymmetry of information: the fact that the supplier knows more than the buyer about the service. The market exists because the supplier has technical knowledge that the buyer needs to pay for. The value of this knowledge, the price the professional can charge, depends on the scarcity of the skill, perceived quality and how critical the service is to the client. But superiority of knowledge also extends to knowledge of the industry and performance of service, both of which affect the nature and structure of the market.

Asymmetry of knowledge is at the heart of an unarticulated tussle between the buyer and the professional services provider. At the most simple this is reflected in the changing attitude of the general population in the developed economies to professionals over the past few decades. In the postwar period, there was a value and reverence for professionals, particularly medical practitioners, which has been eroded as society in general has become better educated. Buyers are much more willing to question professionals and get second opinions.

However, when buyers approach professional services markets for the first time, the very nature of these services gives them difficulty in buying because they lack knowledge of the various suppliers. As professional services are intangible and heterogeneous, buyers are unable to assess their quality and value by examining them in advance. This causes the buyer two risks: 'adverse selection' (they may choose a poor or expensive supplier) and 'moral hazard' (a term covering post-contract opportunism by dubious suppliers).

Professional services markets must therefore evolve mechanisms to induce trust and counter these problems. These include: regulation, personal reputation of principals, industry associations and the firm's reputation or brand. A buyer might gain information about future suppliers directly from industry sources or from discussions with contacts who have experience of the industry. In fact, research demonstrates that 'word of mouth' is transmitted through networks of buyers. The buying process itself might also mitigate the risks of this lack of knowledge. Many buyers use a selection process, asking firms to present their credentials and approach. During this, suppliers can explain their understanding of the problem and propose methods to tackle it. This will enhance the knowledge and the decision-making of the buyer.

The willingness of the client to pay different fee levels is also affected by this asymmetry of knowledge. If the buyer is unfamiliar with the industry and is confronted with a small number of elite suppliers, fees are likely to be high. If, however, the market contains a plethora of competing suppliers offering a familiar and easily understood process, prices are likely to drop and services commoditise.

As buyers become familiar with a sector of the professional services industry through repeat purchase, they become familiar with the individuals, processes and characteristics of competing firms. They then seek to get better value for money by cutting parts of the process, facilitating competition or doing some work themselves. The ultimate expression of this is the introduction of specialists into the buying process. They are more able to judge the nature of the technical skill offered and its value to the buyer's firm. When a human resources (HR) director buys training or recruitment, or when a marketing director buys research or advertising, or when a purchasing manager negotiates a formal contract, prices will tend to go down and quality up.

It is thus in the interests of professional services firms to maintain a degree of mystery and restraint about themselves and their approach. This has to be a balance. The suppliers need to give clues as to their quality while retaining their intellectual property and competitive advantage. They must maintain a degree of mystique about themselves and their processes. By guarding their publicity and controlling communications, they exploit the buyers' lack of knowledge (within ethical boundaries), thus maintaining a price differential. Brand is a device which does this for many firms. The fact that a partner is a member of a large, branded, professional service allows him or her to allude to industry knowledge or technical skill which would be questioned more closely if operating as a sole practitioner.

The leaders of a professional firm should ensure that research is conducted into this issue. Segmenting clients according to their insight into the industry can lead to an understanding of the basis of differential pricing.

The market as relationships or networks

Relationship marketing theory began to develop in the 1980s as the importance of human relationships in the buying process began to be understood. When this thinking was applied to business-to-business markets, research focused upon the interconnection of business relationships in a network. Researchers and theorists were beginning to substantiate the experience of professionals in developing profitable business-to-business relationships. Their work has covered the fact that, in a project-based industry, working relationships may only occur during the duration of a project, whereas personal relationships have to continue over time. They distinguished between 'bonds' between key participants, links over activities and ties over resources.

This is a behavioural view of markets. It sees a market primarily as a set of personal networks within which these mutually profitable business relationships occur. Professional services firms can therefore examine their markets by profiling these relationships and introducing methods to build on them – for example, by encouraging referrals. In fact, for business-to-business professionals, a market profile based on a relationship or network profile could yield better strategic insights than some of the more accepted economic approaches developed by marketing theorists. This is examined in more detail later in this chapter.

Means of gaining an objective market perspective

The market research study

A research project can be constructed to give insights into changes in the market, client needs and business opportunities. (Different research techniques are detailed in Part III). To be successful the study must be properly managed. An idealised process is outlined in Table 2.1.

Engagement of the leadership team at an early stage is essential to success. Leaders should be consulted before the project is started and be engaged in selection of interviewees. They are then more likely to support the insights revealed by the research and consequent actions. However, client research is only one aspect of market dynamics. Other forces, such as regulation or technological change, also affect the market. Limiting analysis to just field research will miss the potential insights from a broader analysis.

Table 2.1 *Marketing process tip: an idealised market research process.*

1. Agree objectives and research needs.
2. Write brief for agencies. Brief includes:
   - Research objectives
   - Summary description of the market
   - Description of the research problem and desired output
   - Description of existing knowledge and previous research
   - Budget constraints
   - Time scales
   - Report requirements
   - Constraints (e.g. interviews must be arranged via client relationship managers)
3. Shortlist agencies from industry directories.
4. Contact and invite to pitch.
5. Create selection criteria. These might include:
   - Technical skills
   - Previous experience
   - Interpretation of the brief
   - Proposed approach
   - Team fit (will the firm's people be able to work with them?)
6. Hold presentations by agencies to selection team.
7. Choose and confirm agency.
8. Negotiate contract.

The full market audit

A more thorough and objective way to gain an economic perspective on a market is to carry out a full market audit, as illustrated in Table 2.2. This is a concept pioneered largely by Professor Malcolm McDonald (McDonald, 2002). Properly conducted, it is as objective and thorough as a financial

Table 2.2 *Marketing process tip: conducting a full market audit.*

Step 1. Analysis of external forces affecting the market
This helps the firm to understand the macro-economic forces shaping its markets and which are creating or destroying opportunities within them. They include:
- Understanding the raw forces affecting the market. Changes in economics, social demography and technology affect the prosperity of the market, and there is little the firm can do to influence them.
- Understand 'moderating forces'. Politics, law and industry-specific regulation moderate the impact of raw forces on the market. These can be influenced by the firm.

By trawling through published data on these issues and drawing them into a perspective on change, surprisingly powerful insights can be found. They could, for instance, highlight an issue on which firms might need to lobby regulators.

Step 2. Understand market structure
- Proper market definition. Many companies miss opportunities because they think too narrowly. The market is 'shareholder assurance' not 'audit' or 'grooming' not 'hairdressing'.
- Plot the maturity of the market. A service must be managed differently at different phases of market evolution. The market will either be in development, growth, maturity or decline.
- Determine purchasing power. What is the balance of power between suppliers and buyers?
- Examine competition. Who are they and what are their tactics?
- Analyse substitutes. Can clients get the benefits of the service in any other way?

Step 3. Buyer analysis and research
This involves analysis of research into the needs and aspirations of existing and target clients. It is wise to start by collecting all published research and previously conducted research projects in order to identify gaps in knowledge. The team may then come to the conclusion that a market-based research study is needed. If so, this is likely to be the most costly and longest aspect of the audit, yet the most valuable.

Step 4. Internal analysis
This is about understanding the internal position of the firm within its market by detailed analysis of both the firm's own competencies and the profile of its clients. This includes the source of business, revenue and income trends and the potential for growth. This analysis can yield surprising insights. Some firms, for example, believe that their buyers are chief executives, when analysis shows them to be lower-level specialists. Others have been surprised to find that larger corporate accounts are less profitable than mid-market, smaller clients. Such insights can yield real benefit for the firm's approach to its market.

audit, and provides a firm basis for planning. The process can take between two and three months to complete.

Data about the market is gathered under key headings, using analytical techniques to tease out insights which can be the basis for strategic direction and competitive advantage. The information needed is surprisingly easy to obtain. There is a gold mine of valuable information within business libraries, professional institutes and government departments on almost any market in the world, and which can be obtained at relatively low cost. With the advent of the internet and search engines, the main cost is personal effort and time.

The market audit can be conducted by a specialist engaged by the firm or, with assistance, by a sensible, experienced employee. If the culture of the firm is resistant to an analysis of the market, and it is not prepared to spend time gathering data, the process can be run as an interactive session with the leadership team. A half- or one-day session, working through the various subject areas, in data-assisted discussions, is likely to yield insights which can improve the quality of subsequent strategic decisions.

Scenario planning

Scenario planning is another analytical tool. It helps firms to think about potential futures in the face of change, complexity and uncertainty. Less linear than the market audit, it allows management teams to explore likely scenarios. With its roots in the military and first developed for the business world as an integral tool in the strategy process of oil giant Shell, scenario planning creates a framework in which potential strategies can be developed and tested in the light of future uncertainties.

Scenarios can be thought of as stories which help managers to develop different potential futures based on both knowledge and people's assumptions about the present. They are not forecasts, but help provide a common language (Ringland, 1997).

Usually, a team comprising people from across the firm is formed to construct scenarios. In a session led by someone experienced in the process, the participants brainstorm potential futures for their firm. Input to their debate might include evidence from futurologists, client views and pertinent data. The team is normally encouraged to think widely before scenarios are grouped and ranked.

Strategic imperatives: determining priorities

This approach focuses on gaining a consensus among a team of leaders or by helping intuitive business leaders make issues explicit. It has natural appeal to professional services partnerships. Leaders brainstorm and discuss strategic challenges the firm faces. Identifying them is best done using some form of market-based stimulus, such as a research report or scenario planning session. Once identified, issues are ranked and the impact upon the firm discussed.

Porter's 'Five Forces'

This famous model for industry analysis, shown in Figure 2.4 and detailed in Part III, was developed by Michael Porter (Porter, 1979) based on his 'five forces'. These include: supplier power, buyer power, barriers to entry, threat of substitutes, and degree of rivalry. This is both a useful analytical and communications device.

The actors–activities–resources model (ARR)

Most professional services firms which think about the growth and health of their business have some form of relationship mapping approach to key

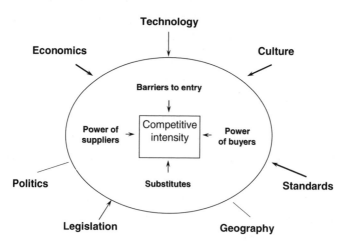

Figure 2.4 *Porter's perspective.*
Source: Porter (1979). Reprinted by permission of *Harvard Business Review*. From 'How competitive forces shape strategy' by M. Porter, March 1979. Copyright © 1979 by the Harvard Business School Publishing Corporation; all rights reserved.

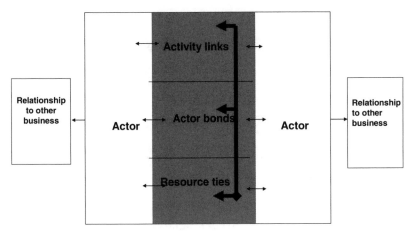

Figure 2.5 *The ARR model.*
Source: Hakansson and Snehota (1995)

clients. This model, developed by academics, substantiated in research and seen in Figure 2.5, formalises this thinking into a useful construct. The model divides business relationships into three levels: actor bonds, activity links and resource ties. It is explained in more detail in Part III but is a reasonably well-developed tool to plot, rate and understand the relationships a professional services firm has with its clients.

Opportunity analysis

The reason for undertaking an analysis of the market is to gain insights into new opportunities or to find justifications for closing down declining areas of business. It is then necessary to draw the analysis into an agreed view of the opportunities facing the firm to which resources need to be allocated. In this area, above all else, it is essential to combine such analysis with market insights and the experiential judgement of the leadership team. While a powerful perspective can be gained from informal discussion, there are a number of formal tools which can be used to structure thinking and debate. Used properly, they lead to a consensus and healthy perspective. Detailed further in Part III, they are:

- The 'SWOT' analysis.
- The Ansoff matrix.
- The directional policy matrix.

Figure 2.6 *SWOT analysis.*

The 'SWOT' analysis

The best known and most straightforward tool is the 'SWOT' analysis, which helps a firm identify internal strengths (S) and weaknesses (W) along with external opportunities (O) and threats (T) (Figure 2.6).

This information can be used to construct the SWOT matrix by plotting the opportunities and threats against the strengths and weaknesses. It can be done interactively, in discussion with the leadership team. However, it is more useful when it is used in conjunction with the market analysis for reference. A surprising number of management teams start out with a 'SWOT' brainstorming session and no analysis. If they have a distorted or mistaken perspective on their market, this is counterproductive, since it builds that entrenched view of competitive position into the firm's strategy.

For the more systematically minded, the 'TOWS' prioritisation system (see Part III) is very powerful. This enables the team to match opportunities with strengths and construct clear strategy in a systematic way.

The Ansoff matrix

Igor Ansoff (Ansoff, 1957) developed the matrix, represented in Figure 2.7 and described in detail in Part III, to help businesses examine both current and potential offers in current and potential markets. The matrix helps leaders think through four different growth strategies. They are presented below in ascending order of risk:

- Market penetration, or increasing market share with existing propositions to current markets.

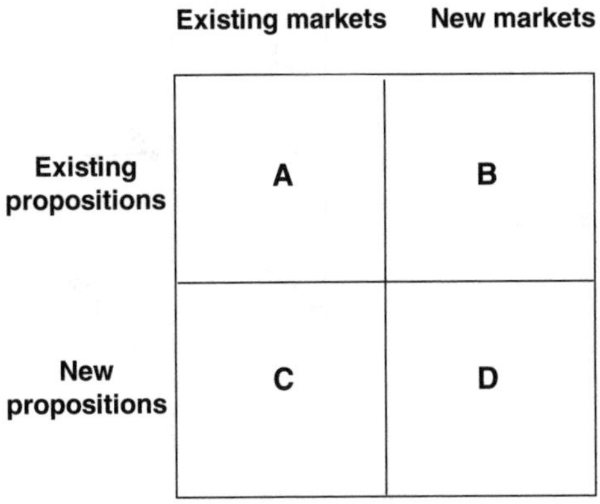

Existing markets   New markets

Existing propositions	A	B
New propositions	C	D

Figure 2.7 *The Ansoff matrix.*
Source: Ansoff (1957). Reprinted by permission of *Harvard Business Review*. From 'Strategies for diversification' by I. Ansoff, Sept/Oct 1957. Copyright © 1957 by the Harvard Business School Publishing Corporation; all rights reserved.

- Market extension, or targeting existing propositions at new markets.
- Product development, or developing new propositions for existing segments.
- Diversification, or growing new businesses with new propositions for new markets.

The matrix helps to clarify leaders' thinking and to illustrate the very different strategic approaches needed for each of the four strategies. Ideally, an operational marketing plan should be constructed for each strategic option approved.

The directional policy matrix

The directional policy matrix, developed by McKinsey for its client General Electric in the 1970s, is shown in Figure 2.8, and detailed in Part III. It helps the firm balance its strengths against the attractiveness of a market. The power of this particular technique is the ability to create criteria unique to the firm, which can form the basis for prioritisation. For example, it could be that a particular market offers potential growth, or that it contains clients willing to pay healthy fees, or the ease with which the firm can access it.

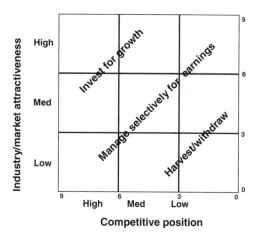

Figure 2.8 *The directional policy matrix.*

Russell Reynolds defines its markets

Russell Reynolds Associates is one of the five leading international executive search firms in the world. Founded in the latter half of the twentieth century (1969), it specialises in finding executives for the top jobs of leading companies. It has 31 offices around the world and more than 40 specialist practice areas.

Historically, the firm had grown by the creation of local geographic offices as teams in major cities established and developed client relationships. However, like other professional services firms, the partners found that clients tended to come back to search consultants who had expertise in their industry sector. Also, as searches became increasingly international, clients valued search consultants who knew their industry sector (and key individuals within it) more than a local geography. So they naturally grew specialisms in certain industry sectors such as 'investment banking', 'technology' and 'consumer products'.

Debate grew within the firm about how to prioritise opportunities and where to invest. How should the firm decide whether 'global telecommunications' had more potential than, say, 'consumer products' or geographies such as the newly liberated Eastern European markets? Where should the leadership team invest partners, staff and marketing programmes? What was the mechanism by which scarce resources would be allocated?

By the mid-1990s the firm had reached the point where it needed to reach a consensus on how to prioritise the approach to industry sectors. It decided to use the directional policy matrix as a tool to structure its thinking.

Understanding industry sectors

The first step was to define each industry sector, something which the firm hadn't done before. Partners were surprised by two things: the actual number of claimed industry specialisms and the difference in the understanding of what comprised such sectors. The discussion among the industry leaders in the firm revealed differences about which clients would belong to which sector. After debate, the group produced an agreed, defined list of the main sectors.

Lead partners then began to consider the criteria which made any of those markets attractive to them. The technique required the group to produce a clear, ranked and graded set of criteria. Again, this was a very useful debate because it helped to make explicit different assumptions made by partners about what made the markets attractive. The debate produced criteria about what made a market attractive to the firm, which had previously been unarticulated and diverse.

The final list included criteria such as 'potential growth', 'client size', 'ability to earn fees' and 'sector turbulence'. Once the criteria were agreed, each was then rated out of 10 to produce a prioritised list.

The next step was to decide what characteristics make a practice (whether belonging to Russell Reynolds or its competitors) strong in each of the markets. After debate, the final criteria included: 'brand strength', 'dominance in sector' and 'partner expertise'. As with market criteria, the final list was ranked out of 10.

Plotting each practice

The industry leaders then ranked each practice against those criteria. So, for example, the industry leader for investment banking (the firm's strongest practice) was asked to indicate how the practice stood against each of those criteria by giving marks out of 10. By multiplying each practice's score against the criteria score, a plot on a matrix was produced.

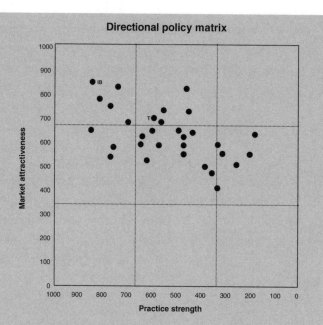

Figure 2.9 *Russell Reynolds Associates.*

Once all the practices were plotted, a final matrix, seen in Figure 2.9, was agreed.

The final matrix proved to be a useful basis for debate and decisions. Investment strategies were naturally discussed and agreed by the group. For instance, at the time, the technology practice was seen to be in a highly attractive market but it was weaker than investment banking. The group therefore decided to invest partners, staff and marketing programmes in it. Other, less attractive areas were denied funding or had resources depleted.

The power of the exercise was the use of the tool to generate debate among the leaders of the sectors and to reach consensus about investment strategy. As each practice was ranked, colleagues challenged their peers and reached a workable consensus.

These tools and techniques help create a framework to structure the leadership team's thinking about its markets by developing a common language, by testing assumption and by helping to reach consensus. Using these tools over a day or a period of months won't guarantee success or eliminate risk. But they will provide the basis for a more thoughtful and potentially lucrative approach to strategic market issues. They will also reduce risk and improve the quality of decision-making.

Summary

It is essential that the leaders of firms gain a thorough and objective view of the market, the competitive forces, and what opportunities (or dangers) it offers. This chapter has discussed a number of tools and techniques available to help firms do this. Used properly, they provide leaders with a deeper understanding of the market issues they have to deal with as a basis for decision-making. More importantly, perhaps, they do so by giving leaders a common language with which to debate and discuss.

3

Client segmentation

Overview

Segmentation is an important strategic issue for firms to resolve. It helps them to become more effective and more efficient. However, in a number of industries, including the professional services sector, the approach is often far too rudimentary and based on faulty analysis to make a real difference to performance. Good segmentation groups buyers according to their common, human needs. This chapter describes previous segmentation methods and gives detailed advice about how professional services firms should tackle this important source of competitive advantage.

The importance of segmentation

The segmentation of buyers into groups which can be easily reached by a firm is a powerful marketing concept which has improved the profit of many businesses. It suggests that buyers can be grouped around common needs. Then, by customising the firm's offer to meet these common needs, suppliers can both gain competitive advantage and save costs because they are only addressing a portion of the market. Periodically, as markets change or fragment, this becomes a major strategic issue which affects the way a supplier relates to its market.

Segmentation is a concept which is covered in almost every marketing course and text book but, unfortunately, it is often misunderstood. In addition, very few suggest *how* exactly to go about segmenting a market. Whereas there are clear and accepted processes to create, say, a balanced portfolio or to manage customer research, there are no accepted processes to identify effective customer segments. As a result, very few firms use a well-worked segmentation in their day-to-day marketing.

In addition, very few service marketing specialists have considered the unique issues involved in segmentation of service markets. The different approach needed to market service businesses gives new opportunities for segmentation, some of which are directly relevant to professional services firms.

Reprise of relevant segmentation concepts

Poor segmentation

In the past, excellent segmentation has been developed in some industries and has produced demonstrable competitive advantage for some suppliers. These have largely been manufacturers of fast moving consumer goods (FMCG) which have had marketing at the heart of their organisation for some considerable time. In other sectors, such as business-to-business suppliers, IT providers or services industries, segmentation is rudimentary, often wrong and largely ignored as a source of competitive advantage.

Some simply group their buyers around the products and services they have bought. But a 'small system' buyer might be a big buyer of other firms' products and may become a bigger buyer if approached in a more relevant way. Or a 'tax' client might be more profitable if a full advisory relationship is built. It is crass, sterile and ineffective to try to segment markets on the basis of product or service propositions.

It is also surprising how many organisations group their buyers according to size. Many companies still categorise their buyers as: global accounts, corporate business, small to medium enterprises (SME) and consumer. This is stunningly arrogant and displays off-handed disregard for both their own buyers and the subject of segmentation because it is virtually impossible to identify useful common needs from such a broad categorisation.

For example, grouping all businesses under a certain revenue level as 'SME' fails to recognise the different buying motivations of these businesses.

The growth rate, management talent and business strategy of small businesses are as diverse as the ideas they are built on. The needs of an IT startup with venture capital backing are very different than those of the local pharmacy, even if their initial revenues are similar.

Another example is the hugely profitable set of businesses which are family owned. These can range from a tiny corner shop up to major corporations. Each has similar issues to tackle (such as how to handle their professional managers and succession planning) which arise from their unique culture. An approach by a professional services firm, focusing on the size of services bought, is likely to miss opportunities in this field.

Industrial sectors are another frequently abused categorisation. Many professional services firms, of all shapes and sizes, have 'line of business' or 'industry' specialists who focus on an industrial sector, try to understand issues within it and customise the firm's offer to them. This is often an informal grouping of professionals across the firm who take an interest in an industrial sector. Frequently there is little investment or output of real significance to clients.

However, such a perspective can be limiting. For instance, industry sectors are breaking down as new technologies change categorisations. It is increasingly difficult to tell which company is in which industry sector. For example, some retailers are moving into banking, so are they now in the financial services sector? And, with the convergence of telecommunications and computing, exactly what sectors are internet retailers or publishing companies in?

Often, the definition of industrial sectors to handle these changes is so broad as to make it meaningless in terms of common issues. In addition, not all businesses within the same industry sector will have the same requirements. For example, a professional services firm trying to sell training, outsourcing or management consultancy might be better placed to identify 'innovative' companies receptive to new ideas. Yet this promising segment could be in any industry sector.

One of the main difficulties with current practice is not with these simplistic categorisations that may work for some suppliers. A far greater problem is with the analysis on which these are based. Most segmentation is based on data which is retrospective. Suppliers examine buyers' past purchases or previous social habits in attempts to create convenient groupings. This says a lot about where buyers have been but not their future buying intent. This is a risky way of setting the firm's direction; similar to driving along the road using only the rear view mirror for direction.

What is good segmentation?

Segmentation is the grouping of buyers by common, human needs. Whether the supplier is operating in the business-to-business or business-to-consumer environment, it is important to consider the characteristics of the people targeted. Good segmentation is the method which groups those buyers by their common needs, wants or aspirations, emphasising their humanity in a way which encourages them to respond to an offer. Properly done, it can be predictive, highlighting the future buying intent of the people in each group.

One word of warning, however: human beings are unpredictable, difficult and irrational. The academics write about segmentation as though the marketer is doing this to the market and manipulating the people involved. This is not something the company should do for administrative convenience. In the real world, markets segment themselves. Human beings tend to group naturally.

Previous segmentation types

There are many segmentation types which have been pioneered by firms and which have given them competitive advantage. They include:

Previous consumer segmentation types

(i) **Demographics and socioeconomics.** The grouping of people according to physical characteristics (age, sex) or circumstances (income, occupation or education). This is commonly used in developed nations. In the US and Europe, for example, there is currently much emphasis on the design of product and marketing programmes for the ageing population.

(ii) **Psychographics.** The grouping of people according to various personal characteristics such as personality or social class. In 1981, for instance, the 'British National Readership Survey' categorised the population as 'A' (higher marginal), 'B' (middle class), 'C' (lower middle class) and 'D' (working class). Fortunately, this is now completely breaking down.

(iii) **Context.** Proposed by Dr Paul Fifield in the early 1990s (Fifield, 1992), this method groups customers according to the context in which they use a product or service. It focuses attention on things that bring people together, exploiting shared interests. For instance, one cursory glance at people on a fishing bank will show that they have little in common other than the sport itself.

(iv) **Geographic/location.** Grouping people according to their country of birth or area of residence. This can focus on the region, population density and climate. It can involve county, town or even street.

(v) **Life stage.** This is a more precise form of demographics and groups buyers according to the phase they have reached in their life such as 'married', 'home building' or 'retired'. They might become 'freedom seekers', 'dropouts' or 'traditionalists' according to their phase of life.

(vi) **'Tribal'.** Grouping customers according to the social groups or cultures with which they identify. For example, in the early 1990s one of Europe's premier television companies started to commission programmes for tribes in society (such as young, independent women) based on how they communicate and live.

(vii) **Behavioural or attitudinal.** Grouping according to a particular behaviour which may affect product usage or price sensitivity, or values and attitudes. A good example of attitudinal segmentation was created by the direct marketing agency McCann-Erickson. It identified: 'avant guardians' (concerned with change and well-being), 'pontificators' (who have strongly held traditional views) and 'self-exploiters' (who have high self-esteem).

(viii) **Benefits sought.** The grouping of people according to the advantages they are seeking from the product or service. For instance, as early as 1968, Russell Haley (Haley, 1968) published a segmentation for the toothpaste market based on this approach. Customers were in the 'sensory' segment (seeking flavour or product appearance) or the 'sociable' segment (seeking brightness of teeth) or the 'worriers' (seeking decay prevention).

(ix) **Lifestyle.** Grouping customers by a common approach to life. One famous example of this type of segmentation was developed by Young &

Rubicam in the 1980s. It was this advertising agency which developed, among others, the famous, but now defunct, term 'Yuppie'. Incidentally, this also illustrates an important point about customer segmentation: it dates easily. Whereas people revelled in being a Yuppie in the early 1980s, it is now considered out of date and unattractive.

Previous business-to-business segmentation types

(i) Industry sector. Grouping businesses according to the industry in which they specialise. These sectors are often formally set by government economists as a means of defining and recording activities in different areas of the economy.

(ii) Context. As with consumers, grouping businesses according to the context in which they use the product or service.

(iii) Organisation style. Grouping businesses according to the culture or prevailing climate of the company. They may be centralised or decentralised or 'innovative' versus 'conservative'. The Myers Briggs organisational types ('fraternal', 'collegial', 'bureaucratic' or 'entrepreneurial') have, for example, been used as a basis for segmentation.

(iv) Organisational size. Grouping businesses according to the number of employees, assets or revenue.

(v) Company life cycle. Companies, like products, have a 'life cycle' through which they evolve. They go from birth to death at different rates, struggling to get through 'inflection points' to increase revenue and margin. They have similar characteristics (e.g. management style) in each phase and this has been used as a basis for segmentation.

(vi) Industry maturity. Industries also move through different phases. For instance, in developed economies, their agricultural or manufacturing industries are at a different phase of evolution compared to, say, biotechnology. The phase of growth affects the behaviour of suppliers in it and has also been used as a basis for segmentation.

(vii) Needs/benefits based. This is based on underlying needs or benefits sought by the company from its suppliers.

Segmentation of individuals at work

Straddling between the two types of segmentation are firms which have attempted to segment people at work. There is, for example, the 'bully' (who tries to dominate), the 'exploder' (who blows up over trivial detail) and the 'wet blanket' (who contributes little and expects the worse). This type of segmentation has teased out the emotional characteristics of people at work that affect purchase decisions. For instance, there are open-minded suppliers who delight in new ideas and play a role in bringing them into a company. Such a manager is likely to be an ideal target for the professional services firm prioritising training or consultancy in the latest new idea.

Tests of effective segmentation

Each of these previous segmentation types has advantages and disadvantages. Clear tests have therefore been developed to check whether a particular segmentation is appropriate for a particular company in a particular market. They include:

- **Homogeneity:** how far will the members of the segment act in the same way?
- **Measurability:** how big and valuable is the segment?
- **Accessibility:** is it possible to reach the segment with marketing or business development programmes?
- **Profitability:** is the segment substantial enough for the supplier to make profit from?
- **Attractiveness or relevance:** is the segment something customers will want to identify with?

The last point is particularly powerful. If the target group can be expanded by people who aspire to belong, demand for the proposition will be increased.

Segmentation issues specific to service markets

As services are different from products, there are various issues specifically involved in marketing services which may be used as a basis for segmentation. These include:

The new and the experienced client

One of the major differences between the purchase of a product and the experience of a service is the process through which the buyer moves. When someone buys a product, they are in control of it. They can do whatever they like with it. They can break it, give it away, or ignore the instructions. However, when they use a service they must submit themselves to the service provider's process. In doing this they cede control of themselves to the service provider. And human beings hate being out of control.

As a result of this, new clients, using a service for the first time, become anxious and look for reassurance. Reassurance can come from the reputation or brand of the firm providing the service, the simplicity of the service process or the behaviour of people who are part of it.

The strategy for providing good service to new, inexperienced clients therefore includes:

- A clear corporate brand strategy.
- Careful management of the behaviour of people.
- Simple process design.

However, once the client has experienced the service process a few times the situation alters altogether. Experienced clients try to take short cuts and try to improve on the service supplier's process. Their emotional dislike of being out of control drives this need (Bateson et al., 1999).

The demands of frequent business flyers show how different the values and expectations of the experienced service user are. Service for experienced clients is more likely to be about streamlined processes or even self-service. The secret to excellent service is to allow them to do more, rather than to perform the service for them. For the client this is better service and for the supplier it reduces costs.

The strategy for providing good service to experienced clients is therefore:

- Self-service.
- Special treatment.

- Streamlined process.
- Use of technology.

Services for experienced clients are beginning to evolve in the professional services sector. Many leading firms have, for example, dedicated extranets for clients. Through these they are taking the first tentative steps towards a self-service model for professional buyers. The first firms to succeed will grasp substantial market share.

High tech, high touch

Some people prefer a service which is 'high touch' because they like contact with people. They gravitate towards services which are highly customised and use human beings as part of the service offer. Often they are attracted by the fact that the people involved give them high status during the service. Higher end management consultancy is an example of this.

Other people prefer a technology-based service. They like to use technology or tools to investigate and deliver their needs. They are self-reliant and prefer to meet their own needs.

Cultural expectations

Chapter 6 explores the issues involved in international marketing and the impact of cultural differences. These differences straddle geographic boundaries and can be used as a form of segmentation. A professional service targeted at Germanic or Hispanic communities will, for example, have a wider audience than just Germany or Spain.

Mind sets

Customers have different 'mind sets' when they approach a service. Their attitude will be different if they regard it as 'day-to-day use' or 'an emergency'. Some people, for instance, regard a taxi service as a normal part of their day-to-day life. Others use it only in dire need, when other modes of transportation have let them down.

Valarie Zeithami (Zeithami *et al.*, 1990) suggested that one basis of segmentation is compatibility between segments due to the fact that service is often delivered in the same environment. People have different styles they prefer from services. Some like an elegant restaurant and others a noisy, fast bar.

Willingness/ability to cooperate in getting service

Some people are pleased to share the service task and to participate in the service process. Others are not. Some might diagnose faults themselves, while others regard it as a performed service that saves their time.

Each of these differences means that segmentation for service companies can be based on issues unique to service marketing. Service marketing professionals therefore have powerful extra tools by which they can create competitive advantage for their employers.

The benefits of segmentation

There are enormous benefits in conducting a proper segmentation programme and working through a careful investment strategy.

(i) Cost effectiveness. By targeting only a clearly defined group, the supplier keeps costs low.

(ii) Better communication and marketing. It establishes channels of communications which reduce the risk of failure in marketing programmes or new propositions.

(iii) New services. Segmentation aids the creation of a unique value proposition because suppliers get to know a group of buyers in depth.

(iv) Competitive advantage. Segmentation also builds barriers to entry for other competitors. They find it hard to copy this approach because they lack the in-depth knowledge of the target group.

(v) Increased profit. Good segmentation should increase market penetration at the same time as reducing marketing costs.

Table 3.1 *Suggested evolution of buyer management.*

1850–1930	Mass marketing	Standardised products
1930–1990	Market segmentation	Differentiated products
1990+	Relationship marketing	Differentiated products/individualised service
2000+	Adaptive marketing	Individualised products and continual improvement

Source: Rust *et al.* (1996)

Customer relationship management (CRM) as a challenge to the segmentation concept

Some marketing thinkers are suggesting that segmentation is a concept which has been superseded by technology. Their view is that it is impossible to group modern consumers because they are so individual. They combine this with two advances in management thought: the concept of relationship marketing and the ability of properly deployed technology to learn individual buyer requirements. Some suggest that there is a new phase of marketing history, as shown in Table 3.1.

But this relatively new thinking has yet to be proven in the reality of the market place. At the time of writing, for example, many firms are reporting failures in CRM implementation. There will undoubtedly be companies that gain advantage by using technology to offer highly tailored offers, but this is nothing new. There have always been industries which have taken this approach at the high end of the market (tailored clothing, custom cars or personal banking). What is happening is that technology is allowing customisation to move down market. But how far will this undermine the need to segment? There are a number of reasons to believe it may not:

(i) **The need to create a clear proposition.** In any market, in any part of the world, suppliers earn profit by making a proposition (service or product) to buyers. Often this is something the buyers had not realised they needed. It may be that the proposition needs to be customised or adapted, but a clear proposition, at a price, is essential, and this proposition cannot be assembled without a group of people in mind.

(ii) **Human nature.** People like to belong. In a frightening and fast changing world, brand allegiance gives warmth, familiarity and reassurance. There will always be suppliers who will make profit in this way. People also like privacy. Some will eventually react against what they consider to be the intrusive information gathering techniques behind some of these approaches.

(iii) Capability to handle technological evolution. It is apparent that data mining techniques are beginning to make available a vast array of buying data. In some industries (such as telecommunications) these can be combined with operational technologies (for example, intelligent network services) to make highly customised offers. However, in many industries it will be some time before either the technology or the firm is in a robust position to manage a customised offer to each buyer.

(iv) The robustness of the relationship marketing and loyalty concepts. These concepts are both relatively new and may turn out to be insubstantial management fads or to need adaptation if forming part of long-term managerial processes. For instance, there is clear evidence that customers are 'loyal' to brands. However, they can be stunningly disloyal in other circumstances. Satisfied or even 'delighted' customers will buy from competitors if they get a better offer.

A method of segmentation

Each firm has its own culture and its own unique market position. In order to gain real competitive advantage it should develop its own segmentation to take advantage of this and differentiate itself.

It is more important to use a process to create a unique segmentation than to steal a previously designed segmentation type. The process in Table 3.2 has been drawn from the academic community and tested in the reality of several projects, conducted in service marketing environments, over the past years. It has produced, for the firms involved, a practical method of segmentation which has given them competitive advantage through a unique approach to their customers.

Table 3.2 *Marketing process tip: a method of segmentation.*

Step 1 – Review all known segmentation methods. A group of experienced leaders should be drawn together to discuss segmentation as a subject and the types previously created, their benefits and drawbacks.

Step 2 – Create an hypothesis. In discussion the team will create an idea of how they think their market might segment. They will need to think about their own clients and how they behave. They may also have to examine market research or industry reports to get to the heart of this. In particular, they will need to discuss different attitudes or behaviours that they have observed. Eventually they will reach an idea of which previous segmentation type best fits their clients in their market and how it has to be adapted. In doing this they are creating a hypothesis which can be tested.

Step 3 – Create segmentation dimensions. Segmentation dimensions represent the ways in which the clients will behave towards the firms and its services. As far as possible these segmentation dimensions should be values, beliefs or cultural biases (whether consumer or organisational) because they determine behaviour. If the segmentation is effective, each client group will manifest these in different ways.

For example, if a supplier was segmenting a business-to-business market on the basis of 'organisation style', they might hypothesise that there are centralised and decentralised organisations. This would manifest itself in different business practices, one of which would be purchasing style and this would become a 'segmentation dimension'.

For a centralised organisation buying would be controlled by a central purchasing department, whereas in a decentralised organisation it would be devolved to business units or local countries.

Other dimensions might be: stability of board, planning style, attitude to technology and geographic scope. Through discussion the team should create a set of segmentation dimensions by which these differences will manifest themselves. These can then be scaled using sensible scoring of the extremes.

Step 4 – Test 1: Use existing client data to test the segment dimensions. By examining existing clients and scoring their behaviour against segmentation dimensions, it is possible to conduct a fast, inexpensive test, on the validity of the dimensions and where different clusters appear. If no clustering appears in this first test, then new dimensions, or maybe a new hypothesis, need to be created.

Step 5 – Test 2: Research. Having identified the segmentation and its dimensions, and having tested it on a few existing clients, the clustering should then be confirmed with direct research. This is best conducted in two phases: first, a qualitative phase, testing the dimension in depth; second, a large quantitative project using a 'trade-off technique' such as conjoint analysis (see Part III). Through this method different clusters of client groups will become evident. Again, if clustering does not appear the team should revisit its initial hypothesis.

Step 6 – Test 3: Test marketing programmes. Research itself is not sufficient to confirm such an important subject as segmentation. Potential segments need to be confirmed in a more practical way, imitating as far as possible the rough and tumble of the real market place. A number of test marketing programmes should be designed in order to ensure that the clients identify with the proposed groups that they are in and respond to propositions specifically designed for them.

Table 3.2 *Continued*

Step 7 – Create a full investment and communications programme. Implementation of segmentation involves changes to: market proposition for each group, client service methods for each group, method of marketing communication, sales strategy, IT systems, operational processes and pricing. Taken seriously, it is a fundamental change in the way the firm approaches its market place.

In a large organisation this could take up to four years to implement properly and incur huge costs. Each of these aspects therefore needs to be defined and costed, with appropriate budgets set up. In addition, a clear positioning strategy needs to be developed which states clearly how the firm will be perceived by each client group.

Step 8 – Gain approval for the investment. This needs to be treated like any other hard-headed investment strategy. The pros and cons, benefits and return on investment need to be assessed and drawn together into a business plan, which should be submitted to the leadership team for formal approval.

Step 9 – Implementation. This involves not only setting up the processes to engage with clients in a new way, it also involves full internal communication. Everyone in the organization will eventually need to be familiar with the new segments and how they should be handled.

Case study: Unisys

In the early 1990s, computer manufacturer Unisys, which now derives 80% of its revenues from IT services, was primarily a hardware vendor and wanted to derive more income from its IT services organisation. It was already serving large corporate organisations by offering support mainly on its own products, such as ClearPath servers. Its service was high quality and it invested heavily in processes, people and technology to improve it still further. However, the large organisations that it served (such as banking and telecommunications companies) were big bureaucracies. The IT departments of those companies were filled with people who were experts in computing. Some were so expert that they understood the supplier's hardware and software as well as the supplier itself. As a result the service support was seen as a commodity and these customers were often challenging the support provided, arguing over value and price. Using the method outlined above, the supplier segmented its market by organisational shape (Figure 3.1).

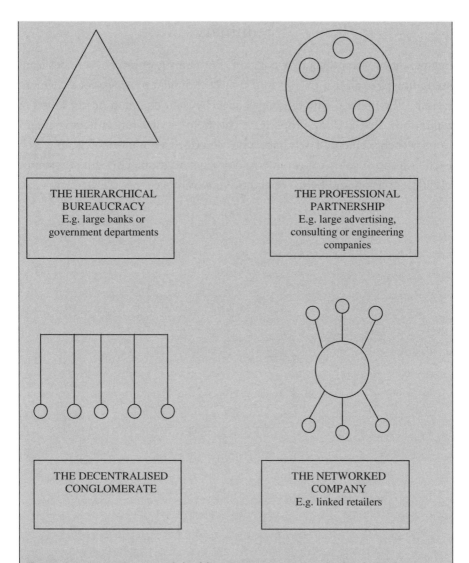

Figure 3.1 *A representation of the different organisation types developed in a business-to-business segmentation.*
Source: Unisys

The company decided to target professional organisations because often their IT people had similar needs as large organisations but few resources. They were able to reconfigure services and offer them at a different price to new buyers.

Summary

Segmentation is hardly a new concept. But many professional services firms are failing to exploit it except in the most rudimentary way. Good segmentation is the method which groups buyers by their common needs, wants or aspirations. If it is done properly, it can help predict future buying intentions of each segment. This chapter has described a framework within which each firm can develop its own method of segmentation. This will be a source of differentiation and hence competitive advantage.

4

Creating and managing a professional services brand

Overview

Brands, whether they are the products a company offers, the service it provides, and/or the name of the organisation itself, are the most enduring, yet often least tangible, assets a company possesses. Managed carefully, brands can be the basis of a firm's sustainable competitive advantage by building strong, profitable bonds with loyal buyers. For services, this means creating a branded proposition that stands out from the crowd and consistently delivers what it promises. However, professional services firms have, on the whole, failed to get to grips with strategic brand management. This is in part because of the nature of service itself, where every employee has to embody the brand values. However, with the right visionary leadership and political will, firms can manage the branded proposition in such a way that it gives a clear direction to everyone involved. This chapter shows how to develop a successful brand management programme, from understanding the strategic issues through to design, communications and measurement.

The power of brands

A brand is an entity that engenders an emotional response from a group of human beings so that they pay more than they probably should for the purely physical or rational components on offer. It is a changing, multifaceted entity which creates a variety of impressions in the minds of different human beings through many different stimuli.

As the respected advertiser Jeremy Bullmore, a director of marketing services group WPP, said in the British Brands group annual lecture in December 2001: 'Brands are fiendishly complicated, elusive, slippery, half-real/half-virtual things. When chief executives try to think about them, their brains hurt.' A brand is also a very valuable intangible asset comprising the goodwill of buyers and nurturing their future buying intent. Or, as Tim Ambler of London Business School has argued, it is 'the future cash flow of the business' (Ambler, 2003).

Brands are among the most valuable and powerful business propositions for which the marketing community has been responsible. They differentiate an offer from competitors, they create a price premium, they enhance margins and encourage buyer loyalty. Moreover, their effect is enduring. There are several brands in existence today that were created over a hundred years ago.

Effective brand management is more common in the consumer goods sector than in professional services firms. Yet professional services brands such as 'McKinsey', 'Deloitte', 'Bain' and 'Clifford Chance' earn enormous value for their owners. They affect the price of every job the firm undertakes in every part of the world. They set expectations of quality and communicate subliminal messages of the firm's *raison d'être*. They are the firm's major intangible asset and should therefore be one of the prime strategic issues for professional services firms to address.

It is surprising, therefore, that brand management is not more generally recognised to be the powerful tool that it is. It has certainly had more impact on profit than many things attempted over the past 20 years by different management teams. During that time companies have reached for changing management fashions (such as 'total quality management', 'process re-engineering' or 'globalisation') as a means to create profit. It is astonishing that more firms have not invested resources and attention into this proven and enduring approach.

One reason for this is that brand work involves such a wide spectrum of activities. At one end, creative companies help to design new images or new names. These projects attract public attention and, sometimes, criticism or even ridicule. At the other end, journalists like Naomi Klein (Klein, 2000) have challenged the ethics and integrity behind brand building. They have suggested that brands exploit workers and trick buyers, causing them to pay more than they should for the goods on offer. Moreover, the range of experts operating in the field of brand management proliferates by the day. In addition to professional brand managers in large corporations, there are strategists, design consultants and valuation specialists.

Despite the disparity of work, it is beyond dispute that a carefully designed image rests in the memory of buyers and helps them to choose products and services. Numerous firms have proved that, by managing that image carefully, a product or a service will appeal time and time again to a group of interested buyers. It becomes a familiar part of their life, giving them consistent benefits in their day-to-day activities.

As a result, they will pay a premium for this offer and develop a loyalty towards it. Over time, they become fond of these entities and, if they think about it, regard them as part of the landscape of their life. What starts as simple reassurance about quality or consistency becomes, on a deeper but hard to measure level, an emotional bond in a hectic modern lifestyle of constant pressure and change.

Consequently, there are people who feel warmth towards a tin of paint, a sugar-filled drink and sports shoes. In fact, these items mean so much to them that they can be as upset and unforgiving if they think a favourite brand has been damaged, as when a favourite soap character is killed off. This simple, yet hard to manage, strategy has created enormous wealth over the past century for both product and service companies with either a consumer or business emphasis.

Yet it is hard for inexperienced firms to identify and manage all the components of an effective brand programme. As a result, many companies have ignored, to their detriment, the precious role that brands can play in the life of both companies and buyers. It is therefore possible that professional services firms might miss a very powerful, proven source of enhanced profit.

A reprise of relevant brand concepts

Brand integrity

The concept of brand integrity is the basis of the success of all brands. It means that the promise and expectations created for buyers by the brand name is always delivered when they use the product or service. Consistent delivery of an offer is the fundamental principle from which brands originated. In pre-consumer times, at the start of the industrial revolution, most buyers could not rely on purchases of any kind to be consistent, reliable or safe. As in the undeveloped world today, a brand thus gave a much-needed promise of quality and delivery. An advertisement from the *London Illustrated News* of 1880 for Pears soap refers to the fact that the company had then been offering the product to the London market for over 100 years. (It is still a healthy brand today.) The key claim of the advertisement is not based on differentiation, nor is it focused on identification with aspirations or health issues. It is about consistency. It has been an 'honest' product.

So, successful brands have to deliver the promised function of the product or service, time after time. Many of the enduring brands became market leaders through consistent delivery to the expectations of buyers. Admittedly, expectations change over time and there is a need to keep pace. For instance, some food products reduced their sugar content dramatically in the last half of the twentieth century. However, this has happened step by step as consumers' tastes have changed, moving in line with expectations so as not to lose the precious brand franchise.

Consistency of delivery is also important for service brands. For a service brand to be successful and flourish, it is essential that the promises of the advertising and the expectations raised by promotion are properly reflected in the service experience. This means that the cocktail of service components (the way people behave, the process through which the clients move, the environment in which the service is experienced and the technology deployed) must embody the brand promise. Moreover, this must happen every single time that people experience the service process. This is probably the most challenging and difficult aspect of marketing experienced by any specialist in the field, for two main reasons.

First, the delivery of all services is unpredictable and variable. It is hard enough to translate research insights into product propositions. It can also be difficult to communicate the essence of a brief to design agencies and production people in order to create or change a physical product. Once done, however, the factory can normally continue to produce the product proposition without difficulty.

It is much harder to ensure that a service delivers the promise time and time again. While many mass services (in the airline, fast food and car hire industries, for example) achieve this, there is even greater complexity for professional services firms because they comprise sophisticated employees who do not wear uniforms or adopt any of the behaviours of mass services. The firm has to understand the common values that its professionals employ in their work and embed them in the design of the brand.

The second reason is scope and responsibility. Service delivery is the responsibility of the operations side of the business. Marketing or brand specialists are rarely given the power to affect these operations directly. They must therefore work through influence to achieve the desired experience for clients.

In short, specifying, designing and managing consistent service to meet a brand position is both very important, because brand integrity rests in the service experience, and very difficult, because the people who deliver the service and the environment in which the service is experienced must match the communications to the market. It is much more than designing a corporate logo, a 'strapline' or choosing a snappy name. Brand specialists have to focus on attitudes, principles and values that run through the organisation and which clients experience.

In fact, it is normally best to start by understanding what clients experience on a day-to-day basis and engineer that back into the communication to the market about the brand proposition. All of the components of the service must be integrated in one programme in order to reinforce the brand claim.

Fame

A phenomenon of modern society is the cult of fame. Actors, musicians, singers, politicians and even criminals are admired and followed for their recognition as much as for their particular skill. Some are even famous for little more than continual appearance in the media: famous for being famous. Alongside favourite TV shows and magazines, these celebrities become a familiar part of everyday life. They are intriguing, beguiling and incredibly valuable as a result. People feel a sense of warmth and interest in them. They tend to follow their own package of celebrity, magazine, style and soap opera.

Brands also occupy this arena. Their fame and their familiarity to different groups of buyers is part of their success. In the same way that a consumer might buy Burberry and be a fan of Tom Cruise, a business buyer might buy Pink's shirts, read the *Economist* and choose McKinsey. The wide knowledge in the general population of what these brands stand for enhances their appeal to those that buy them.

Often politely called 'awareness', fame is, then, a major ingredient in the success of brands. Firms that have been successful in exploiting this phenomenon have invested, over years, in marketing programmes aimed at improving awareness, or recall, in the minds of a wide range of people. These might comprise a range of activities from 'brand awareness advertising', through product placement in feature films to high profile sponsorship. All are aimed at the very simple objective of helping both the potential buyers, and the larger population, to remember the brand and to aspire to have its benefits. In fact, research suggests that sales and revenue decline over time, as memory fades, when these programmes are stopped or paused in difficult times.

Aspiration is also an important aspect of the fame phenomenon. People mimic their favourite film stars or sports heroes because they want to be associated with the success represented by their lifestyles. This is often subliminal, but nevertheless very powerful. A young woman styling her hair like Jennifer Aniston or teenagers dressing like British soccer star David Beckham are all associating with perceived success, and buy associated merchandise as a result.

This extends into professional services. Sometimes the choice of a well-known professional brand is a badge of honour. A particular hairdresser or counsellor might be *de rigour* in certain social circles of London or New York; just as a leading law firm or the latest management guru is the natural choice in some management circles. Both have normally achieved recognition from a combination of publicity and word of mouth.

Association with fame is also evident in business-to-business services. The leader of a modestly sized business who wants a Big Four firm as their accountant, the director who stands on an awards platform with a well-known academic guru and the chief executive who basks in the glory of the latest acquisition led by one of the big merchant banks, are all reflecting this phenomenon to a certain extent. Even at the very highest levels fame, or brand awareness, plays its part. A chief executive might choose a professional services supplier because they trust an individual in it as a result of a long and healthy business relationship. However, they may regard the quality of the firm's brand as a mechanism to legitimise the decision, communicating to their staff that their enterprise will receive quality work.

The creation, maintenance and exploitation of brand awareness is, therefore, a key component of brand strategy.

Brand essence or personality

Each brand has a simple truth or essence which it leaves in the mind of its target buyers. This is a promise that creates expectation and demand. For example, the essence of the Disney brand might be 'childhood magic', whereas the essence of an accountancy brand might be 'financial rigour'. In clarifying this brand essence, the firm seeks to understand the fundamental truth about the firm's promise to the client and to build its presence in the market around this truth. This is sometimes called the brand message, the main idea communicated to the market about the whole firm which creates a reason to buy. Over time, this brand essence develops depth and different aspects as buyers use it. It creates a brand 'personality', to which buyers relate.

Experience suggests that it is enormously difficult to create such sophisticated simplicity in professional services firms. Each professional in the firm sees levels of complexity in the promise of their business and seeks to have these included in its presentation to the market. Creating a simple, compelling idea which communicates the essence of the brand claim, but which is also a consensus of all the leading players in the firm, is therefore very hard. A lack of understanding of the huge value in producing such a claim often means that there is a lack of political capital to drive such a project through its formulation stages.

The concept of the 'corporate brand' and its importance
for service companies

One of the major differences between product and service marketing is the way in which a brand is managed, illustrated in Figure 4.1.

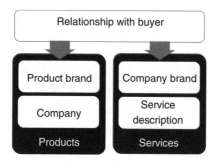

Figure 4.1 *Difference between product and service brands.*

A product company can create a brand entity which has its own presence in the market. When a brand is properly managed, buyers respond to the proposition, incorporating it into their purchase habits and returning again and again. The corporate entity behind the product proposition can be irrelevant to them. The dynamic with service brands is completely different, however, because the emotions engendered by the buying process are different.

Every service, from a mass consumer service to customised or sophisticated professional services, has a process through which the buyer moves. They must surrender themselves to the service provider, and this yielding of control creates anxiety (Bateson *et al.*, 1999). As a result of this anxiety, service buyers reach around the service proposition itself to seek emotional reassurance from the entity in charge (without being aware that they are doing so). Thus, the great service brands tend to be corporate brands.

This has implications for many aspects of brand development and naming strategy. For instance, a product company can organise itself so that brand management is handled by a division of specialists, sometimes under a director of brands. While being integral to the health of the company, it can be managed as one function within it. However, brand management for a service company is about dealing with the corporate brand, or the company itself. It therefore involves a different set of stakeholders, including the firm's leadership. Competitive positioning and brand essence involve the whole firm. Naming strategy is also different because service names have to be simple functional descriptors. (Business class from Virgin or American Airlines or audit from KPMG versus audit from Grant Thornton.)

QinetiQ builds its brand

QinetiQ is a defence research business, formerly backed by the UK government, which positions itself as a global advisor on defence and security technology. Previously called the Defence Evaluation and Research Agency (DERA), it became QinetiQ in 2001 when the UK government decided to put its defence laboratories on a commercial footing (see the case study in Chapter 9 on creating new services).

In February 2003 a 32% stake was sold to the Carlyle Group, a US private equity firm, to capitalise on QinetiQ's research and development expertise, with the British Ministry of Defence (MOD) retaining the principal shareholding. (A public flotation is intended when market conditions allow.)

Becoming a brand

This is part of a major transformation in how the company has defined its approach to its market since it was part-privatised. Before 2001, most marketing activity was sales led, with the marketing team involved in 'business development', trying to sell what the divisions offered.

But when the company was renamed QinetiQ, and hired its first marketing director, it began the transition to a brand- and marketing-led organisation. For the first time the focus would be on developing one corporate brand, rather than operating through a number of different brands.

Increasing brand awareness and understanding both externally and internally has been the major thrust of the marketing strategy of the last few years. Because what QinetiQ does is relatively unique, it has been putting a lot of effort into explaining to the outside world just what the company does and what the brand stands for in terms of its defence and security proposition.

The main challenge has been aligning the corporate culture with that external brand promise, since the company is not selling physical products but its people, knowledge, know-how and expertise. This has meant working to instil a more commercial mind set among the scientists while keeping them motivated to continue their leading edge research.

There are three ways the company has gone about this. The first is by improving the physical environment, in terms of the buildings and offices. Second, it has worked on enhancing the intellectual environment, making sure the experts are given ever more interesting and stimulating problems to solve. The third strand, which is the most difficult, is to create emotional engagement, which the company is encouraging in a variety of ways, including a share scheme.

The concept of financial brand value and brand equity

Historically, businesses focused upon their ownership of tangible assets (plant, buildings, IT, etc.). However, a trend over the past few decades, in parallel with the move from manufacturing to service dominance in the economies of most developed countries, has been the decline in the relative value of a number of these assets and the rise in importance of 'intangible assets' such as intellectual property. In fact, many businesses now consist mainly of intangible assets and it is very common that one of the most valuable intangible assets is their brand.

A brand's value or equity is based upon the response it commands from a group of people willing to buy. The emotional response it engenders causes them either to pay a premium price for the perceived benefits or to remain loyal to the brand (buying again and again) or, in fact, both.

David Aaker (Aaker, 2000) defines brand equity as the brand assets or liabilities linked to a brand's name and symbol that add to (or subtract from) a product or service. Those assets are brand awareness, perceived quality, brand associations and brand loyalty. This means that a brand is much more than simply a design concept or a name.

A brand's equity can be managed and improved in a similar way to other business assets. An indication of the hard financial implications of this is the fact that the accountancy profession has had to create methods of valuing intangible assets, including brands. Having its roots largely in mergers and acquisitions work, brand valuation is now used in calculations (or disputes) on tax, in licensing or royalty agreements, in trademark defence and in post-deal disputes.

In the past, marketers and strategists have found it hard to translate brand strategies into clear numeric data which wins the respect of senior management. Investment in many brand programmes, particularly corporate brand strategies, has therefore been based on little more than faith. As a result, worthy brand strategies have not received the investment they warranted and some non-brand literate companies have not even begun to venture down this path.

However, while there is still an element of judgement involved in these valuation techniques, it is now possible to estimate the likely success of different brand strategies and the likely future brand value based on those strategies. In other words, it is possible to put numbers behind brand strategy and calculate the likely return on investment (ROI). To do that it is essential to merge marketing and financial techniques in a profound way. Valuation and economic modelling can be merged with brand positioning tools to give a detailed, manageable route map for what is now one of the firm's most important areas of investment.

For example, using conjoint research (see Part III), it would be possible to understand the role that brand plays in a client's decision-making process when compared to a non-branded item. (A branded search company might compare itself against a boutique, a premier league law firm against an 'ambulance chaser' or a niche insolvency firm against a single practitioner). This would reveal the price premium of the firm's brand and its value in the work the firm undertakes.

A strategy might be agreed to increase this price premium by, say, 3% over three years using internal marketing, training, redesign and market promotion at a cost of, say, $10 million. By estimating the future value of the brand, a judgement on the return of this programme could be made. For instance, if a brand is estimated to be currently worth $80 million, and an investment of $10 million over three years increases the price of every single job the firm undertakes so that the brand is now worth $150 million, the investment pays back. (There is then, of course, a further discussion as to whether this $10 million could be better invested in another area to get a better return, by comparing the rate of return against other proposed investment projects.)

Some companies, from consumer goods through to utilities and oil companies, are already managing their brand in this hard, analytical way. Some formalise the ownership of the brand as a corporate asset, for which business unit managers must pay a royalty to use in their operational budgets. This creates a discipline throughout the firm which causes line managers to pay due regard to the management of this major asset. It can also be tax advantageous. Such an approach by professional services firms will increase margins and, in partnerships, partner returns. In the professional services industry, financial management of the brand is generally an unexploited strategy to increase the wealth of the firm's partners or the company's shareholders.

Brand issues unique to the professional services industry

Partners/'stars' and the brand

In a large partnership, employees work their way through their career, conducting client projects, until they 'make partner'. For many, this is a defining moment of their career. They are included in meetings and discussions that they did not know occurred before and they become part of an inner circle of colleagues. Reward is different but so too is responsibility. In many firms, one of the main characteristics of a partner is the ability to build a book of business and to win work.

As a result, after years of performing at this level, they will gain an external reputation for a specialist skill. At this point, the client weighs both the firm's reputation and the high quality or specialist skill of the partner when buying. In fact, part of the strength of the company brand becomes the leading partners in its offer. The brand of the firm and the reputation of key partners become inextricably linked.

It is dangerous, however, for the partner to discount the power of the firm's brand because of their relationship with business leaders, their experience of advising on major projects or their personal reputation. Some become so enamoured with their own position that they discount the support of the brand that grew them. In fact, there have been cases of partners leaving thriving firms to set up on their own and finding, too late, that their former firm's brand was a major part of their fee value. Some find that they are no longer on client short lists and many find that they are expected to charge a lower day rate.

There is thus a symbiotic link between the brand of a professional services firm and the reputation of key practitioners. A balance needs to be maintained. Individual practitioners should not be allowed to rise too far above the brand or to damage it by deviant behaviour. On the other hand, the firm's brand consists of the experience that clients receive from the partners more than the design concept or professed set of values. They must feel that it represents them. It is much more important that the presentations to the market represent their aspirations than some vague, esoteric whim of the leadership.

The brand in employee behaviour

Service marketing academics have, for some time, suggested that employees of a service business are a very important aspect of its approach to market. In many ways they are part of the service, part of the value that the client is buying. Their appearance, language and behaviour affect buyers' views of the firm and their willingness to buy again. If they disappoint or underperform, part of the value proposition of the service is destroyed. The living representation of a professional services brand is therefore the behaviour of employees towards clients. Their day-to-day activities in client work are, in fact, probably the most influential aspect of building a professional services brand.

Employees of the firm, whether partners or 'staff', therefore need to be the first focus of the brand manager or planner in a professional services firm. They need to be considered carefully in the design stage. When creating the brand position and brand values, designers should derive their work both from attitudes of employees and clients' perception of their values. Too often brand designers working for or in professional services firms start with a blank sheet of paper and build brand concepts around the leaderships' perceptions or aspirations ('quality', 'integrity', 'innovation'). If, however, these are not dominant attitudes and behaviours at the client interface, the brand will seem remote and irrelevant. It is better to start with a hard-headed audit of what is experienced by clients and make that the foundation of the strategy. Aspiration can be built on that.

Once a concept is created it should be tested on groups of employees to check that it is credible. Designed properly, this is an opportunity to unite the firm in a clear direction and motivate all the staff. Done badly, it will demotivate and undermine the credibility of the leadership. The design and strategy should be adjusted in the light of employee discussion groups and dialogue with clients.

Once the concept is finalised, a detailed launch and communications plan to employees should be constructed. This should be executed before it is launched to clients. If the firm has 1000 employees, there are more than 1000 opportunities every day for the brand to be communicated and, more importantly, demonstrated to clients. This, in turn, will affect client perception, causing them to buy again, develop relationships and refer to others. In short, it will increase revenue. An investment should therefore be made in a carefully crafted communications programme which is credible and sustained.

Adopting brand strategy and management

Political will and leadership vision

So why hasn't this powerful approach been more fully adopted by professional services firms? Bear in mind that all the famous branding exercises look good in retrospect. To take a non-professional services example, before Nike emerged as a leading sports brand, people bought gym shoes or sneakers. Teenagers (and their parents) would have been astounded to be told that they had to pay over $100 for a pair of running shoes and would wear them in a social context. Similarly, before Intel, microprocessors were just 'chips'. It took visionary leaders to invest in the development of those brands, to invest in brand strategies which turned a near commodity into a value proposition. The leaders of firms as diverse as Nike, Intel, Body Shop and Virgin had to put their personal political capital behind the risk of a commitment to brand (Joachimsthaler and Aaker, 1997).

The world of professional services is, however, generally very poor at investing in such strategies. Ironically, even the experts in this area, the advertising agencies, are woefully deficient when it comes to managing their own brands. Most professional services brands like Bain in management consulting, Farrer & Co. (solicitors to the British royal family), McKinsey and so on have evolved from years of quality work reinforced by repeat purchase.

The brand has emerged naturally from reputation rather than by strategic intent.

There is thus an opportunity in the industry as a whole to create distinction and differentiation through focused brand work. The problem is that large firms do not typically have the political commitment to radically alter the balance of power in their internal operations in order to achieve this longer-term benefit. They often have to be driven there by relentless market forces, going through traumatic management change en route. Smaller companies, for their part, can be daunted by the power of better known consumer brands like Coca-Cola or Nike. They forget that many successful brands (like Unilever, Virgin or Body Shop) were built from scratch by business leaders with very modest initial resources.

Whether brand success has resulted initially from vision (Mars) or luck (Virgin) or the ravages of the market (the car industry), the steps needed to succeed are well established. Truly adopting brand management involves both visionary leadership and a change of organisational emphasis. The brand, once created, should give direction to everyone in the business.

In order to thrive in the changing professional services market, firms of all sizes need to take a hard-headed look at brand management. This has been shown in different sectors of the world to produce real value over time and guard against the vagaries of the market. It is time that professional services firms became less supplier driven and learned to create true branded value propositions, just as many predecessors, some in the professional services industry, have done over the last century.

Steps in creating a brand

It is possible for professional services firms of any size to create a brand which clients prefer and pay a premium for over many years (Table 4.1). First, they

Table 4.1 *Marketing process tip: steps in creating a brand.*

1. Decide which client segments to serve.
2. Research: determine rational and emotional needs of clients. Also, understand employee views.
3. Create brand strategy, including: architecture, values and essence.
4. Create brand implementation programme: design framework, internal and external communications, financial rationale, measurement.

must decide which client groups they wish to focus upon and concentrate on those clients. This is hard because it means choosing not to serve certain other clients. Second, the rational and emotional needs of the clients must be understood in depth, together with the views of the firm's employees. Third, a brand strategy needs to be developed and a clear, unique proposition needs to be designed. Finally a brand implementation programme needs to be constructed and launched which will deliver consistent, reliable benefits over time.

Developing brand strategy and architecture

One of the main considerations of brand strategy is the architecture of the brand. This needs careful examination by specialists. It has the following components:

(i) A monolithic, master brand strategy or sub-brands strategy. In other sectors, companies have a range of different brands and sub-brands. However, as professional services brands are normally corporate brands, it is common for a firm to decide that it will invest in one major 'master brand'. This allows it to focus on the building of one intangible asset and to communicate that one entity through all points of contact with buyers. To succeed, all identity and communication pieces must reinforce the values and image of the master brand.

Some firms might consider branding particular services such as consultancy, or taxation advice, by trying to create easy-to-remember names. But this is normally a failure because of the emotional dynamic in buying services explained previously, where, because of the anxiety involved, buyers want to feel reassured by the entity behind them. However, a form of sub-branding that *is* open to professional services firms is to apply the brand to organisational groupings. A group of competing practices which might be described as 'KPMG Advice' or 'McKinsey Strategy' or 'IBM Business Insights' (all fictitious) signal different approaches to buyers. They each subliminally communicate a different 'flavour' in terms of the service offered based on the main brand's essence. So the brand architecture can reflect different organisational groups and their positioning.

(ii) Brand extension. A firm with an established brand might decide to extend its business into new areas by developing its brand franchise. By doing so it is saying that it is applying its established business approach, resources and skills to that new business opportunity. Product companies have been very successful at this. Cosmetics companies extend into ranges of products and confectioners into different types of chocolate bars and ice cream. Buyers seek a familiar taste in the new category of product. Many service companies have also succeeded at this. Companies like the Virgin Group, run by British entrepreneur Sir Richard Branson, have moved with their buyers from entertainment to airlines and trains.

It also happens in professional services. For example, accountancy firms did this in the last century when they decided to enter the mergers and acquisitions market. Their brands suggested that their analytical and financial approach to work would be applied to this field of business.

(iii) Positioning. Chapter 2 introduced a generic perceptual map of a market as an analytical tool (detailed further in Part III). Positioning tools are used to understand client values in a market and the franchise held by suppliers to the market. Such maps can be used by the leadership of the firm to position its brand in the market. They may, for instance, decide that one of the viable market positions is vacant. This might entail setting out to be 'premium' or least-cost provider in the market. They then need to construct a well-rounded brand programme to move the firm in that direction.

The design elements of a brand management programme

The success of a brand rests on the fact that it creates a shorthand in the minds of the clients. Crucial to this success is a clear and professionally managed design process. The elements of this includes the following:

(i) A colour scheme for the entire 'public face' of the organisation. This is not as straightforward as it sounds. A designer needs to be employed to create a colour scheme which reflects the mood and style that the firm's leaders want to achieve. For instance, a 200-year-old law firm may want a 'classic' style, whereas a high end search firm may want a premium quality image, or a management consultancy may want a modern, open-minded fresh approach.

Colour gives this subliminal message. A designer should first produce a palette of colours representative of a 'mood and style' which reflects the firm's objective. There is added complexity if the firm is international, because colour gives different subliminal messages to different cultures. For example, to British eyes pure white means freshness and cleanliness. To a Japanese eye, on the other hand, it is the colour of mourning. The firm must therefore take on board the subliminal message of the intended colour scheme and not just its aesthetic appeal.

(ii) Scope. The design scheme must cover all of the 'public face' of the firm in every physical manifestation of the firm's presence. This encompasses such things as: signs on buildings, design of client reception halls, letterheads, fax headers, business cards, invoice formats, email, presentation slide format, the website, proposal documents, report covers, conference appearances and so on. Some organisations even apply it to staff briefcases, PCs, Filofaxes, and other items regularly seen by clients. Large firms often have to undertake an extensive audit of all of the points of contact with their public and are frequently surprised by the extent of the project. A useful technique here is the 'contact audit' (see Part III) which ensures that all points of interface with clients are identified.

A designer needs to apply the colour scheme to representations (or 'mock-ups') of all these items. These must be tested in discussion with clients and employees to gauge their reactions to the design before finally being implemented. Some partners are hesitant to put unformed propositions about their own business to clients. However, experience suggests that clients are often willing to help a worthy supplier to find their way and the risk of launching an unpopular or negative design is worth the much lesser risk of imposing on a client's time a little.

(iii) Straplines. Very often a firm uses a strapline, which is a short statement intended to communicate the essence of the brand, to reinforce the thrust of its approach. For example, at the time of writing, PricewaterhouseCoopers (PwC) uses 'connected thinking', Goldman Sachs uses 'every catalyst elicits a reaction' in its annual report, and Morgan Stanley has 'one client at a time'. Such a strapline should reflect the brand essence. If the strapline and its claim isn't truly reflective of the firm's approach, then neither staff nor clients will see it as having any relevance and it will have no effect on the brand's asset value.

(iv) Linguistics. It is absolutely essential that any words associated with the brand or names are checked before implementation. This might seem to be common sense, but some firms fail to do it. The opportunity for mistakes in this area are legion. Choosing a name, for instance, where the web address (URL) is already owned by someone else, or means something obscene in a foreign language, happens more often than is usually admitted publicly. Choosing a strapline that will not translate into other cultures is also very common. Before the project is implemented all names should be trademarked, URLs tested, and translation into key cultures of the world undertaken.

(v) Ongoing management: the 'brand police'. Once the brand design is agreed and implemented across the firm, it is critical that someone in the organisation has the responsibility for ensuring brand compliance. Initially, this will be almost entirely about completing the implementation of the design project. It is a huge task to ensure that all contact points with clients in all parts of the firm are subject to the redesign. Once implemented, however, it is essential that someone is responsible for controlling the integrity of the design.

Professionals are creative, entrepreneurial and restless souls. There will always be a reason why they feel they need to adapt a colour, a piece of design or a strapline. This should be resisted at all costs as it undermines the subliminal message of the brand and damages the financial value of the asset. Even a slight change in Pantone colour will create an impression of confusion and diversity in a client's mind once a number of pieces of collateral are produced differently in different parts of the world. Corporate firms are normally disciplined about such policies but partnerships ought to control this closely as well. It could easily be added to legal and regulatory compliance requirements.

Current practice is to develop an internal website where all standards and materials, together with an explanation of the importance of compliance, are set out in full. Professionals across the firm can access and download materials from the site. This helps ensure that all aspects of brand design are produced in accordance with the overall design scheme. It is absolutely essential, however, that leaders at all levels of the firm reinforce this necessity. If they do not, they are damaging a valuable intangible asset of the firm and are being negligent.

Communication aspects of a brand management programme

One of the inhibitions that professional services often have about brand building and brand management is a wrong perception that these are based on advertising alone. In fact, several well-known and successful brands have been built without relying on expensive television advertising (Joachimsthaler and Aaker, 1997). There are several ways to communicate a brand promise to a market.

The first is through the experience of the service. If a firm has a particular style and approach in its work, it will cause a reputation to evolve through word of mouth which will, in turn, create its brand positioning. The primary way of building a professional services brand, then, is to manage internal marketing so that employees and partners are clear of the firm's position in the market and speak with a common voice to clients. Yet few professional services firms create a consensus around a succinct brand message, or 'elevator pitch', which all employees and partners understand and support.

One episode of the hugely popular television series 'West Wing' shows the US President's staff excited because the rival candidate was asked 'Why do you want to be President' in a debate and waffled meaningless, forgettable nonsense. This occurs daily in the professional service industry as sophisticated and consummate professionals stumble over opportunities to answer the question: 'What is your firm about?'

The second tool is public relations (PR) to enhance competitive reputation. There are good examples of brands built through PR and publicity. Companies which started with a modest budget have created a huge intangible asset in terms of their brands through targeted reputation management. This must be based on a measured and detailed knowledge of the competitive reputation in the mind of key clients. It should be designed to enhance and grow that natural reputation over years. The techniques might include media relations (proactive work with journalists and editors), sponsorship, and publicity.

The third tool, denied by law to many professionals until recently, is broadcast marketing communications: advertising consistent marketing messages in TV and radio. The latter can sometimes be more effective than the former. A sophisticated buyer listening to a jazz station in the car on the way home may be more influenced by this cheaper media than by a national press advertisement. This needs to be sophisticated and carefully planned communications which manages spend judiciously and targets closely the intended audience. In the very large firms this is very often a question of marshalling existing budgets and resources to give a consistent approach rather than new money.

Whatever the chosen method, the firm should ensure that regular funds are set aside to enhance its brand through building fame by direct communication to the market.

Deloitte designs its brand

Deloitte is a global professional services firm present in almost 150 countries and with 120000 people worldwide. The geographic member firms operate as separate, legal entities within the auspices of the global membership organisation Deloitte Touche Tohmatsu. Deloitte offers services in four main areas: audit, tax, consulting and financial advisory services. It had revenues in 2003 of around $15 billion.

The firm has developed into one of the 'Big Four' accountancy firms over the years through a series of mergers. Growth through merger had led to a proliferation of multiple logos and other brand characteristics over the years. In 2002, Mark Allatt was brought in as UK director of brand and image development, a new position, and was given a global project to begin the process of making the imagery more consistent in all of its manifestations across the local firm.

Redefining its approach

Initially, this consisted of refreshing the existing identity by eliminating many of the contradictions. However, a combination of circumstances led to a far more ambitious international brand redevelopment project. First, the firm decided, unlike its competitors, not to separate out its consulting business and instead to integrate it fully into the business. Second, there was a change of global leadership and a growing realisation that the firm had to be far more ambitious about explaining its position to the market, and do so within the context of a strong worldwide brand.

Having seen a number of possible alternatives, the leadership gave the go-ahead to the chosen approach in August 2003. They set a tight dead-line of October of the same year to begin the global roll-out. Such speed was possible because a lot of the thinking that had already gone on during the early phase was still relevant to the agreed approach. For example, a master brand strategy had been agreed, ensuring support throughout the firm to investment in one approach, with no sub-brands. The brand attributes were 'insightful, principled, inclusive, straightforward, multi-dimensional and leadership'.

The brief for the redesign was to be 'classic with a contemporary twist'. The classical elements included the long heritage of the firm, and the quality and integrity that stemmed from its origins in accountancy. The contemporary twist was to come from the firm's more modern advisory activities (for instance, the work being done in e-commerce and human capital) and drew its inspiration from the firm's new brand positioning. Central to the redesign has been the focus on the single word 'Deloitte'. There has also been an emphasis on the firm's ability to tackle clients' problems laterally, and from multiple perspectives, by drawing on the broad and deep range of skills it can offer.

The redesign has already had an impact on the firm, both externally and internally, as it is rolled out across the world. Externally, it has started to give Deloitte a single face in the market for the first time. It has also given it a strong base from which to refine its recognisable and distinc-tive 'voice'. The aim has been to make sure this voice is both explicit and implicit any time the firm communicates with its audiences.

Getting employees on board

Internally, the big challenge has been to have every single person in the firm embrace the brand philosophy. Allatt has described this as getting people to march to the same drumbeat in a bid for coherence rather than conformity. The rebranding itself has been instrumental in sending the right message, while relevant training has also been put in place.

The aim is to have everything, including the physical environment, reinforce the brand values and bring alive 'The Deloitte Difference'. This extends from the look of the buildings themselves, to the approach to exhibitions and events. It extends to the use of photography (of Deloitte's own staff working in the community and with its clients) rather than anonymous corporate art to hang on the walls and even to the flower arrangements.

This is all part of a much bigger shift in the understanding at Deloitte that, as markets become more complex and demanding, the brand is much more than a logo. It is an integral part of reputation management.

The tools used in brand management programmes

There are clear and well-developed tools used by experienced brand-oriented companies which make explicit the features of a brand which need to be managed or improved.

Brand attributes or brand values

It is possible to identify a number of 'attributes' or 'brand values' which resonate with potential buyers. These will be functional attributes (such as 'diagnoses', 'solves problems', 'advises') or characteristics which are judgements of value (such as 'integrity', 'quality', 'innovation' or 'excellence'). Some of these will be characteristics, called hygiene factors, that the firm must display in order to compete in the market. These might include the approach to projects, the approach to business or even technical skill.

For instance, in the current suspicious climate after the Enron and Andersen débâcle, it is tempting for surviving accountancy firms to emphasise their integrity. However, as demonstrated by the Andersen experience, that is an attribute necessary to compete in the market. It is something that the clients expect the firm to have in order to qualify for work. It is a hygiene factor.

Senior experienced buyers tend to take the same attitude to technical skills. They often regard the technical skills of high quality suppliers as identical because recruitment, resourcing and training approaches are very similar. A brand programme built on hygiene factors alone will create little added value and will, over time, contribute to a commoditisation of the firm's offer because it is emphasising issues which the client does not particularly value.

'Motivators', however, are brand values which are meaningful to clients. They might include soft factors such as 'generosity'; describing the tendency of a supplier to give insight and help which is not always charged but is part of a professional approach. On the other hand, they might be matters of style, such as the way relationships are conducted. Or it might be a particular approach, like the way merchant banks bring market insights or opportunities. Emphasis on these will, over time, differentiate the brand from competitors.

If this technique is to be successful, it is essential that the values are really experienced by the clients using the firm's service. If not, it will be merely a theoretical and meaningless corporate statement which is unconvincing to clients, partners or staff. The firm should use properly conducted diagnostic research techniques with each of these audiences to understand how the service can be crystallised into a few 'extant' brand values.

This is the reality of the firm's competitive reputation as experienced by clients. For every four or five real values the leadership might then choose one 'aspirant' value in order to take the brand into a new, competitively advantageous position. This is sophisticated and carefully engineered work, which must endure over years, not a meaningless, changing wish list.

Brand development models

The model in Figure 4.2, developed by the research firm Research International, represents the key elements of a brand, as discovered by their practitioners in many projects over their firm's life. This model, typical of those used by many brand managers, represents the fact that a brand has both rational and emotional components. The rational elements might be connected with the service that a professional provides, such as financial analysis in an accountancy firm or eye testing at an opticians. The emotional aspects of the brand are as, if not more, important.

For instance, one of the most profitable dynamics of the buyers' relationship to a brand is 'association'. The trainer and sports shoe brand Nike became enormously successful by understanding teenagers' desires to be

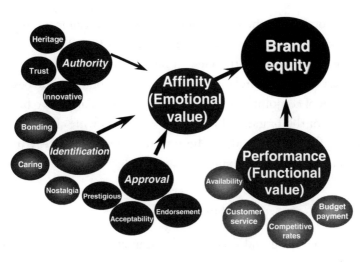

Figure 4.2 *Research International's model.*
Source: Research International

associated with both sporting heroes and a group of peers. Similarly, chief executives might engage McKinsey in order to be part of the group that uses such high quality advice for their company's success or to communicate the importance of a piece of work to their own staff.

The brand manager should identify, in detail, clients' attitudes to different aspects of their firm's brand and those of competitors. Using a model, investment must be made into programmes which will emphasise those aspects of the brand, either rational or emotional, which will give clear competitive advantage. If a firm wants to win business from a group of target clients, or induce existing clients to spend more, it has to understand the aspects of its brand which will appeal most, and invest to improve those elements.

Measurement techniques

As the brand is such an important asset of a professional services firm, it is sensible to establish measures of its health in the market place. It is normal, therefore, to establish some form of brand tracking survey. This can either be by buying into one of the many brand tracking surveys run by large marketing firms, or by creating a proprietary survey. For example, the Brand

Asset Valuator, run by the advertising firm Young & Rubicam, has tracked 20000 brands in 40 countries on common metrics for 10 years.

The firm needs to know the view of both clients and non-clients in the target market of its brand relative to its competitor brands. The best surveys use some form of conjoint or trade-off technique (see Part III) to break down the elements of the brand and the way it resonates with clients relative to competitors. Such surveys allow the firm to adjust the strategy in light of changing client views and competitor actions.

Financial tools

Apart from budgeting and financial planning approaches it is possible, as discussed earlier, to use brand valuation techniques in the firm's brand management programme. Historically, a 'residual' approach to brand value has been taken. The company's intangible assets were valued by subtracting its intangible assets from its market value and anything remaining was the 'goodwill' which included brand.

A number of different approaches are now used regularly:

- **Price premium:** this compares the branded offer against 'own brand', commodity and non-branded equivalents to assess the premium that the brand earns for its owner.
- **Market based:** this estimates value based on the sales of similar businesses or brands between companies in capital markets.
- **Replacement costs:** the costs of creating the brand since its inception are estimated at current values.
- **Royalty relief:** this estimates the price that would have to be paid if the firm licensed the brand. Interest which will derive from the brand in future years is estimated by forecasting likely sales and applying a royalty rate. Discounted cash flow (DCF) is then used to get net present value.
- **Earnings-based approach:** this is by far the most useful, but most thorough and costly, approach for day-to-day planning and management. It is the basis of many of the proprietary services provided by the firms who specialise in this field. It involves creating a view of the market in which the brand competes, the 'economic value added' that the brand contributes now to its owners and then projecting this into the future to get future value.

Summary

Effective brand management is a very powerful tool that the leadership of professional services firms can use to enhance both revenues and margins. It can communicate the firm's approach to clients, engender client loyalty, distinguish the firm from the competition and contribute to the firm's endurance. As more and more professional services firms are responding to changing market conditions by instituting brand programmes, it is likely that good brand management will become commonplace in the industry and firms will have to develop a competence in this area in order to thrive. Specialists in this field, with careers that demonstrate a successful track record in brand building, should be hired to use the tools and strategies necessary to reap these rewards for the shareholders or partners. They can only succeed, however, if forcibly backed by the personal political capital of the firm's leaders.

5

Competitive strategy

Overview

Professional services firms have been inclined to judge their performance according to the expertise with which they serve their clients rather than the competition they face. They have been able to do this for some time because they have enjoyed a healthy market for services where demand has often outstripped supply. But this is increasingly no longer the case. As markets get tougher and clients more demanding, firms need to think carefully and explicitly about the competitive framework in which they operate, or in which they would like to operate. This chapter outlines the tools and techniques that can help a firm develop the appropriate competitive stance to succeed in its market. It also describes sources of competitive advantage which professional services firms can usefully exploit.

The competitive challenge

The ability, style and will to compete are issues that the leaders of professional services firms of any size (from single practitioners through to large networks) need to consider. There are times when the actions of individual competitors are of real concern, such as during a proposal to clients. More important, however, are the times when changes in the business or the market allow actions by other firms to threaten the health of the business. Competitive response then becomes a major strategic issue which the leadership needs to address urgently.

Professional services firms have had a tendency to focus more on the improvement and presentation of their own work rather than any specific attack on vulnerable competitors. This is not surprising: professionals take pride in their area of technical expertise, and are often motivated by interest in their own field, so that the quality of the work they execute for clients has often been their main priority. There are, therefore, few firms that are really motivated by a desire to take work from others or that have focused competitive strategies which run through the organisation, as they do in suppliers within more mature industries.

This has been made possible by the boom in many professional services in the Western world over the last few decades which has ensured that there is plenty of natural demand. Many professionals have been able to earn an excellent living by offering their services in a benign market. However, the experience of other industries suggests that, as markets tighten and professional services proliferate, the leaders will need to think more explicitly about their competitive strategy. They will have to concentrate on how to attract business to them rather than to other firms. Even more importantly, they need to find processes whereby that competitive strategy, once developed, can be implemented throughout their organisation.

For example, it may be that a professional services firm which has been number two in its market decides that the time has come to challenge for leadership. This means taking the position of the established market leader in a deliberate and planned way, backed by proper investment. The rewards of such a move are great and explored later in this chapter. It implies that this 'challenger' will seek to gain the leading clients in the market and will aim to have the dominant share of the budgets of those clients. It must also offer the value proposition which appeals to most of the clients in the market and keep it in line with changing needs. The firm will become the leading authority on technical matters and policy issues within its own market place, advising regulators and industry advisors. In short, it must behave like the market leader. However, such a strategy will not be viable if the leadership espouses it but the firm itself carries on as it has always behaved.

Alternatively, a professional services firm may settle on a niche position based on some source of differentiation. A differentiated service will enable it to earn greater margins and attract more clients than the industry average. However, this will simply not be feasible if the experience the clients have of the service is much the same as it always has been and is no different from other providers. The service experience has to be truly different.

The challenge of competitive strategy, then, is not just to set strategy or to deal with ad hoc competitive threats as they occur but to implement a competitive stance throughout the organisation so that it becomes an effective guide to day-to-day management decisions.

Reprise of relevant concepts

For many professional services firms, competitive response is primarily tactical. They might consider competitor tactics in a beauty parade or in an acquisition battle. Yet changing market conditions suggest that competitive practice and strategic focus on the management of competitive competence in this industry will sharpen in the future. Visionary leadership of professional services firms in tightening markets ought to be building clear competitive strategy into their firm's processes now.

There are a number of approaches adopted in other industries and techniques postulated by theorists. Some of these, set out below and detailed in Part III, have proved effective over time. However, caution should be used when applying them to this industry. Many are, for example, based on assumptions about market share and growth which may not apply to some professional services markets. There does not yet seem to be the depth and quality of research into their applicability to the unique dynamics of professional services firms as have been applied to other areas of marketing.

Porter's three generic strategies

Michael Porter (Porter, 1980) has made a major contribution to the thinking on competitive strategy over several decades. Among other things, he has argued that firms should focus on one of three generic competitive strategies, all of which appear to be relevant to professional services firms. They are:

(i) Overall cost leadership. The organisation concentrates on gaining the lowest costs of production and distribution, and thus has the capability to set lower prices. Whether it does the latter or not depends on its objectives in its market. Some set lower prices to gain volume share; others maintain higher prices to increase margins. Cost leaders achieve their aims by very tight cost control across all areas of the business. This is helped by having a large scale of operations and opportunities for economies of scale, perhaps internationally.

The basis of cost control is the 'experience curve' (see Part III), globalisation of operations by focusing production in cheaper parts of the world, labour efficiency and the rewards of global brand development. Clearly, all these options are open to professional services firms. Some leading providers, for example, have sought to create global brands and global delivery to shut others out of their market. There is also some evidence of back office production being moved to cheap labour markets, although the wide margins in the industry have not yet pushed suppliers as far down this route as others in other industries.

(ii) Differentiation. In this, the supplier focuses on a component of the offer which is important to buyers and emphasises it in its business dealings. Normally it is brand, quality, innovation or technology. In the professional service industry there is evidence of differentiation through brand, technical heritage, client relationship, fame of key individuals and geographic knowledge.

(iii) Focus. Here the firm concentrates on one or more market segments. By doing this, it is able to gain in-depth knowledge of the segments and tailor its approach in detail. This best suits small firms, able to focus on a portion of the market. Professional services firms which are dedicated to one particular expertise are an example of this.

Clearly these ideas can be used to shape the firm's strategic focus. Their strength is that they can be developed and implemented internally using resources and information within the firm. A drawback might be, particularly with the insular focus of many professional services firms, neglecting the perspective on the external market and the responses of competitors.

Positioning as a competitive tool

Chapter 2 introduced the concept of market positioning based upon client views of value, which is a derivative of quality and price (see also Part III). Each company involved in a market takes its own position in that market, whether by design or default.

They may take the following positions:

- **Market leader:** typically the largest firm with the largest share; able to offer a value proposition which sets the price and quality expectation of the whole market. All other buyers and suppliers tend to compare their offer to that of this firm. It is the benchmark for the industry.
- **Market challenger or follower:** a smaller firm than the leader but with a similar offer. It typically uses pricing and other tactics to gain business from rivals.
- **Premium supplier:** typically a low volume supplier with a long heritage. It is able to offer a features-rich, high-priced offer.
- **Niche:** typically a number of smaller firms able to survive through specialisation, offering a truly unique and different proposition.
- **Least cost:** offering a streamlined, no frills service to budget buyers.

This is the competitive position of the firm and ought to be the orientation of everyone in it. Also, the price and features of the offers ought to be different. For example, the service of a least-cost supplier ought to be very different to that of a features-rich premium supplier. Each earns money in a different way from different groups of clients.

The power of developing these perceptual maps and the resultant positioning strategies is that they are built upon clients' value perceptions. If constructed using client research, they can clearly indicate what the firm needs to do to its offer in order to move to one of the market positions which is viable in the long term. If, for example, clients perceive there to be no 'premium' supplier or no 'least-cost' service, then the leadership has discovered a vacant position into which to move its firm. They can also be used to anticipate the moves of competitors or to understand shifts in the whole market. However, as with Porter's ideas, they advocate that the firm focuses on one position rather than vague aspirations that give it no clarity in the market.

Military analogies as a guide to developing competitive stance

It is possible for the leadership of a firm to give it a competitive emphasis, or a 'stance', which permeates the organisation. Several academics have suggested that military language and approaches are useful analogies in the development of this competitive stance (see, for instance, Wilson *et al.*, 1992).

They suggest:

Market leaders are in the most powerful position but are constantly under threat from the various competitors. Their competitive strategy is therefore largely defensive. The firm can adopt a 'position defence' (holding on to a supposedly impregnable fixed position), although this is thought to be the weakest defensive strategy, causing the firm to retreat progressively. A 'mobile defence', on the other hand, is to move into other areas which might prove to be leading offers in the future, whereas a 'flanking defence' means attacking vulnerable area such as an unaddressed part of the market. 'Contraction defence' is a withdrawal from a certain area in order to use resources more effectively, 'pre-emptive defence' is to make a move before that of a competitor and 'counter-offensive defence' is a response to an attack from a challenger.

Whether the market leader thinks in these militaristic terms or not, it needs to maintain its lead by consolidating its brand, client relationships and employee loyalties while honing its offer over time. Although it will be assailed by most of its competitors, it can, if necessary, affect all of them by changing the rules of the game. If it changes its price and offer, all others will also have to move. The market leader can, for example, initiate a price war in order to damage competitors. Before doing so, it should estimate how far it can afford to reduce margins and how low competitors can afford to go in response. An alternative is to invest in new uses for its skills or to seek to grow the whole market.

Challengers, being strong competitors with abundant resources, have a number of competitive strategies open to them. They can attack the market leader, attack peers, attack smaller firms or seek to maintain the status quo. Their attacking strategies are: 'full frontal assault', a direct challenge for leadership needing superior resources; a 'flank attack', using technology or market opportunity to focus on a vulnerable area; an 'encirclement attack', striking in several areas of business at once and a 'bypass attack', competing against indirect or less important parts of the market.

Whether or not the strong competitor thinks in these terms, it will need to consider its market position and how it affects the health of its business. It may be that it can hold its position and maintain its earnings by seeking to preserve the status quo in a steady market. However, it may be forced to take business from others to maintain earnings or to satisfy the ambitions of the business owners. In which case, it is sensible to consider the benefits of focusing its resources on one particular competitor's offer.

Niche suppliers are normally smaller and more focused firms which, again, have several options. They might adopt an 'alliance strategy', working with another firm to challenge the business of others or they might adopt a 'guerrilla strategy', gaining the loyalty of one market group. Both involve using the strength of being small and fleet of foot against the larger competitor.

Again, whether or not these smaller firms use this approach to plan their business development, they need to be obsessive about their point of specialisation and use their smaller resources judiciously to secure their business growth.

It is clear that strategy is valued by the military and is thought to pay off in success in battle. The direct applicability of these tactics to management and leadership teams while they are constructing day-to-day strategy or policy seems to be less evident. Many of the anecdotes and case studies used in work by theorists on this subject appear to be more post-event application to illustrate an interesting thesis rather than practical business thinking.

Service quality as competitive strategy

It is surprising how many companies, which consider the quality of their client service to be an important part of their offer, do not think through the place of service in their competitive strategy. Service programmes are often imprecise and vague, thereby losing any potential competitive advantage. It is essential to develop a clear, competitive strategy for the service of the company which matches the general business strategy and for the service style to reflect market position. If the firm is a least-cost, premium or niche supplier, its competitive position is reinforced if its client service is undertaken in a style similar to that positioning. This is explored in more detail in Chapter 11.

As important is to recognise the moments in the evolution of a market when there is a strategic opportunity to gain ground by offering a new style of client service. Industries appear to develop through an evolution of thought and strategy with regard to service standards. Suppliers in other industries have reaped enormous rewards when taking advantage of those moments.

The first phase is to reach national par. This is a common expectation of service quality which is shared by the population as a whole. It is assumed, ill-defined and emotionally based, but is a common value nonetheless. For various reasons (such as a historic monopoly or legislative distortion) the service provided by an industry may be below this expectation. (Incidentally, a service which slips far below par will eventually become the subject of national ridicule and the target of comedians and journalists because they recognise that there is a common experience which can be exploited.)

In an industry where all suppliers are criticised, the first supplier to move to meet national par will gain market share. This has happened in numerous industries in both a national and international context. The example given in Chapter 10 is the radical improvement made British Airways (BA) in the 1980s, which gained market share and grew for nearly the two following decades while other international carriers floundered. It moved to meet the service expectations of buyers when others in the industry did not. As a result it attracted new buyers, gaining competitive advantage.

These unique strategic opportunities taken by a few suppliers in passing moments of developing industries have become the examples used by many of the service quality and customer care gurus. Few have gone on to look at the opportunities to use service quality as a strategic asset in other phases of market development.

For instance, once competitors notice that a company is taking a lead through quality they begin to develop programmes of their own. As a result, the service of competitors begins to catch up. They then look for ways to communicate the efforts that they have made in order to attract buyers back. The industry goes through a phase where it 'markets' the quality of service it provides.

Once the industry is filled with suppliers communicating common quality of service propositions, it must evolve further. It moves towards 'service differentiation'. This is a process which results from changes in attitude among both buyers and suppliers. If all suppliers are making similar quality claims, then buyers choose on the basis of service style along with price. They are attracted to an ambience, design or behaviour which suits their taste. Suppliers therefore respond by developing different service offerings for different groups. Clearly, if the industry is not yet at this stage, a supplier can gain competitive advantage by anticipating it. It can choose the most attractive segments and design a service which appeals primarily to them.

There is then a stage of service evolution when 'added value' services are offered to the market, such as those for the experienced buyer. Buyers are

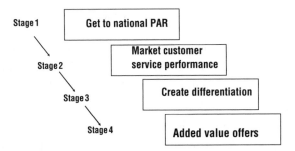

Figure 5.1 *Evolution of client service in a market.*

able to recognise the value of the base service and are thus willing to pay extra for added value service features. This evolution of service standards is represented in Figure 5.1.

Competitive advantage can be gained by launching packages of added value services for the segment that the firm is targeting. The difficulty is that the incremental value of the added value features is eroded over time as standards improve. Buyers then expect them to fall into the base service. Suppliers must continue to create new added value features to distinguish them from the core service in order to maintain their competitive lead in their chosen segments (see Chapter 9, Figure 9.5).

An example of competitive advantage derived from service quality is the difference between naive and experienced clients as described in Chapter 3. In an industry where all services are designed for naive clients, the service standard comprises: good client care, clear process, smiling people and a reassuring brand. However, because of the need for emotional control, frequent purchasers can become frustrated with this approach. For them, good service is self-service and streamlined process. By constructing a service which has, at its heart, the sense of privilege of joining a club, the supplier can provide better quality service at less cost. If a professional services supplier introduces a new standard of service for experienced clients, it will attract them from other providers.

This can be seen in the deployment by leading professional services firms of extranet facilities to their clients. Very often these facilities are for experienced, repeat clients, allowing them to be a member of that firm's service and receive a steady flow of information and updates. They also transact some service themselves using the supplier's technology.

Critical success factors

Any market has established rules of engagement by which the participants in the market survive or prosper. These rules may be imposed by regulatory or market pressures, and usually by a combination of the two. For example, in a professional services industry all of the participants must meet the necessary legal or industry standards of qualifications and behaviour in order to be able to participate. Meeting these criteria is a critical success factor as it is not possible to trade without them.

Beyond these basic requirements for being 'in the game', service providers also face certain criteria which enable them to succeed in the market place. These critical success factors are commercial imperatives resulting from the evolution of forces within their particular market.

Value chain analysis

This concept suggests that business leaders view their businesses as a series of activities, linked in a process or 'chain', each of which adds value to raw materials, as Figure 5.2 illustrates. The concept is familiar in manufacturing businesses and is used to find items of extraneous costs. However, it can also be used to identify areas of potentially greater added value and areas of competitive advantage. Theorists have now developed a generic value chain

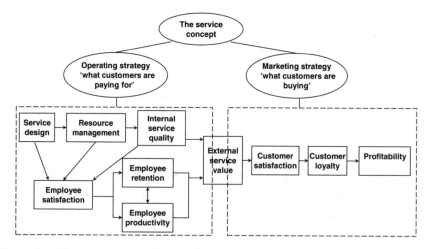

Figure 5.2 *The service concept and value chain.*

model for service businesses which can be applied to professional services businesses.

Competitive tracking and analysis

As with other areas of strategy, decisions about competitive response are more likely to benefit the firm if based on market insight and good analysis. Unfortunately, many service firms rarely have the reliable and objective measurement systems that have evolved in other markets. (Some other markets, for instance, have research systems which are supplied with data by key suppliers to inform all involved about the market performance.) Some larger professional service firms have dealt with this by either buying research surveys or having small competitive research units establishing a perspective on competitors. They will gather published reports, interview employees who have joined from competitor firms, trade information with competitors and interview consultants who specialise in their market.

Information which is typically sought about competitors is:

- Objectives and plans.
- Performance.
- Structure and organisation.
- Senior management changes and the decision-making track record of those assuming leadership roles.
- Strengths and weaknesses.
- Marketing materials and campaigns.
- Wins and losses.
- Response profiles (i.e. are they opportunistic or targeted in their selection of business targets).

Without such a system to inform leadership about competitor response, this information can be anecdotal and, quite simply, wrong. More than once, a practice has thought itself to be the market leader in a field of work but, once objective analysis was undertaken, discovered that it had been overtaken. It is sensible to establish a system to gather objective knowledge about competitor moves.

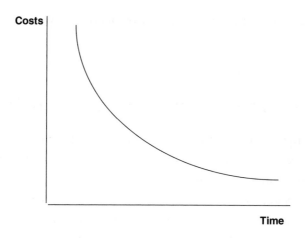

Figure 5.3 *The experience curve.*
Source: Boston Consulting Group. Reproduced by permission of The Boston Consulting Group.

Sources of competitive advantage

One of the most important aspects of competitive strategy is to find sources of competitive advantage. They are likely to include:

The 'core competence'

Each company has a skill or function in which it invests over time because it is seen as the most important task of the organisation. Often this is made a priority unconsciously because it is so obviously the most important task. It is the area of responsibility which always receives time, attention and investment, almost without question, in comparison to other functions. Because of investment in both people and resources, this area is likely to improve in both performance and cost. It is represented as an 'experience curve' (Figure 5.3). This concept was highlighted by the Boston Consulting Group and used as a basis for the Boston matrix (Boston Consulting Group, 1968).

Unfortunately, despite the fact that many strategy experts emphasise the importance of the core competence, there are few recognised techniques to define it. Ultimately it can only be determined in discussion, or brainstorming, with senior management. Such discussions can seem vague and difficult but, once the 'blinding flash of the obvious' occurs, the simple heart of the company's performance can be exploited.

The corporate brand

The corporate brand (see Chapter 4) is a source of competitive advantage. It will appeal to the target market of clients, causing them to relate to it in such a way as to purchase it over time. Client loyalty is fostered by this corporate brand because it gives reassurance in the intensely emotional experience of buying or using service.

Client relationships

The relationship between a company and its clients is also a source of competitive advantage. The heritage of contact between the people, processes and systems of the two organisations cannot be duplicated. Ideally, relationships are best served by a client experience which is both responsive and consistent, and in which expectations are always met. A service company's relationships will include some clients who are very loyal and others who could be made more loyal. They are a source of competitive advantage because they are more inclined to purchase and repurchase. They are also likely to be advocates of the supplier's service. This might be turned into highly profitable growth through a structured relationship programme.

Distribution

The way a firm reaches its clients is a source of competitive advantage. For retail professional services, this might be the location of a shop to attract the best flow of clients but a similar dynamic applies in business-to-business professional services. A firm might decide that it needs to open an office in a city or region where it identifies potential demand for its services. It will need to secure a facility, assemble resources and launch the new presence.

However, it may also mean ensuring that there are sufficiently skilled senior people representing a specialist service to clients or a sector expertise. A number of successful professional firms attribute their growth to having the correct skills in place to meet untapped demand. Clearly, then, it is important to decide whether resources are in place to meet key opportunity areas as part of a regular strategic business review.

Improving the firm's competitive competence

There is almost complete unanimity among marketing specialists that one of the main roles of the chief marketing officer (CMO) or marketing leader is to maintain a perspective on the market and articulate that to the company, acting as the voice of the market into the organisation. It is less frequently argued (but more frequently experienced by those who do the job) that the CMO has a responsibility to ensure that the firm has the organisational competence to meet the demands of the market.

This has two elements. The first is highlighting to the leadership of the firm those areas where it needs new skills or processes, in any part of the firm, to tackle competitive threat or market opportunity. The second is developing the competence of the marketing function itself to tackle strategic imperatives (explained in Chapter 7).

The first is likely to arise from the firm's strategic planning process. The leaders need a clear perspective on three things: market trends, competitive moves and the firm's competence. These are likely to reveal changes which need to be made in order for the firm to thrive. For instance, some professional services firms have had enduring contracts with large multinational clients disrupted by regulation. These organisations need to develop skills in international relationship management for the first time. Others have been able to grow their business without any mass communication. However, as their leading competitors are investing in broadcast advertising this may erode their position and undermine their health. They may need to revise their approach. Both need new organisational competencies.

It is the role of the marketing leader to identify these issues and illustrate how their absence threatens the firm. While the development of the organisational capability to meet the problem might not rest with the marketing function, the facilitation of a strategic debate does. Similarly, the function has a responsibility to review the result of the project and to ensure that the new skill is established and able to meet its intended objectives so the firm can compete effectively.

Summary

It is no longer enough for professional services firms to take a tactical approach to competition. It is imperative that all firms bring a more strategic focus to the management of their competitive competence, including developing processes to ensure that this is embedded throughout the firm. As this chapter has shown, there are a number of techniques which firms can use to develop a successful competitive positioning that evolves over time as markets change. What is essential is that firms base their decision on market insight and good analysis to secure a sustainable source of competitive advantage.

6

Handling international operations and cultural differences

Overview

The professional services industry employs a number of different models of international business with different growth and marketing strategies. Whatever approach the firm decides to take, there are a number of organisational and cultural challenges that need to be addressed, not least ones of technical and linguistic differences. For example, will the firm service clients in other countries from the home territory or set up an office in chosen countries? What degree of local expertise will be needed? Does it have a perspective on each international market? As this chapter argues, using the right tools to find answers to questions of internationalisation is critical to success.

The challenge of working across borders

In the modern world it's hard for any professional service firm to avoid international work. Almost any client, large or small, has international needs, particularly if it offers its products and services on the internet. Even those serving consumers can become involved in international projects as their reputation and scope grows. Professional services firms therefore need to think about how they approach requests for work across geographic borders. They might travel to service that demand themselves, they might have relationships with local partners to whom they refer work, or they might extend their firm into another country where there is frequent demand.

Unfortunately there are a number of complicating factors for professional services firms moving on to the international scene. The first and most obvious are the differences in regulatory and legal requirements for professionals undertaking cross-border work. Although much has been done by many professional bodies to standardise practices across the world (e.g. in international accounting standards) there can be large and significant differences in national law or regulation. Some firms, for instance, are surprised about the restrictions placed upon the use of client information outside by some European countries. Professionals therefore need to take extreme care to ensure they have local knowledge if their work is going to be technically correct.

International operations complicate much more than technical content, though. They affect almost every aspect of approach to market whether strategic, tactical or managerial. While another country may look misleadingly similar to home territory, there are underlying attitudes to life and business that mean different criteria are used to make judgements. These differences in lifestyle, values, behaviours and business practices between different geographies and cultures are difficult to digest and manage. While stereotypes and clichés are often exaggerated, there are genuine differences in taste and approach which can cause real problems.

Language is an obvious example. Although English is generally accepted to be the international language of business, different words have different meanings. Mistakes can be made in the use of English alone. However, they are even more likely when a supplier is working, through translation, in a client's local language. Even worse, culture and upbringing give different meaning to words which can dramatically affect understanding.

For example, while the English word 'lunch' refers to food taken in the middle of the day, what this signifies varies enormously in Europe. In Sweden, it is generally a meal at 11:30 am which comprises fish, potatoes and salad accompanied by a light beer; to the English it means sandwiches soon after midday, often 'in the pub'; to the French it is generally a three-course meal at 1 pm with red wine and, to the Spanish, a big meal at 3 pm.

The cultural context gives different meanings to the word, complicating life. If an inexperienced Swedish business person says to a Spanish client, 'we'll discuss this over lunch' obvious complications arise. This cultural heritage also has an enormous affect on business language and understanding. 'Quality' to a New Yorker, for example, can mean speed of delivery while to the English it means sincerity and to Germans, thoroughness or accuracy. Similarly, 'client relationship management' can be very different in America, France and parts of Asia. The same words have very different meanings according to their cultural context.

If technical and linguistic differences can complicate international work, other factors, explored in this chapter, can cause enormous difficulty if not properly managed. More than one professional services firm, large and small, has been damaged by international or 'global' strategies and adventures. Leaders should therefore think through the strategic and managerial aspects of international market approaches with real care.

A reprise of relevant international marketing issues

The exporter, the network, the multinational and the global firm

There are different models of international business which adopt different growth and marketing strategies. Each is successful in different circumstances and each occurs in the professional services industry.

The exporter, for example, is primarily a domestic firm. Its offer, approach and underlying business assumptions are a reflection of its domestic culture and perspective. In moving abroad it is normally responding to unsolicited demand or opportunities. Its strategy is to reap new revenue streams with little customisation or cost. If it cannot visit foreign clients itself, it normally chooses local representatives (whether individuals or firms) who can service demand. Many small professional services firms export through links with trusted fellow professionals into countries where there is healthy demand. The marketing of the exporter normally involves the use of domestic campaigns through established links and relationships with international clients. Any separate marketing into foreign countries has to be carefully examined and justified.

An international network, on the other hand, is a group of companies or individuals working under a similar brand or proposition. This might be a formal franchise structure with very strong controls on local operations, a holding company owning many different decentralised firms or a federation of locally owned practices which contribute part of their earnings to a central organisation for some greater benefit (usually a shared brand or the ability to service large international clients). Again, all these structures occur in the professional services industry. In fact, some of the world's largest professional services firms are actually little more than international federations of different national businesses.

A franchise normally has a clearly defined offer and image. Marketing is funded primarily from franchisees' contributions but is centrally prepared, packaged and launched. It is highly controlled. Marketing in a federal network, however, is almost completely the opposite. Central guidelines and marketing policies can be very weak. The approach is frequently diverse and defuse, driven largely by the local businesses. The holding company, on the other hand, will vary its approach according to its policy on the effectiveness of brand impact. Some might play down the corporate centre, while others might promote it heavily, depending on the relevance to client need.

A multinational is a large firm operating on several continents. It has one consolidated set of accounts, one profit pool and a corporate function which directs or leads policy. While it seeks to optimise costs (by streamlining processes, locating facilities in areas of cheap labour and standardising offers) it also tends to configure its marketing approach to local nationalities and culture.

In fact, the proponents of a global approach cite the degree of product standardisation and similarity of marketing as a fundamental difference between the multinational and global firm. They are different in policy and approach and, again, both styles have been adopted by the professional services industry.

It is important that the appropriate marketing and growth strategy should be adopted for the firm's culture, structure and mentality. Muddled thinking has, for instance, confused federal networks with global policy, damaging the earnings of partners in some large firms over the past few decades. Because they were a network of independent firms, they had to build another layer of management to create a global identity. But, as the power of decision-making belonged to the individual countries, these networks never became truly global. It was therefore unnecessary and ineffective extra cost which reduced the profits the partners could take from the business.

Cultural differences and their affect on client expectations

Different cultures create different expectations and attitudes in clients. People around the world have different languages, mind sets, preferences, attitudes and prejudices. This 'collective programming of the mind' occurs during childhood and adolescence. It is often so subtle that people themselves can be unaware of their own cultural perspectives and biases. Yet it affects their attitude to life and business.

It also affects their demand for different professional services. Some cultures value strategy and consultancy more than others. Some rank various professions more highly than others and some regard certain services as professions while others do not. This means that the demand for a professional service, and the price people are prepared to pay for it, is different in different cultures of the world.

What is not often understood is the vast difference that cultural heritage makes to quality expectations. People approach every service with a set of expectations which are both emotional and practical. They will only think that a service is good quality if both the technical content and the client service meet those expectations. Yet they will not make any effort to explain these expectations to the service supplier and, in fact, are often unaware of them themselves.

However, they are ruthless in the way they criticise and judge a firm if it does not meet these articulated and unarticulated expectations. If, therefore, a service supplier is designing a service which will be received in Scandinavia, Germany, Spain and France, it needs to research the expectations of that service in each of those cultures. The outlook, attitude and assumptions will be different in each culture and the service must be customised to suit those different tastes.

To use a consumer example, even the ubiquitous American fast-food service McDonald's has to be customised in different cultures of the world to deliver satisfaction. (In fact the franchise dynamic of the firm's international operations has not only ensured that the service is varied around the world but also that the fast-food menu itself is customised to some degree.)

For instance, in the early years of its expansion into the UK, their people were trained to say 'have a nice day'. In America this is a polite, unremarkable phrase which is part of day-to-day life. However, this was not natural to employees in the UK and their uncomfortable tone of voice implied insincerity. Unfortunately, one of the key service assumptions in the UK is sincerity. (British people will tolerate many other aspects of poor service if the service supplier is sincere or polite.) It therefore caused dissatisfaction and had to be changed. In fact, McDonald's publicly apologised to the country.

Excellent international service is therefore the customisation of a service proposition to meet cultural expectations. For the service provider, this has serious implications. It may be that, in one culture, the delivery of service is a performance designed to serve the client and take care of all of their needs. In another, however, excellent service may be self-service. In yet another, excellent service may be delivered through high technology. The creation of service propositions needs to be customised to suit the culture concerned.

The effect of cultural differences on business-to-business practices

It is often wrongly assumed that, in the business world, attitudes and expectations are very similar. As a result, cultural differences are less important. However, there is much evidence that differences occur and affect all aspects of business. For example, one of the most useful studies of international variations in culture was undertaken by Gert Hofstede (Hofstede, 1980, and see Part III). He identified five significant cultural variations and devised matrices by which business affairs can be planned and managed. Interestingly, his research was conducted in one company (IBM) that perceived itself as having one consistent global culture. So, even in a perceived monoculture of one large international business cultural variations have a large influence.

This has implications for many aspects of business practice. International account and relationship management practice is a good example. Some cultures seem to emphasise one ubiquitous offer that is managed across the world. For example, many American companies work on the assumption that a similar management style, with similar policies and processes, is the way to deliver excellent 'global' performance.

However, some other cultures – for instance, some Japanese firms – want their values and standards to be delivered through local subsidiaries which have freedom to express those values appropriately to local countries. Yet again, the management of Swedish companies tends to reflect the consensus and debate (seeking fairness) which is at the heart of Swedish culture.

International functions have to persuade local operating companies to take on new ideas. A professional services supplier to IBM, Hitachi and Ericsson is therefore likely to have to vary its relationship management approach with each of these clients.

In fact there is very little business practice which is not influenced by cultural diversity and, as a result, impacts on professional service suppliers. For instance, different cultures respond differently to colour and music. This affects the work of international design, advertising and brand companies. Similarly, there are indications that business innovation occurs differently in different cultures, which means adapting the styling of products and propositions. Finally, there appears to be a difference in attitude to the adoption of new ideas, affecting the demand for management consultancy based on thought leadership or innovative thinking.

The concept of globalisation

In the early 1980s Theodore Levitt published an influential article in the *Harvard Business Review* (Levitt, 1983) on globalisation. This pointed out that people around the world have similar aspirations for their life and family. He argued that this was an opportunity for international firms which were able to create common processes in brand management, advertising, and distribution to create a new style of profitable international businesses: the global firm. The global approach is owned by no culture but serves all equally well with a common offer.

The crux of the globalisation argument is that technology is a powerful force, driving the world towards convergence and commonality. While demonstrating his sophisticated understanding of cultural differences, Levitt argued that these were declining in influence in the face of standardised products which derive from commonality of preference. In fact, he suggested that 'different cultural preferences, national tastes and standards . . . are vestiges of the past. Some die and some become global propositions (Italian food, American rock music, French wine, etc.)'.

In this view, multinationals which accommodate national preferences in their approach are thoughtlessly accommodating poor marketing which 'means giving the customer what he says he wants'. A global strategy is to create a cheap, reliable ubiquitous product which appeals to a universal need and also to 'create markets' for that proposition by investment in marketing communication or brand advertising. Some well-established global offers (such as Coca-Cola) are cited as leaders in this approach.

In the subsequent decades, particularly in times of economic growth, many companies in different sectors attempted a global strategy. In fact, some city analysts marked down the shares of those which did not have a 'global brand' or were attempting a 'global strategy'. However, the reality is that some damaged their companies by undertaking huge investments in global strategies that did not pay back. Some large professional partnerships committed themselves to a global, multidisciplinary strategy. In the process they created a costly layer of management on top of their federal structures, much of which has since been cut back in the light of changed priorities and regulatory threats. (An independent national partnership is thought to be less threatened by lawsuits facing other firms in the same network, as it is not seen as part of an integrated global firm.)

At the time of writing, there is a resurgence of national identity and a dislike of some Western offers in much of the world. This, combined with a number of failures to achieve global positioning, has caused all but a few established global firms to attempt risky investment in truly 'global' strategies.

Tackling international strategic market issues

International growth strategy

The professional services firm has several strategic options to consider as soon as it receives significant opportunities for international work.

Is it going to refuse international work and remain a domestic practice?

The unarticulated assumption that demand should be serviced is at the heart of many firms. There is, however, the option that international demand could be refused. The leaders of the firm could take the view that margin, not growth, is their prime strategy and that international work risks damaging their margin. In these circumstances it is advisable to know international firms to whom clients can be referred. This will safeguard reputation and the potential for future work from them.

Is it going to service demand entirely from the home territory?

If the firm is only going to service international demand in an opportunistic way, or as a service to domestic clients with international needs (i.e. without an explicit drive for significant international growth), it has a number of options. It might recruit an employee from the foreign territory and allow them to travel there to service clients. Alternatively, it might make an arrangement with a local agent or partner firm. With the former, the firm needs to recruit an experienced professional with both technical and business development skills. If the latter, it needs to choose carefully who their local agent is and decide the nature of the relationship. This might range from a simple percentage reward for work referred, to a tightly defined franchise agreement. All will involve risk, however, because any poor service or variation in technical standard will damage the reputation of the firm.

Is it going to actively target chosen countries or international markets?

If the firm decides that it wants to actively pursue international growth, then it needs to think through and prioritise its investment. It needs to conduct an initial strategic review and opportunity analysis to decide which are the most interesting opportunities. These might be based on geographic proximity, cultural fit or overriding opportunity for its services. It then needs to conduct detailed analysis of the markets it is considering and decide on the first areas it wants to focus on. Like any area of investment it needs to decide the amount it is prepared to invest and the time it is prepared to give for payback.

The style of overseas investment can be affected by the reason for the approach. Many work internationally because of demand. Others move because of slowing home markets, declining business or intense competition. However, as there is increased risk in international work, those moving abroad due to significant problems in home markets need to ensure that they have secure investment funds for a long-term approach.

The 'follow the client' strategy

The international growth of many small firms begins with large international clients. A small firm, or a partner in a large firm, might service a division of a large international client. As the work and relationship develop, it might find demand for work in many parts of the world from the same client. This might become the foundation for international offices and employees.

What degree of local expertise will it employ and when?

There will come a time when the leaders will judge that there is continuing demand from an international market. The firm then needs to plan how it intends to provide local resource to service that demand. It may set up an office using expatriate employees from the home firm. The intention in these circumstances is eventually to hand over to talent developed locally and reap earnings from the profit of the new entity. Alternatively, it may combine recruited talent with an acquisition to create a new firm.

International market analysis and perspective

Any debate about international expansion is better conducted in the light of analysis and insight into that market. The processes and techniques described in Chapter 2 (market research, market audits, etc.) are essential for this. All apply equally in international market analysis as they do in domestic markets. However, there is increased risk of error in international analysis. Whereas published research reports and industry data can be freely available, a lack of real local knowledge can be very costly if the firm is considering a serious investment. At the very least, there should be a visit to the target countries, discussion with local professionals and even a visit to the commercial representatives of embassies in that country. Each will round out knowledge and yield insight prior to any strategy debate.

Segmentation of international markets

It would be dangerous and wasteful for any firm to attempt to 'target the world' with a broad and amorphous approach to expansion. All have to start by choosing a portion of the international market, a group of clients, to concentrate upon. The most obvious international segmentation method is by country. This has allowed many firms to grow businesses inside national borders until they are flourishing mature businesses.

Yet choosing a country or a geographic market can also be a limitation. The firm is, in fact, restricting itself to agreed borders and legal frameworks (many of which resulted from long forgotten peace conferences which followed centuries-old wars) that are irrelevant to some modern business needs. Some firms have therefore created a broader grouping of clients based on cultural groups.

For example, a Spanish emphasis is likely to appeal in Spain, South America and certain Spanish-influenced areas such as Miami in the US state of Florida. This segmentation approach might also lead to an emphasis on 'Anglo-Saxon', Germanic and Chinese groups, which involve similar cross-border opportunities. Some firms have found that successful penetration of cultural groups in this way has led them, through trade relationships, into valuable groupings of diasporas which have developed from previous migrations of trading peoples. Others have followed ancient trade routes into new geographies. For example, some professional services firms relate to clients in South America through Spanish offices.

In fact, many of the segmentation approaches outlined in Chapter 3 can apply in the international context. If, for example, a consultancy firm has decided to grow by penetrating a few international clients, it might concentrate on managers or firms with cultures that make them 'early adopters' of new management concepts. These might be large firms in many different countries which would be attracted to leading conferences. Leaders should, therefore, define the most relevant segmentation for their firm using a method similar to that described in Chapter 3.

International or global brand strategy

The leadership of professional services firms has several strategic decisions to take with regard to the positioning of their brand internationally. Each has serious implications to the health of the firm, to the development of brand equity and to the ease with which revenues will grow.

*Is the brand going to be perceived to be indigenous to
each country in which it operates?*

It is possible to create a brand which makes the firm appear native to each country in which it operates. It will be American in America, British in

Britain, and Australian in Australia. It will be familiar to locals in every country in which it becomes established. This multinational brand strategy can evolve naturally for professional services firms which have strong offices established in countries that are staffed with good local professionals. The reputation from excellent local work will, as described in Chapter 4, create a local brand in each country. This strategy can be maintained by following the same approach as new countries are penetrated.

Is the brand going to reflect the culture of the corporate or domestic headquarters?

The brand can simply reflect the values and image of the country in which the firm originated or is headquartered. IBM Global Services, for example, is unquestionably American, while the professional services teams of Ericsson are unquestionably Swedish.

This has both advantages and disadvantages. First, it is relatively easy to maintain the integrity of a brand which reflects national identity. It also resonates with some cultures, creating opportunity. In recent years, for example, the countries of Eastern Europe have been very open to American professional services firms because they have thought that they needed to catch up after years of communism.

On the other hand, some Asian countries have been cautious of Western advisors after the last collapse of their economies. Some professional services firms have had to let locals lead work to overcome this prejudice.

Is the brand going to be presented as what a national culture is perceived to be?

Clients in different countries have perceptions of foreign cultures and their business practice, some of which are unrealistic images based on media received in their home country. If the brand reflects a dominant culture, the firm needs to decide whether the positioning should embody the reality of that culture or what the local market perceives that culture to be. The 'perceived culture' can be aspirational and help the firm's brand. For example, in some markets American business is perceived to be efficient, process driven and modern. This may not actually be the case, but the brand positioning which exploits the indigenous market's perception of American business is a strategy open to the firm.

Is the firm going to attempt to create a 'global' brand?

A global brand is an entity that commands allegiance from buyers in many parts of the world. It has equity and the same identity in many markets. Proponents of the approach argue that the commonality of design, distribution and advertising allows its owners to reap efficiencies of spend which competitors are unable to achieve. This is based on a number of global brands that have achieved enormous benefits from scale.

There appears to be, however, very few clear definitions of a global brand. If simple criteria (such as being present in at least three continents of the world and having more then 40% of revenue outside its originating country) are applied, then there appear to be very few global brands in existence. The risk here is that the brand will be perceived to be Western rather than truly global. This strategy is also hugely expensive because the firm has to invest in all markets in which it operates to create a consistent impression.

International marketing management issues

All the marketing management issues, outlined in other chapters, need to be handled in the international context but, like international strategic market issues, they are made more complex in a cross-border context.

International market communication issues

A firm working on the international stage has to communicate with both individual clients and with markets of clients. Just as with domestic market communication, it needs to use communication techniques to plan and execute its messages so that they pave the way for personal dialogue between clients and service staff. It needs a strategic communications plan, good message management, clear media selection, programme management processes and response mechanisms.

In the international context, however, differences in language, taste, colour preference and humour need to be accommodated. The design and message of all communication pieces need to be checked with internal representatives of different cultures at the planning stage. There need to be clear processes which engage communications representatives of all the firm's organisational units in the development of both strategy and programmes which should be developed to influence the thinking of local clients.

International business development and account management strategy

Many of the approaches to personal business generation described in Chapter 8 apply in the international context. It is possible to use the pipeline management tool to focus thinking on the internal management of business development processes. It is also possible to build a personal network of international clients and handle them effectively while, at the same time, managing the implementation of a personal marketing plan.

However, 'relationship management' is one of those phrases that, although it uses the same words, is heard differently by different cultures. The way an American or British professional manages business relationships is different from the way the French professional manages them and different again from the way some Asian firms work.

For example, Western professionals feel at ease approaching all levels of a client organisation and would expect to receive honest, clear feedback about the client firm. In fact, professionals will often recommend to senior clients that they visit and collect data from front-line employees in order to get a true picture of how a company is performing in its market.

By contrast, however, in some Asian cultures there is a sense of people having their place at certain levels of society. Junior employees will not therefore express any view which appears to be a criticism of senior management, even if those views are strongly held. Very often they will be uncomfortable spending any time or developing any relationship with professionals serving top executives. Approaches to relationship management and some client consulting work must therefore be different in different cultures.

International service design

New service design (NSD) also has to be adjusted when working on the international stage. There is both an international and local management dynamic. For instance, innovation is most likely to occur in local firms or countries because they are close to the client. Local leaders are likely to spot developing needs and to deploy resources to meet individual client opportunities. They are unlikely, however, to be successful at spreading that innovation across the firm because they will be limited by their own time constraints, by a lack of local perspective in foreign cultures, by internal politics and, sometimes, by petty jealousy.

It is therefore effective to have a small international NSD team who are responsible for service innovation across the network or international firm. They must have a budget to create or stimulate new ideas and to undertake feasibility studies. Their prime task, however, is to legitimise local innovation and spread it across the firm. They need a clear mandate and international processes to do so.

Similarly, the firm's portfolio management and NSD design process must be managed internationally. Normally new product development (NPD) or NSD processes are managed by a representative team of senior leaders who ensure that proposals reach the various criteria to pass through the 'gates' in the design process. They are responsible for both the encouragement of spend on new idea development and the control of costs. Both are important to success.

There is, however, a local dimension to the design of service components. Different cultures respond differently to process, people, colour, image and technology. These differences need to be built into the NSD process. The international team needs to decide the degree of standardisation or customisation which will occur for each service and in which parts of the world. This will be based on a balance between research into client needs and affordability. Once the policy is decided for each service, tools such as features design or blueprinting (see Part III) can be used to modify the service for local cultures.

Organisational issues

Many of the organisational constructs suggested in Chapter 7 apply on the international stage. Perhaps the hardest time is had by those in international partnerships with national profit pools. In these it can be hard to persuade partners to adopt common human resources standards and strategies toward the marketing function. In many networks, it is difficult to establish high quality resource to manage marketing in various countries. Publicly owned firms, or those with one profit pool, can be more directional, developing structures that engage the whole firm.

Tools to help with international strategy

Market research

Market research studies (see Part III) can yield as much valuable insight into international markets as they can into domestic markets. However, they need to be managed with as much care, with the creation of a clear research brief and the use of proper selection processes to choose properly qualified agencies. Questionnaires and responses should be properly translated, and then normally translated back into the original language to check meaning. The main area of vulnerability is usually the level of spend that a firm will tolerate. Restrictions on research budgets mean that samples in different foreign countries can be ridiculously small. One way of handling this is to undertake an initial quantitative study to make early judgements of potential and then to explore one or two countries in depth.

Hofstede's models

Hofstede's (Hofstede, 1980) models have five axes to define cultural differences: Individualism, Masculinity, Power Distance, Uncertainty Avoidance and Long-term Orientation (see Part III). His data enables strategists to easily identify cultures with similar characteristics which might be candidates for similar strategies.

The ARR model

Academics have used the ARR model (see Chapter 2 and Part III) to research the strength of international relationships between professionals and their clients. They have used it to yield insights into potential theory and approaches. For example, Sharon Purchase and Antony Ward (Purchase and Ward, 2003) used it to study the strengths of relationships between Australian engineering consultancies and their Thai clients. The tool seems robust enough to use in a commercial context in order to plot strategy and plan international relationship marketing programmes.

International value chain analysis

A number of professional services firms are structured as decentralised organ-isations. Some own separate international firms whereas some are a network of different national firms. Moreover, if they are a partnership, it can be difficult to get partners in different firms to cooperate effectively. Often the resources to create and run international initiatives have to be provided from the profit pools of these individual firms. Maintaining a perspective of the value chain of the network (and thus areas where client needs or com-petitor actions require the firm to change) provides a rational and relatively objective perspective on which to base arguments for international action or initiatives.

Summary

Many professional services firms, whatever their size, will find themselves at some point faced with the possibility of having to work across borders, thanks to a combination of modern technology, with its erosion of time and borders, and the expansion of clients to new markets. Understanding the issues involved in working across borders has thus become imperative. This includes having a clear view of what is the same and what is different in each market in terms of client expectations, and what impact international work will have managerially and operationally. As this chapter has shown, it demands that firms resolve some difficult questions if they are to succeed in profiting from cross-border business.

PART II

Making Marketing and Business Development Work

Once the strategic marketing issues have been resolved, firms need to develop effective processes to execute them. Understanding the role of marketing and how best to organise it in a professional services setting is integral to this. It involves crafting thoughtful answers to questions of personal business generation, creating and relaunching services, communicating with the market, servicing clients and the attraction and retention of the best people. This part offers a detailed guide to these critical topics.

7

The organisation and management of marketing in professional services firms

Overview

All professional services firms carry out some form of marketing, whether they do it formally or informally, to grow their business. But too many firms fail to capitalise on the powerful impact service marketing activities can have on profits and revenues because they don't build them into their business effectively. This chapter examines how the marketing function should evolve as firms grow, and the questions of organisation and skills that need to be resolved to make marketing work. It includes a functional model of marketing for the professional services firm, as well as detailing the processes that characterise good marketing. It also suggests ways to measure its effectiveness.

Marketing counts

As all professional services firms have to draw in revenue and all professionals have to gain work, all undertake aspects of marketing. Presenting credentials to clients, hosting seminars and giving presentations at public conferences are part of the marketing mix. So, whether they call it marketing or not, whether they have specialist marketing managers or not, professional services firms do undertake marketing activities to grow their business.

In publicly owned firms or retail chains these are likely to be primarily the responsibility of a relatively small specialist unit comprising people who are qualified in marketing. They will be responsible to the management team for creating strategy, plans, budgets and programmes to grow the business. They will also be expected to balance the skills, resources and processes of the function to optimum effect and for the benefit of the business in its market. They will have delegated responsibility to manage the function effectively.

They will therefore need to ensure that their marketing community has good knowledge of service marketing, has relevant competencies, and uses appropriate techniques and robust processes. They will also need to engage with the whole firm to ensure that client experience is appropriate to meet the firm's objectives. In short, the function needs to keep up to date and act as a catalyst for the whole firm in its approach to market.

In partnerships or networks of professionals, the situation tends to be more fluid and less clearly defined. Different partners will have initiated different marketing activities, which are frequently handled by people who have no specialist marketing knowledge and often, in large firms, are not linked to each other. Even if a marketing manager or marketing department exists, they are not likely to have exclusive responsibility for all business generation tasks.

As in all aspects of business life, these activities can be made more effective by using the right techniques, deploying relevant skills and designing effective processes. Experienced marketing specialists can advise on the most effective approach and methods to link activities together for the benefit of the whole firm. Managing marketing in a more consistent, concerted fashion is likely to reap enormous rewards for these firms. Leaders of partnerships can therefore improve the margins of their businesses, generating more revenues at less cost, if they institutionalise service marketing skills and technology in a form which is applicable to their firm.

Unfortunately, prejudice and misunderstanding frequently deny professional services firms the chance to use marketing techniques to their full advantage. Some think that, as the professionals themselves have to execute work, they must therefore undertake all the activities to win it and so there is no place for specialist marketers. Others confuse marketing with advertising and are thus sceptical about its usefulness. Still others think that marketing is exclusively associated with consumer goods and are unaware of modern service marketing techniques.

If leaders of professional services firms want to optimise their approach to revenue generation, it is important to understand exactly what marketing is and work with representatives of the specialism to make sure it is effectively deployed in their business. This chapter concentrates on the responsibilities, organisational structure and managerial processes of the marketing function in a professional services firm. It seeks to show how leaders can align the development of the function to the strategic needs of the business.

One more time: what is marketing?

Marketing has been variously called an art (because it is creative, requiring judgement and experience), a science (because market-oriented companies use data and analysis to inform decision-making), a management discipline (one of the functions of many firms), an academic field of study and a profession (because it requires deep knowledge of techniques with the experience to know how and when to apply them). In reality it has all the elements of all of these. Opinion formers have defined it as follows:

• Marketing is the process of planning and executing the conception, pricing, promotion and distribution of ideas, goods and services to create exchanges that satisfy individual and organisational goals – American Marketing Association (AMA).
• Marketing is the management process that identifies, anticipates and satisfies customer requirements profitably – UK Chartered Institute of Marketing (CIM).
• Marketing is the social process by which individuals and groups obtain what they need and want through creating and exchanging products and value with others – Philip Kotler (Kotler and Armstrong, 2003).

Marketing is therefore a management process by which leaders of a firm draw in revenue and grow the business. These activities can be undertaken using common sense by anyone in the firm. However, the firm will be more effective, and generate more income in a more cost-effective way, if the right techniques are used and if experienced specialists are engaged using management processes that enable them to contribute appropriately to the health of the firm.

Marketing activities relevant to professional services firms

The aspects of marketing relevant to professional services firms, in no particular order, are:

- **Competitive intelligence:** understanding what competitors are doing and adjusting the firm's direction in the light of that.
- **Opportunity analysis:** agreeing which opportunities in the market are likely to create more revenue for the firm and how they might be addressed.
- **Client management:** the approach by which the firm gains new clients or relates to existing clients.
- **Internal communications:** creating and managing messages between the employees and the leadership.
- **Pitch or bid processes:** the process by which the firm presents its credentials or specific proposals about an engagement to potential clients.
- **Press management:** the way the firm handles its public appearance in the media.
- **Sponsorship:** any paid involvement in sporting/entertainment/arts events to improve the reputation of the firm.
- **Corporate social responsibility (CSR):** engaging in the support of community projects to encourage a positive reputation for the firm.
- **Client events:** hosting social or issue-based events in order to attract new business.
- **Thought leadership:** presentation at public conferences, producing reports, books or other projects to demonstrate the skills of the firm and draw in new business.
- **Collateral design:** the production of leaflets, brochures and case studies to illustrate client issues.
- **Advertising:** using paid advertisements in TV, radio and print to spread awareness of the firm.

- **Client database management:** using technology to ensure that client details are assets of the whole firm.
- **Networking:** managing relationships with a wide range of individuals in order to generate a book of business.
- **Pricing:** setting charges for the time of the firm's professionals and specific services for clients.
- **Creating new services:** designing and launching new concepts or offerings.

In addition, for consumer retail services in particular:

- **Point of sale:** displays on premises.
- **Premises selection and design:** layout of shops to create the optimum traffic flow and sales.
- **Sales promotion:** campaigns designed to make certain products or services attractive in order to increase sales.

All professional services firms, of all sizes and ownership types, will undertake some aspect of many of these activities.

The evolution of marketing in an organisation

Much of the academic work on marketing focuses on issues of marketing theory, concept or practice. By and large it makes assumptions about the way the function works in a firm. It is assumed that there is a well-developed organisation led by a marketing director or chief marketing officer (CMO), able to call on financial and human resources to undertake research, manage advertising or adjust product features in the light of rational, justified arguments. There is little talk of the need to convince organisations of the need for marketing, of competing for resources or of organisational politics.

The situation is rarely so clear cut. Whereas some large mature firms have elite and impressive marketing units that lead the firm's approach to market, much marketing is done in small firms with only one or two marketing specialists. In others, the marketing function is undeveloped. It has to argue for its role in the organisation and has to invest in processes, as well as running projects to generate revenue. In some, the company itself does not understand its own need for certain marketing skills and restricts the contribution that the function can make, limiting it to, say, a minor promotional role.

Professor Nigel Piercy's research (Piercy, 2001) showed that there was rarely consistency about what functions marketing leaders have responsibility for. Nor was there consistency in the shape of organisations. He observed four types of marketing departments:

- **Integrated/full service:** closest to the theoretical models and with a wide range of responsibilities and power in the organisation.
- **Strategic/services:** smaller units with less power and integration. Their influence is in the area of marketing support services or specific policies or strategies.
- **Selling overhead:** often large numbers and dispersed but primarily engaged in sales support activities.
- **Limited staff role:** small numbers with few responsibilities and engaged in specific staff support such as market research or media relations.

Also, it appears that marketing departments evolve (from a limited staff role to fully integrated) as firms grow and marketing grows in importance within them. When a company is initially formed much of the marketing role is undertaken by the founders or specialist subcontractors. Some time after that a marketing specialist will be hired to manage activities such as brochure production, new product launch and perhaps some advertising. As the firm grows, marketing specialists are recruited into different places in the organisation, such as public relations (PR) and sales support.

Later, this develops into the fully integrated marketing function, seen in many corporate firms, including those with professional services branches. A large corporate entity might have up to 500 marketing specialists running campaigns, integrated by both a hierarchical senior management team culminating in a marketing director or chief marketing officer (CMO) and by the use of common processes and technology. In some (largely mature product) companies the marketing function is an elite group of specially recruited and trained people who lead its approach to market and develop into its dominant leadership group.

There appears to be a similar evolution of marketing in professional services firms, which reflects the need of leaders to ensure that the growing firm engages with the market. In most young professional service firms, much of the 'business development' work is led by the partners themselves. They develop a reputation for good work, they present the firm's credentials, they create a network of trusting potential buyers and they finalise deals. However, there comes a time when the demands of work mean that all these activities cannot be handled by one person. Some try to maintain the pace, undertaking business development work erratically during lulls in client projects. Some enjoy the variety this gives to their professional life alongside client work. However, many will eventually bring in 'marketing people', as support, to help the firm grow.

In the first phases of growth, a firm's first marketing resource will often be someone who is a good administrator, who is able to organise functions such as social events or seminars for clients. The partners decide what to do and this administrator manages it. There is little specialist input to strategy, direction or ideas. As the firm grows a little further, it may engage a few specialists such as a PR professional to manage media contacts, but the marketing function is still largely administrative 'support'.

The next phase is when the leaders become conscious that they need to generate their income in a new way and seek help from 'professional' marketers. Their logic is that, just as they engage lawyers to advise on legal issues and human resources (HR) specialists to advise on human capital, the firm would benefit from qualified marketing experience. They will often engage consultants (if margins are small) or hire practitioners from 'classic' marketing backgrounds (i.e. consumer goods companies). Unfortunately many of these people find it difficult to make the transition to the world of professional services. The techniques they have used in their product background and the culture of the organisation are both very different. Also, they often find it to be an environment in which marketing is not valued and it is therefore difficult to find a voice for their arguments which will carry weight with the firm's leaders.

Another phase follows when leaders engage with marketing specialists who have an understanding of both state-of-the-art service marketing techniques and the unique characteristics of the professional services industry. This may be in a role which supports a group of partners with marketing programmes or as part of the senior leadership team for the whole firm. At the time of writing, for instance, several leading multinational professional services firms are seeking CMOs for the first time because they are conscious of dramatic changes in their market. Partnerships are therefore beginning to employ marketing skills within their firms to have greater effect and to maximise their contribution to business growth.

Berwin Leighton Paisner: embedding marketing into the culture

Berwin Leighton Paisner is a full service law firm based in London. Its expanding international network includes its own office in Brussels and alliance partners in New York, Paris, Milan and Rome, along with relationships to firms in other key areas around the world. Its revenues in 2004 of £102 million ($182 million) placed it 13th in the City in the listings of the UK's top 100 law firms by turnover.

But its goal is to become a top 10 firm in the City through a strong marketing orientation. Recognition of its progress so far came in 2004 when it was named Law Firm of the Year at the profession's premier annual awards ceremony.

The emphasis on a more strategic approach to marketing to build the business began to gain momentum in 1999, with the installation of a new managing partner at what was then Berwin Leighton. At the same time, Gillian Khan arrived from another leading law firm, DLA, as marketing director. While there was very little in the way of marketing infrastructure, she found that because the firm already had a good strategic understanding of what marketing was about, she was knocking on an open door.

The first big step in the firm's decision to move into a different competitive league came in 2001 with a merger with Paisner. Berwin Leighton had originally been a real estate specialist, and still earned roughly half of its fees from that area. To bring profitability in line with the top 10 firms and to continue to cater for an increasingly finance-driven real estate market, however, the firm would have to strengthen its corporate and finance capabilities considerably. The merger brought corporate expertise, while the firm beefed up its financial skills through hiring the appropriate professionals.

Another key part of the strategy has been to offer an increased international capability. The firm had its own office in Brussels and then, in September 2002, formed an exclusive alliance with the US law firm

Kramer, Levin Naftalis & Frankel LLP, which had an office in Paris, to mount a joint attack on the European market. A further alliance in February 2003 brought Italy into the fold, and penetration into other key European centres continues. Alliances were judged to be preferable to the expense and potential cultural conflicts from full-scale mergers, although a much closer relationship could develop further down the line.

Finally, along with rebalancing the portfolio and becoming international, the managing partner put in place a firm-wide review covering every aspect of the firm from the bottom up and including both the practice areas and support departments. Well over 100 taskforces were set up with a wide mix of people from across the firm. For example, the taskforce on brand which Khan pulled together included five partners, a couple of marketing people and the IT director. These all produced action plans as a basis for the firm's development.

As of 2004, Khan reported to the managing partners and sat on the board. She managed a central marketing team overseeing functions such as client management, new business, public relations, marketing communications, international marketing and marketing technology. There were also marketing 'mini-teams' in the four key business categories of real estate, finance, corporate and litigation. These four divisions were further divided into 16 practice areas, while industry specialist groups cut across the practice areas in a matrix structure.

Making an impact

Marketing has become more deeply embedded in the firm's culture in a number of ways.

(i) **Client service.** There is a constant focus on providing excellent client service. For example, workshops have been run with each practice area. An entire practice group (including support and secretarial staff) is taken way from their work for three hours to make sure everyone understands just what their role should be in constantly improving client service.

There is also an established client relationship management (CRM) programme, including client relationship partners for each client.

Many value added services are offered to clients including tailored extranets giving clients access to various work status reports, tailored newsletters, briefings and updates and often allowing them to ask legal questions online.

(ii) New business. The firm is actively targeting bigger clients with bigger briefs in its bid to grow. There is widespread training in pitching for new business, including an online 'pitch' library, with templates. The sales director and the head of new business both help the partners go and sell to new clients. For very large tenders, initial meetings are held with everyone involved where the strategic thrust is decided.

(iii) Brand strategy. This has been an integral part of the firm's overall strategy. It encompasses every aspect of the culture, from the words that are used to describe the firm, the behaviour of the staff and the main messages to the market to the visual brand in all its formats. Marketing makes sure they are all consistent with the firm's strategy, culture and values.

(iv) Client research and analysis. Clients are interviewed on a regular basis, with the results tracked against a set of standard key performance indicators. Findings have shown that, increasingly, clients are taking quality as a given and instead are looking for responsiveness and partnership from their law firms.

One major initiative the marketing team has undertaken was a detailed analysis of the top 200 clients over a three-year period to see to what extent fees were rising, staying the same or decreasing. The results have been eye-opening for the partners and had a positive impact: not only has the value of each instruction risen, but the number of clients from which the firm receives a larger amount of work has gone up. It has also underlined to the partners just how important a role marketing can play.

(v) Market planning. Each practice has a marketing plan which is developed in alignment with the firm's overall business strategy. Each plan includes the strategy toward existing clients whose business the firm wants to grow, the new clients to target and the sectors to focus on. These plans are the basis for 12-month action plans.

(vi) Marketing programmes. The firm doesn't spend a lot on advertising as such. Instead, it puts much of its effort into developing a range of different events geared to specific clients. This includes educational events such as seminars and workshops. However, the firm also experiments with other formats. For example, it has signed up a high profile UK rugby player, Lawrence Dallaglio, both to promote the firm and to provide motivational events for staff and clients to focus on physical, mental and emotional fitness.

Lessons learned

Khan has learned a number of valuable lessons in how to improve the perception of marketing in a professional services firm:

* Professionals are bright people. Marketers need to explain a possible course of action, logically and in detail from the outset in order to gain buy-in.
* The big initiatives can't be achieved in a short timeframe. Most large projects require some kind of cultural or behavioural change which always takes time.
* Marketers need to persuade a significant proportion of partners to back their initiatives. It helps to win over some of the more influential partners first. Stress test the proposal by talking to people first or trial with a pilot group. And be prepared to modify the original plan.
* It can take anywhere from one to three years to change behaviour in a professional services firm.

Managing the organisational competence of the marketing function

The marketing leader in a firm needs to ensure that the marketing function evolves appropriately so that it is able to handle all the tasks that the strategic position of the firm in its market demands that it should. Sometimes the firm is unaware of these needs and they have to be argued for in the policy development process.

For example, a new marketing competence might be justified by a new market insight. If approved during the planning round it will then be resourced. Initially, it may take time to be effective or it may fail, setting the development of the competence back for several years. Alternatively, the firm might take a cautious approach, investing in a small trial before the new competence is fully deployed. It may, in fact, set up a marketing competence in another part of the organisation for, say, political reasons. But in all these ways the competence of a good marketing unit should evolve and develop in line with the firm's market needs.

It may be that the unit needs to embrace new skills. For example, some professional services businesses are owned by product companies, where the predominant approach to market will be through using product sales and marketing techniques. But these communication, product development and financial management styles will be inappropriate for a service business. The marketing team will therefore need to learn service marketing skills, educate their colleagues in their relevance and institutionalise them in their company. (In leading consumer goods companies, new graduates often serve a year long apprenticeship where they are taught the firm's marketing techniques because general marketing training is so superficial. There is now such a growing body of knowledge about how to market services that there is an argument for a similar approach to marketing training in professional services firms.)

Similarly, the tightening of some professional services markets might mean that the marketing department, or specialists within it, need new processes. For example, a number of firms are currently investigating structured relationship marketing programmes. Outlined elsewhere in this book, these involve a new mind set and an emphasis on a behavioural approach to marketing. It needs new systems to map networks, and new communication techniques such as viral marketing. The marketing department needs to learn to test and establish such new processes.

The marketing director or CMO thus needs to ensure that the skills, processes and competencies of the marketing function are sufficiently robust to meet the needs of the firm. Many leaders undertake regular external benchmarking exercises or detailed marketing audits (see Part III) to keep their function in line with competitive needs. The necessary infrastructure projects are then costed and specified as part of the normal planning round. Without such a continual review, the unit can fall behind, restricting its contribution to the business.

Different marketing roles

Market management

The market manager is the source and powerhouse of marketing in an organisation. The role is to understand a defined market and construct programmes to influence it. Those programmes will feature in the strategy, planning and resource allocation processes of the business. Market managers will also give briefs to their firm's marketing services arm and to chosen suppliers to execute work. Their prime role is to lead the activities aimed at their portion of the market.

As organisations define their markets differently and shape themselves differently, the nature of market management will differ. Some market managers are specialists in an industrial sector (for example, technology or pharmaceuticals or financial services), some in a consumer group and some in a business unit. In small companies, the marketing manager of the whole firm is likely to behave like the market manager of a strategic business unit (SBU) or industry marketer in a large firm. The job titles of market managers will therefore vary even if the role and approach do not.

A market manager needs four essential skill sets:

- **Knowledge of service marketing techniques:** able to choose which is relevant at which moment in time.
- **Excellent communications skills:** able to act, with credibility, as an advisor to the firm's leaders.
- **Practical delivery:** able to deliver practical marketing programmes which, when executed well, generate leads for the practice or firm. This includes: analytical understanding of research, the ability to design clear programmes and project management skills.
- **Good management skills:** able to deploy people, processes and resources to achieve agreed objectives.

Table 7.1 *Marketing tip: questions to ask marketing specialists at interview.*

1. What are the differences between product and service marketing?
2. How do you determine the competitive strengths of the firm's reputation?
3. How would you enhance our firm's reputation?
4. How would you approach a partner who wanted you to execute a marketing activity that was, in your judgement, ineffective or ill-advised?

The 'practice marketing manager'

This is the market manager role in professional partnerships. Whether a practice is a small firm or a group of industry partners in a large firm or a country firm in a network, it will reach a stage where it will benefit from a specialist marketer.

This person will have several functions. The first is to manage all marketing activities effectively. These will frequently be ad hoc marketing or business development activities initiated by partners between client projects. They are likely to be: large social events with clients, seminar programmes, internal 'town hall' meetings, sponsorship of public conferences and 'thought leadership' projects. A good practice marketer will shape this into a coherent programme which will have a cumulative impact on the market, increasing leads and referrals (see Table 7.1).

It may be that, to date, some of the activities have not been professionally planned and that some suppliers are not providing competitively priced work. Alternatively, some long-standing events may yield few leads while others may not be aligned with the firm's objectives. A good practice marketer can tackle these issues and as a result frequently show cost savings upon starting with an established partnership by shaping an effective programme.

Second, through this work, the best practice marketers win the respect of the practice leaders and become advisors on market-related issues. They will be able to contribute to debate about direction or bring in appropriate expertise to tackle market-based strategic issues. The partners and the practice then gain access to specialist marketing expertise, improving impact in the market. Therefore, in addition to the skills of the market manager, this type of marketer also needs good consultative skills. They need to treat their partner group like clients.

A firm with a number of practices needs to define this role throughout their business and encourage the various practice leaders to seek specialists with the right skills. Once the concept is established, the specialists can be linked either by direct reporting to the corporate marketing functions or by dual reporting (i.e. the marketing function provides career development and mentoring while the leader of the local practice has direct day-to-day management). In the former, practice marketers might report to the central function and be assigned as consultants to different practice leaders.

By linking these people in a clear or virtual organisation, a common language, style and approach to work can be encouraged and a career structure develops which improves overall expertise. This will benefit the whole firm as plans, budgets and timetables begin to coincide. Over time there will be a concerted, greater impact on the whole market and better deployment of resources.

Marketing services

A range of specialist marketing activities needs to be undertaken to complete many projects. Activities as diverse as press releases, printing proposals, managing large clients, securing client hospitality packages and advertising have to be carried out by the firm. In fact, many of a professional services firm's business projects, whether called marketing or not, are carried out by marketing agencies, freelance individuals or employed specialists. Yet it is unlikely that functional marketing will be at its most effective if organised as an erratic array of support for partners across a large firm (although this is not unknown). Such specialist providers are best structured into a service organisation within the firm which manages clear processes with approved external providers.

This unit needs to be organised like an internal agency so that:

- It treats internal practices and business units as clients.
- It understands the firm's objectives (to avoid taking on work which is off-brief).
- It has clear briefing processes.
- It uses proper procurement processes.

Its functions are likely to include: design, bid management, proposal preparation, event management, sponsorship, press relations and advertising in all its forms. Properly executed, this will ensure the best use of resources, optimising spend and improving impact. Just as importantly, it will contribute to progressive organisational learning by becoming a repository of experience and approach.

Creation of 'product managers' for services

A function which has evolved within the manufacturing environment is the 'product manager'. This individual is a senior manager who is dedicated to the management of the features and benefits of a product and its success in the market place. They often have worldwide responsibility for the creation of new products, the adjustment of existing products and the deletion of products from the range. They are invariably people who have either a technical background or a deep knowledge of the organisation. They are trained in new product creation techniques and have responsibility for the business plan of the product, for understanding the requirements of buyers and for the profitability of the whole product range.

Theorists have argued that, if the creation of new services is important to organisations, they should have dedicated 'service managers' who have equal weight and responsibility. The role of a 'new service development manager' would be:

- To create new services.
- To adjust the features mix of existing services.
- To withdraw old services.
- To prepare and manage the business plan for a particular service.
- To be responsible for the profit of the service being brought to market.
- To establish all processes necessary to launch the service successfully and generate revenue from it.

Many organisations have 'service champions', who are senior individuals responsible for the spread of a new service concept through the organisation. Unlike product mangers these are not often dedicated to a service but are senior managers with weight in the organisation who are political champions for the concept of that service. This is necessary because of the difficulty of selling new service concepts inside an organisation. The need to get buy-in from so many different functions and individuals to support a new service concept means that internal marketing is critical to the success of that service in a way that is not necessary with new products.

A champion needs the skill to encourage the members of the new service development team to perform at their optimum level, while addressing the team objectives. They must lead the team and smooth over disagreements and, particularly, give support to the new service concept at all levels in the organisation.

In general the 'service managers' need to have good all-round knowledge of the business and good overall commercial awareness to suit their broad general responsibility. In addition to this, sales and marketing knowledge as well as technical understanding are important. In some companies, service 'managers' are from a marketing and sales background but also have some technical understanding, whereas in others they are technically trained people with good business awareness.

The CMO or partner-level marketer

This person has several roles. The first is to provide experience, judgement and advice to colleagues about the firm's policy to inform decision-making. The second is to lead the function, ensuring that it is properly resourced and contributes to the firm. The third is to be the voice of the market within the firm, challenging it to embrace market opportunities and understand client needs.

This role is most often found in large corporate firms which adopt a functional structure and where marketing people responsible for professional services business units have to report to the group marketing director or CMO. Even those which have changed from a partnership to a corporate entity tend to create specialised sales and marketing functions, with a senior marketing leader in time.

Professor Leonard Berry (Berry and Parasuraman, 1991) suggests that the role of a marketing director or CMO in a service business is different to that of a product company because so many parts of the organisation are undertaking marketing activities in addition to the specialist marketing department. He suggests that the role includes:

- **Change architect:** ensuring a good fit between the organisation and its market.

- **Marketing facilitator:** educating managerial and front-line staff in the marketing skills that will make their interface with clients more effective.
- **Image manager:** using all possible means to establish a distinctive and compelling company identity.

In partnerships, a number of the larger firms have people at partner level leading marketing in much the same role as the 'chief marketing officer' in publicly quoted companies. Sometimes these are partners who are qualified in the firm's core skills, undertaking the role as part of personal development. If they are marketing people they have probably come through a consultancy route, although some might have been recruited externally. (Sometimes, as in the case of some accounting and legal firms, the senior person leading marketing has a special contractual relationship so that they can have partner status and authority without necessarily being a full partner in the firm.)

The decision as to whether the marketing leaders should be a marketing specialist or not appears to depend on whether the firm views it as an important function at that point in the firm's development. Those who form the view that it is critical to their success tend to seek a dialogue with a seasoned specialist.

Different organisational constructs

The classic functional shape

The classic marketing organisation is a clear function in a bureaucracy, depicted in Figure 7.1. It reports to a CMO and has the delegated authority to generate revenue and create all marketing programmes. This type of structure has been criticised heavily by Western management thinkers in recent years, as they have become fans of flat and flexible structures. There are, however, real benefits in terms of specialisation, clarity of reporting, accountability and decision-making emphasis of this type of structure. It is still found in many firms.

The diagram depicts typical functions within the unit but these can vary enormously. For instance, brand management might exist within market management (because it focuses on categories) or in marketing communi-

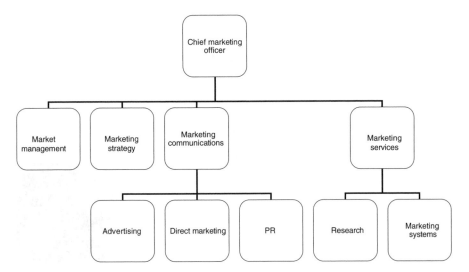

Figure 7.1 *The classic functional shape.*

cations. Also, there may be elements of the marketing mix in other parts of the organisation. For example, some firms place new service or product development and pricing under a separate director. Others have directors of corporate relations responsible for reputation, brand, CSR and PR.

The single marketer or SBU

Another type of organisational structure involves the single, or isolated, marketer, depicted in Figure 7.2. This person might report to the firm's leader, gaining authority to create programmes, strategy and change from the closeness of that relationship. Constrained by lack of resources, the single marketer needs influence to get the wider organisation to take on work and the budget to rely on external contractors. They need the capability to handle a wide variety of tasks and the humility to do much of the work themselves.

In some firms they report to a senior leader who manages all functional specialists. This, however, tends to be less effective because it weakens the assumed authority behind the specialism, reducing the influence of marketing.

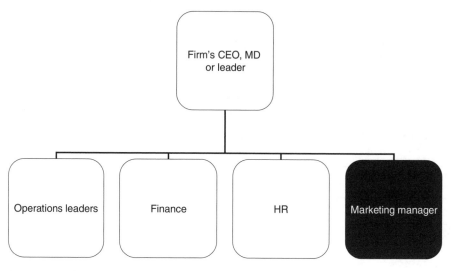

Figure 7.2 *The single marketer or SBU structure.*

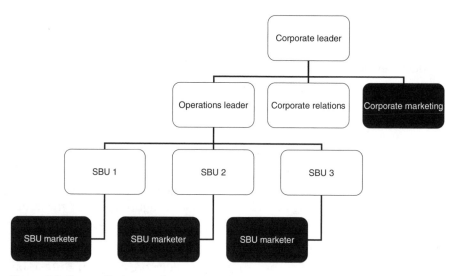

Figure 7.3 *Decentralised approach.*

The decentralised model

Figure 7.3 depicts a decentralised organisation with devolved business units. These might be practices in different disciplines or in different geographic countries. The effectiveness of the approach and the behaviour of the marketers depend on the degree of autonomy of the different units. For example, this structure is often adopted by large technology companies. In these, the professional service arm will be a strategic business unit (SBU) but they will be expected to work within tight guidelines. The marketer is likely to have a clear job description with defined competences and objectives. They are likely to report regularly to the corporate function and participate in clear, firm-wide processes.

At the other extreme, some large partnerships are networks of separate firms with different profit pools. They cooperate in a joint approach to the international market in order to get synergy out of issues like brand, service offers and international client service. The marketers in these firms are likely to have almost complete autonomy from the corporate centre, reporting to local leaders. It is in these networks that a definition of competencies, skill and approach is likely to yield economies for the whole network. In particular, the corporate marketing leader needs to review continually which parts of the function ought to be handled at corporate or local level in order to manage the competitive effectiveness of the whole network.

Shaping the firm-wide function in a network organisation or large partnership

Since the evolution of service marketing as a recognised discipline of marketing study, theorists have challenged the effectiveness of the centralised and specialised marketing department. Apart from a general debate in Western businesses about flatter, decentralised and less hierarchical organisations, they have argued that some of the special characteristics of services demand a new approach.

First, they suggest that, as the production and consumption of services cannot be separated, it involves a much broader interface between the organisation and the buyers than in production companies. Second, because the people who deliver the service are part of the value their clients buy, they are intimately involved in the marketing process.

It is the advocates of a radical relationship marketing approach who have pushed for a fundamental rethink of marketing structures. Some have suggested that everyone in the firm is a 'part-time marketer' due to their involvement in the engagement of the firm with its buyers and their resultant need to undertake many marketing activities. In these organisations, the main marketing task is as much about facilitating a cross-organisational market-oriented culture as it is about managing a relatively small unit of specialists. The CMO is as likely to be concerned with improving the account handling skills of colleagues or the proposal management capability of business units as the creation of a communications campaign or new service.

In many ways partnerships are the embodiment of the decentralised, flat and flexible organisations theorists advocate and have been so for many decades. While their strength lies in autonomy and closeness to the market, a drawback is the tendency towards confusion of the skill and competence of 'support' within them. Some practices might use client service staff to execute all business development work, others will use administrators and others will use marketing specialists. Some networks have no central marketing department, or a very small one comprising inexperienced people, and so lose the input of high quality specialist insight into their firm's direction. The resource then depends on the vision and aims of the partners in the various practices. However, from the perspective of the network, this results in diseconomies of scale and a less than optimum impact on the market.

The organisational shape depicted in Figure 7.4 reflects the thinking among several leading firms to overcome these drawbacks. First, there is a specialist function handling corporate reputation, media relations and chief

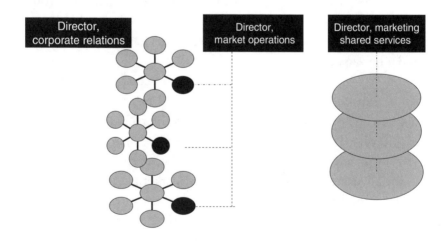

Practice marketers in separate practices

Figure 7.4 *Functional shape in a large partnership.*

executive communications. Second, there is a separation, at both corporate and local level, of practice marketers (who directly interface with partners) and marketing services specialists. The latter are grouped into a firm-wide shared service to maximise effectiveness, budgets and supplier management.

In some firms, practice marketers report directly to the partner group they serve. In these firms, there will be benefits from creating a common approach, defining skills and using senior marketing leaders as mentors. In other firms, all practice marketers report directly to the CMO but work with the practices as consultants. All are linked, however, in a professional community which sets standards and direction.

Supplier management and outsourcing: where to draw the line

Most marketing activities involve a process which hands on work to different specialists in the production process. The market research process, for example, will begin with some form of market manager agreeing a need to understand a part of the market with an operational group. They are likely to engage a research company which will use statisticians, field researchers and questionnaire specialists to produce the work. Similarly, if the firm wishes to communicate with the market it might engage creatives, strategists, designers and printers to undertake a piece of communication. Clearly not all these skills need to be directly employed by the firm. For example, few professional service firms would consider employing their own printers, yet many employ their own designers.

Leaders of the marketing function need to review continually the advantages and disadvantages of direct employment against contracted work. Directly employed people understand the firm and its environment in depth but there needs to be sufficient volume of work to employ them and the managerial skill to run their own specialism appropriately.

A contractor, on the other hand, is likely to charge at market rate and work hard to deliver to its client. This benefit has driven many in the professional services industry to outsource much of their marketing services function. They leave in the organisation a few market managers, to understand the organisation and interpret its will to suppliers, but much else is given to contractors. The success of this approach depends upon the enduring relationship with the contractors. If they understand the firm's strategy and enjoy a mutually beneficial relationship with the firm, then such moves can be effective.

An activity model for professional services marketing

What, then, are the elements of the marketing function that need to exist in a professional service firm and how should they interrelate? Figure 7.5 has been adapted from work by Paul Denvir, Cliff Ferguson and Kevin Walker (Denvir et al., 1998) to suggest that there are three 'levels' of marketing in a professional services firm:

(i) Contact marketing consists of all activities at the point of client contact. It includes activities such as proposals, events, account management, business development and so on.

(ii) Credibility marketing includes industry skills, technical skills (professionals often take their skills for granted and fail to tell the market about them), and thought leadership.

(iii) Corporate-level marketing encompasses brand, go-to-market strategy and CSR.

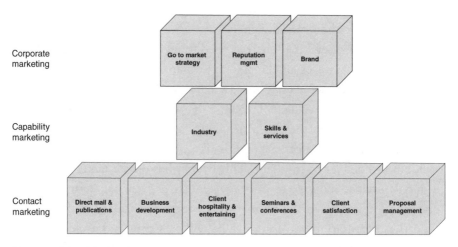

Figure 7.5 *Model of marketing activities in a professional service firm.*
Source: Adapted from Denvir *et al.* (1998)

The firm should identify all activities in these categories and link them in the management structure with common budgets. This might be a 'virtual' team with one common professional leadership or a unitary organisation under a CMO. Properly integrated, this function will enable the firm to generate income more cost-effectively, because the activities will be mutually supportive. For example, a well-constructed 'corporate marketing' programme will explain the brand to the market, while effective 'capability marketing' will promote industry expertise to the target client group. Both of these will save costs when the firm's professionals are proposing work to clients, because they will have no need to explain these two issues.

Marketing administration

The impression that marketing is a creative and intuitive art, rather than a professional management discipline, has caused it to be run as a haphazard series of activities in some firms. In reality, successful marketing relies as much on having good processes and administration as it does on using appropriate skills and concepts. These should cover areas such as:

Marketing planning

Table 7.2 contains an idealised format of a marketing plan. It is typical of the business unit plans found in professional services firms. It is an attempt

Table 7.2 *Suggested format for a marketing plan in a professional services organisation.*

- The leadership team's priorities.
- The firm's objectives.
- Summary of the market environment, insights from client research, competitive position and the firm's position in the market.
- Marketing objectives and targets.
- External marketing programmes and campaigns.
- Internal marketing programmes.
- Changes to services (new services, relaunches, withdrawals) plus associated price changes and communication activities.
- Collateral strategy and associated programmes.
- Infrastructure programmes (training, systems, organisational development).
- Longer-term investment programmes (i.e. brand, new market entry).
- Timetable of events.
- Budget.

to align the resources of the firm to meet business objectives, often in the immediate financial year, and is different to the firm's strategic plans.

Planning is a fundamental process of the marketing function. Some firms plan rigorously as part of an annual cycle while some are more short term, not even committing plans to any form of document. Yet, whether it is elaborate, detailed and long prepared or simply a series of decisions expressed by a leader, all firms should plan their approach to market. A plan aligns marketing resources and actions to both the leadership's priorities and budgets available. It makes strategic objectives achievable.

However it is developed, there are several issues which will round out and make a marketing plan effective:

(i) Strategic context. The plan must take into account the strategic issues which the firm faces, particularly those with direct market relevance such as brand, segmentation and competitive strategy. The strategic imperatives and corporate objectives of the firm must set the context for the plan.

(ii) Market perspective. No market plan is useful unless its approach is based on insight and perspectives on the market it addresses. The approaches outlined in Chapter 2 ought to be used to bring external orientation in the plan.

(iii) Scope. There are a number of issues the plan needs to address in order to give it maximum impact. They range from communication with different audiences through adjustments to service features or pricing, to changes in account selection and revenue targets. The most recognised concept which summarises the elements that need to be drawn into a marketing plan is the 'marketing mix' (see Part III for details). This is a shorthand for the items which need to be adjusted and balanced to influence a group of buyers. It suggests that the firm's marketing plan should comprise programmes in the areas of: product, pricing, place (distribution) and communication (for product companies) with the addition of 'people', 'process' and 'physical presence' (the seven Ps of service marketing) for service companies. This is represented in Figure 7.6.

Yet it is the mix, the right adjustment of components to suit each target group of buyers, which is most important. The marketing team should include all these elements in the marketing plans of the business, even if

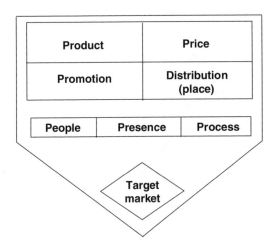

Figure 7.6 *The marketing mix for services.*

their organisation is not directly responsible for them. The marketing plan is the plan for the whole firm, not just their function.

(iv) Dialogue. Marketing plans must be constructed in dialogue with key stakeholders. They should be consulted at the start, during the analysis and as preliminary conclusions are drawn. This communication needs to be two way, engaging them and including their views. It will ensure that the final plan is approved more easily.

The market planning process ought to combine all these features. It should be based on relevant strategy and analytical insight. It must embrace all appropriate activities and create practical budget programmes. A full approach, likely to be adopted by a corporate firm, is represented in Figure 7.7.

Programme management

There is a tendency in companies that are not experienced in marketing for communications projects to be short term and erratic. Poor planning and uncoordinated marketing resource result in many different messages being sent out by the same firm at the same time, which undermine each other. Moreover, a lack of investment in market communications often ensures that such messages are short term, erratic and poorly executed. Yet it takes

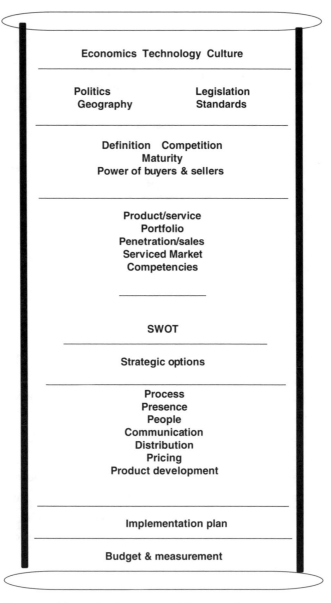

Figure 7.7 *Overview of the market planning process for service businesses.*

time for markets and buyers to grasp a message in the midst of all the other communications that assail them. As a result the messages coming out of inexperienced companies are not integrated and can cause confusion in the market place, if heard at all. Neither the market in general nor the clients in particular have a chance to grasp the message.

The concept of the marketing programme introduces a discipline into a firm's communications with its market. It is the marketing version of project management and ensures that programme managers plan the message, the media and the duration of the communication, together with its integration with other programmes that clients are likely to receive. Programmes tend to be a year to a year and a half in duration. The investment of funds into a few well-planned programmes of longer duration is more effective than multiple, unplanned and confusing bursts of activity. It is a case of less is more.

Each programme has specific objectives, defined scope and a delivery programme manager. In planning the programme, all activities and interdependencies should be identified. It may be divided into different fields of activities (thought leadership, PR, etc.) and could be grouped into 'campaigns'. All programmes and campaigns should then be grouped into a timetable of firm-wide marketing activities to clear any clashes of message to the market or to a client.

Briefing processes

Like computers, first-class marketing programmes are dependent on the data and programming put into them. Garbage in means garbage out. Marketing agencies, of any kind, are unable to produce good work of any impact if not properly briefed. The leading industry advertising agency Saatchi & Saatchi was so concerned about this that it created its own client template for firms that were unclear about their needs.

Firms should develop a standard brief for all activities which is given at the start of a job. This should be discussed and developed by the relevant team members to ensure that it is a clear articulation of the need and required work. A good supplier will take as much care to ensure that it understands the brief and interprets it correctly.

Marketing systems

The marketing function needs its own IT and systems strategy to develop its organisational competence in line with the firm's needs.

The best known marketing systems are databases to store and hold client details. At its most basic, client database management is the systems strategy used to hold records of clients. It is sensible for these systems to have relevant functionality (i.e. the ability to make lists, reminder mechanisms for important events, etc.). Whether this information is held on a Palm Pilot, on an Outlook database or in a sophisticated customer relationship management (CRM) system, professional services firms need systems to hold client data.

CRM is, in fact, a relatively new concept which suggests that the contact between a firm and its clients should be managed and should deepen, to the profitability of both, if responses are properly handled. By analysing purchase data using sophisticated computer systems the supplier learns the purchasing preferences of the buyers and can then respond by packaging further articles and communications tailored to them.

Unfortunately this has been oversold by both consultants and computer companies and led to overelaborate consulting and IT projects. As a result some have shown disputable real return and led to growing cynicism about the concept's benefits. At the time of writing there have been a number of research reports that show that CRM projects have disappointed. In addition, CRM systems were designed by computer manufacturers for use in traditional companies with an hierarchical structure and clear sales organisations. Some of the functionality is not relevant to professional services and costly customisation is often necessary.

There is, however, a need for firms to set a strategy and framework for the sharing and maintenance of client data. This is an important issue for professional services firms in that, particularly in large firms, partners and other professionals tend to keep information about their clients and their network in individual databases. The control of a very precious intangible asset, client knowledge, therefore remains with individuals who may leave the firm, rather than the firm itself. Client data systems, despite the difficulty of implementing them, aim to reduce this risk on behalf of the firm's owners.

Lesser known are marketing systems with other functionality. Systems exist, for example, that can plan and hold data on marketing campaigns, marketing programmes and materials. This means that, in large firms, best practice can be shared and marketing specialists can see potential clashes of programmes at the planning stage. Also, by storing research reports, advertisements, brochures and other materials, marketing specialists in smaller parts of the firm (perhaps in smaller geographies) can use and adapt materials developed by others. One major firm, for example, found large savings in professionals' time resulted from having an online 'pitchbook' available for international practices. This held key facts and case studies which could be customised for client proposals by local professionals once downloaded.

Systems also exist to help with marketing analysis and planning. They can be used to store research and other data. Using electronic versions of many of the tools described in Part III can help to focus strategic thinking and decision-making.

Purchasing

Marketing-naive firms tend to have ad hoc (and hence expensive) relationships with a range of marketing agencies and suppliers. The industry tends to encourage the nonsensical view that these creative agencies should be exempt from the rigours of purchasing and contract negotiations. However, all should be subject to proper controls through a managed purchasing process. (A small firm can hire freelance buyers to handle this for them.)

Michael Page changes the rules of recruitment marketing

Michael Page International is one of Europe's leading professional recruitment consultancies. It was founded in 1976 in London, primarily to recruit accountants for industrial clients. Now publicly quoted on the London Stock Exchange, it operates across a broad spectrum of industries and professions, with over 100 offices in 16 countries around the world.

When Mike Stevenson arrived as head of marketing at the London headquarters in 2000 from car maker Mazda, there was a good-sized marketing team. However, it was mainly concerned with 'marketing support', such as setting advertisements for other parts of the company, for example, rather than using marketing to help develop and grow the business.

His brief from the senior management was to inject far more professionalism into the function. Going public in 2001 had reinforced the need for the company to make sure that professional marketing underpinned its brand, and hence its reputation, for top-level quality and performance. So the first step was to put in place the processes, systems and procedures that would improve the level of service to the department's internal clients. This included basic things such as making sure that phones in the department were answered immediately and the creation of a 'client service' questionnaire to receive feedback from other departments in the firm.

As the more rigorous approach took hold, the second phase was to encourage the marketing team to begin to think more proactively about how they could help their colleagues in the front line. Stevenson had soon realised that the way to spread the marketing message in such a sales-led environment was not to propose big, costly marketing projects but to be patient, be realistic about what could be done and, above all, take a very commercial approach that focused on particular business issues. That included being careful about using any marketing jargon that might alienate other colleagues.

One of the team's first successes was with a direct mail campaign to highlight to chosen clients that Michael Page dealt with temporary as well as permanent appointments. It consisted of a box with the client's name, and with a pair of handcuffs and keys inside (the idea was that the client would like the temps so much they would want to hang on to them).

The hope was that clients would find this so amusing, they would keep the box – and hence the Michael Page brand – on their desks, while at the same time injecting humour into a brand perceived as big and blue-chip but rather staid as well. The campaign, first tested with financial clients, was so well received that it was also targeted at legal and marketing clients. More importantly, it was instrumental in winning a number of new briefs to undertake work.

In 2004 the marketing department scored another hit with a press advertising campaign that stood out from the usual 'laundry list' approach to recruitment advertising by emulating fashion advertising. Created in-house, the ads were run first by the financial division. They attracted such acclaim that other areas of the company were soon asking for versions geared to their markets. The campaigns created quite a stir in the relatively staid world of recruitment advertising, attracting a lot of media attention, including a feature in the *Financial Times* (Figure 7.8).

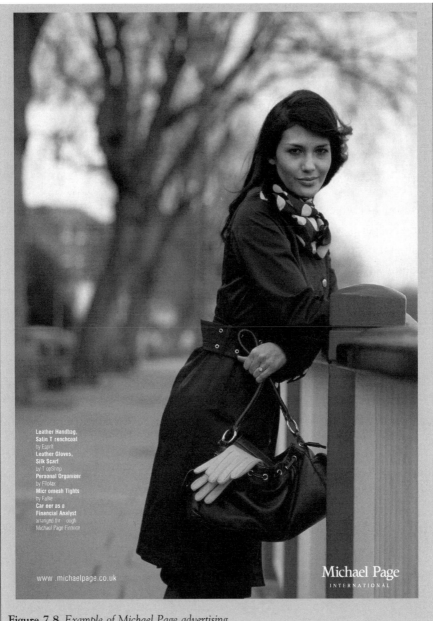

Leather Handbag,
Satin Trenchcoat
by Esprit
Leather Gloves,
Silk Scarf
by TopShop
Personal Organiser
by Filofax
Micromesh Tights
by Falke
Career as a
Financial Analyst
arranged through
Michael Page Finance

www.michaelpage.co.uk

Michael Page
INTERNATIONAL

Figure 7.8 *Example of Michael Page advertising.*

Scoring tactical hits with such marketing activity has helped strengthen marketing's credibility in the rest of the business. On a more strategic level, the marketing team has also been carrying out a widespread brand audit in order to develop the vision, mission and values that the brand encapsulates which, over time, can be rolled out across the world.

Marketing measurement

It is now many years since a leading entrepreneur said: '50% of my advertising budget is wasted but I don't know which 50%' (it has been attributed to several people). During that period marketing companies and marketing academics have tried various mechanisms to measure the effect and return of marketing. So much so that the comment no longer applies and there are many ways to get a view on the effectiveness of marketing, if the firm is willing to invest the effort in progressively developing the necessary processes and systems. It can be measured in three main ways:

Financial measures

The first and most important financial measure to have in place is revenue or projected project sales volume resulting from marketing activities. In a professional services firm, as work is done by client service partners, it is not often possible to isolate the sales resulting directly from marketing. It is possible, though, to record 'leads generated' and then to analyse how many turn into projects. It is also possible to form a judgement of cost-effectiveness and, hence, return on investment (ROI) for certain projects.

Market-based measures

One of the prime market-based measures of marketing activity is 'test' marketing. Groups of clients are either invited to group discussions or are subject to a small trial run. Response is then assessed. Another way of measuring the effect of marketing programmes is by having 'quiet areas'. These are geographic areas where no marketing is undertaken. They are compared against revenues in areas where programmes impact.

However, some of the most effective measures are research based. It is possible to establish research programmes which track changes in the attitudes and intentions of clients. An ongoing survey which takes, for example, a small monthly sample can build up useful trend data. Key issues to track are: brand strength, competitive reputation, propensity to refer and propensity to purchase.

Internal performance measures

The firm can establish its own performance measures. Partners and professional staff can spend both too little time on marketing activities (because they are doing internal or technical work) and too much (because they are having to do work better done by administrators or marketing specialists). The firm can set measures using time sheets of marketing tasks and also measures of marketing output (articles published, conferences spoken at, etc.).

Organisational politics; a final word to marketers on managerial effectiveness

Professional services firms are based on finance and, as economically based organisations, people within them are therefore competing for scarce resources. There is a competition of ideas, policies and ambitions which uses both informal and formal mechanisms to influence the development of the firm. The marketing function has to engage in this continual debate successfully if it is to fulfil its role effectively.

In fact, the marketer has a responsibility to join the fray in order to achieve the outcomes that shareholders or partners have employed them to gain. They must participate in formal meetings and communicate effectively in one-to-one presentations to leaders. Communication, policy development and, yes, internal politics are the mechanisms by which everyone in the organisation influences decisions and contributes to the health of the organisation.

Internal politics are a common experience of every organisation and a prime ingredient in managerial success. They are neither good nor bad. They simply are. It is strange, then, that this subject is so rarely discussed in books

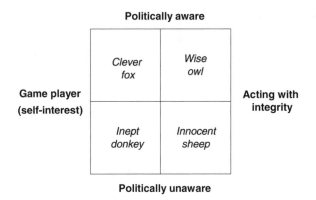

Figure 7.9 *Political effectiveness.*
Source: Baddeley and James (1987). Reproduced with permission from Baddeley and James, in Management Education and Development, Vol 18, p 18, Copyright © 1987, by permission of Sage Publications Ltd.

and business conferences. It is not unprofessional to think about how to achieve the strategies and policies from a marketer's perspective. In fact it is unprofessional not to.

A pair of academics who have studied it, Simon Baddeley and Kim James (Baddeley and James, 1987), created the matrix in Figure 7.9.

People who are politically unaware but put prime emphasis on achieving their job objectives are those that tend to say: 'I don't engage in politics. I just get on with my job.' These 'innocent sheep' want to shelter within their own technical area but are not doing the full job that the owners of the business employed them to do. 'Innocent sheep' tend to get sheared and eaten for lunch.

The employees who are primarily interested in themselves and are politically aware (the 'clever foxes') are the people about whom others say: 'they are very political'. Colleagues sense that their first interest is themselves and that the work to be done comes at least second. Real achievers at senior level, however, tend to be people who are both politically aware and also act primarily in the interest of the organisation. Nobody in any senior role achieves that pre-eminence without an awareness of how to influence organisations in order to get the outcome that they see is right.

Of course the degree of a marketing professional's influence depends also upon the level to which the organisation has adopted marketing orientation. Those organisations which do put marketing at the forefront of their business tend to have senior marketing people as part of board level debate and the function is therefore more influential. Others have a harder journey. However, whatever the degree of marketing, marketers must add the right management, communication and political skills to their technical expertise, if they are to serve the business owners properly.

Summary

For marketing to have an impact on revenues and profits, it is essential that the right organisational structure and management processes are in place. Many professional services firms, however, still equate marketing with advertising, or feel that marketing is best left to the professionals who execute the work for clients. But it is essential for firms to understand what good marketing is: a management process by which the leaders of a firm grow the business. Marketing evolves in firms over time. When a firm is small, it is often undertaken by the founders or is subcontracted to specialists. As firms grow, the way they approach marketing should become more sophisticated, to the point where marketing is developed into a fully integrated function with well-defined roles and responsibilities, processes and proper measurement techniques.

8

Personal business generation

Overview

Practitioners in all aspects of professional services are characterised by the expertise they have gained in whatever area of the industry they work. But if they want to prosper in their career, they have to do more than wait for work to come along. They need to learn how to generate business proactively, whether for themselves as sole practitioners or for their firms. There is a well-established marketing methodology to help increase and manage the flow of business. It includes a range of techniques to encourage client acquisition and retention. This chapter examines the issues, processes and approaches that make personal business generation successful.

Why generating business is essential

For many professionals, their early career is focused almost entirely on technical expertise. They go through university and post-graduate training, then some form of structured professional induction to learn the crafts and techniques of their chosen profession. However, at some stage, they begin to realise that the work they are receiving, and for which they will be paid, needs to be generated by some mechanism.

In some cases there is simply natural demand in the market place for the skill needed or a network of easily renewable contracts; in others there is a semi-monopolistic distortion in the market and, in others, a first-rate reputation or brand draws in the work. Frequently, though, it is also the energy and success of a senior individual that attracts business.

As professionals progress through their career, this issue of personal business generation washes in and out of their lives. Sometimes it demands a focus on a particular client, sometimes on the execution of a major project and other times they are focused on 'the market' in general. Many firms require candidates for partnership to demonstrate the ability to generate work. Junior professionals are therefore interested in business generation activities either as part of their general responsibilities (helping to grow the practice they are part of) or as preparation for partnership.

Reprise of relevant marketing concepts

Pipeline management

This is a management concept and sales discipline which builds the generation of business into the day-to-day life of either an individual practitioner or a group of professionals working in a shared practice. It is the foundation of good sales practice and the focus of sales management in many industries. Sometimes called the 'sales funnel' and sometimes 'the book of business', it is a discipline that translates easily into the professional services industry, particularly in project-based businesses.

Without good pipeline management, marketing activity can be erratic and will only occur after a particular job has been finished. If there is no obvious next job, the professional might keep busy on marketing activities, among other things, until the next project comes along. Unfortunately, this means that business generation is erratic and unstructured. The practice experiences peaks and troughs in workflow because there is no consistent focus on the generation of future work. Pipeline management helps overcome these difficulties. Figure 8.1 illustrates the concept, which should be approached from a hard-headed, numerically driven perspective.

For example, starting from the right-hand side, if a professional has a target of $2 million, and the average value of their projects is $500000, they need to win four projects a year. The next section of the pipeline shows that,

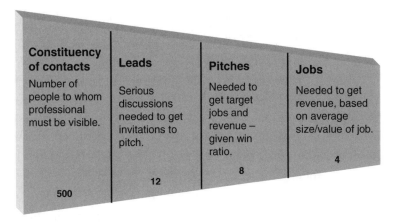

Figure 8.1 *Pipeline management: a tool to manage business flow.*

in order to win four jobs a year, they need to propose a number of projects to potential clients. If, in their market place, the conversion ratio is two to one, then they need to propose eight jobs to win four.

In some professional services markets there are no formal proposals and presentations. Sometimes a client will simply ask the professional to start the work. Other times the project can be loosely defined. Nevertheless, there must be some form of discussion, presentation or scoping of projects which forms the basis of the agreement to go ahead. These all count as part of the 'pitches' section of the pipeline. If the practice is to have work at all, then someone has to conduct 'pitches' of work, however informal, to potential clients.

The next category refers to 'leads' or 'serious expression of interest'. A professional will be known to a number of potential business clients but, at some stage, those clients must express an interest in the practitioner's professional skills if work is to proceed. This might be by telephone, in a meeting or in a social context. The clients discuss their need for a certain skill and ask whether the professional is interested in engaging with them.

That may simply be an invitation to examine the need, or an offer to take part in a 'beauty parade' where the firm has to formally respond to a request for a proposal, or formally present their credentials, or both. Again, if the conversion rate in a market is two to one, there will need to be 16 expressions of interest to get eight proposals to get four jobs. In the example above, the professional needs to receive at least one serious expression of interest a month if workflow is to remain healthy.

The final part of the sales pipeline, the wider end of the funnel, is the 'constituency of contacts' on which the professional should focus. This will have several components. First, there will be those clients, or former clients, who form a professional's intimate business contacts and where there is a close relationship. In some cases the professional finds it hard to distinguish between these contacts and friends. They will be seen in a social context, and there will be a close relationship of trust, built on mutual value that has been given over the years. Many of these will be advocates of the professional, referring them to others. In extreme circumstances (e.g. if there is a cash flow crisis) the professional is able to approach these contacts and ask for work without damaging the relationship. In fact, many are pleased to help.

If a professional has a dozen of these contacts, clearly they can manage the relationships easily. They can, for instance, see one a month for lunch or dinner. However, there is also an outer circle of less intimate clients and professional contacts that knows of the practitioner or sees them in some context. There might be scores of people with whom the professional needs to maintain a wider relationship. Finally, there is the broad market of potential clients, the general constituency of interest, within which the partner needs a personal reputation. In the example above, 12 serious expressions of interest a year need to be generated from this audience of 500.

The size of the constituency of contacts varies. In some professional services markets, it's quite small and focused. For example, the merchant banks focus on the community of chief executives and business development directors, which is relatively small. In others, such as general legal services, it's very broad. Alternatively, it might be primarily in one major organisation, as when, for example, a professional is the lead relationship partner for a large client. If the constituency of contacts is within a major client, then an account development plan is usually necessary (see Table 8.2).

To use the funnel effectively, professionals need to build these processes into their day-to-day lives. For example, with their secretary/assistant, they can make sure they maintain regular contact with their intimate professional relationships. They can schedule personal meetings, send Christmas cards and invite them to ad hoc hospitality or professional briefing events.

In the wider constituency, they can work either with their firm's own marketing people, or a self-employed specialist, to create an individual marketing plan. This will avoid the 'feast and famine' effect of erratic marketing if

Table 8.1 *Marketing tip: suggested personal marketing plan for a professional.*

1. Objectives:
These might be revenues, measured reputation enhancement or increases in referrals.

2. The target clients:
Information about the individuals. How many? Who are they? What are their roles and their issues? Where do they go to learn? What do they read, watch and listen to? What conferences do they attend?

Note: good marketing people are able to access this information through the planning department of large agencies. Given a clear description of the intended clients, a remarkably precise view of the media which influence them is available.

3. Activities:
What mailings will be sent out and at what frequency (e.g. Christmas or other, religious card, birthday card, occasional letter, accompaniments to company publications such as annual report)?

- What hospitality activities are to be held?
- What messages are to be communicated?
- What thought leadership or professional messages are to be participated in?
- What conferences will be attended or even spoken to?
- What is the diarised visit programme?

managed on the professional's behalf. The plan must be based on knowledge of whom they are targeting, where these people go for professional development, and what they read or listen to. This information will guide the media chosen and the activities undertaken. The plan will contain activities such as speaking at conferences, holding social events or publishing articles. A suggested format for such a plan is set out in Table 8.1.

In summary, the professional who needs to generate work should therefore have a clear idea of the constituency of contacts from which work is generated, their reputation among those contacts and the quality of their relationship to them. They must also know the 'conversion ratios' in their own corner of the market and have robust administration processes to handle the various aspects of the pipeline.

Pipeline management is also a powerful tool for leaders of professional services firms and for groups of practitioners in mutual partnership. Both can set up the appropriate administrative processes after a debate about the relevance of the concept to their business. Some build the concept into IT systems so that the pipeline of the business can be seen easily by managing partners. Some build in processes of peer review, to keep colleagues focused on the need to manage future business while conducting client work. It is surprising how effective a regular meeting or conference call among colleagues focusing on actions to follow up contacts can be.

Relationship marketing

Since the early 1980s marketing practitioners and academics have been exploring, researching and testing the concept of relationship marketing. This focuses on the buyer as a human being and gives attention to the interaction between human beings in transactions. It suggests that organisations seek to understand their buyers' purchase habits through, among other things, research and analysis of buying data. They then create communications programmes directed at these buyers which are more targeted, personalised and relevant. As buyers respond to these, the supplier can adjust their plans further, creating a virtuous circle of improved profitable engagement.

It is based upon the assumption that long-term mutual value is created for both sides if the buyer, and the interactive relationship with the buyer, becomes a focus of the supplier's policies, processes and people. The marketing of the firm then stresses enduring profitable relationships with buyers, rather than individual random transactions.

Many successful business leaders have taken such an approach. For instance, Lord Sieff, one of the leaders of the famous British retailer Marks & Spencer, was asked why, in the mid-twentieth century, he put such emphasis on service and offered no-argument refunds on defective goods. He is reported to have said that, if a young couple marry and move into an area, there is the likelihood of many years of profitable purchases from their growing family. Why damage that over an argument about one defective sweater (Sieff, 1988)? This early example of what later became known as the 'lifetime value of buyers' epitomises relationship marketing. The lifecycle of the buyer's engagement with the firm is the priority, rather than one transaction.

The leading marketing academic Evert Gummerson (Gummerson, 2002) suggests that relationship marketing 'is based on interaction within networks of relationships'. In other words, effective marketing needs to emphasise communication between people who know each other to varying degrees.

From this perspective, markets are a set of networks comprising relationships between people. They need to be understood, mapped and enhanced.

The concept, which started largely in the consumer products industry, led to the creation of tools such as customer relationship management (CRM) systems and data warehousing. It has been applied to many different markets, including professional services. For many it fills a large gap in marketing theory, recognising the role of human relationships and communications in the buying and selling process. It has proved particularly relevant in business-to-business markets.

Most professional services suppliers, when they become familiar with the principles and techniques of relationship marketing, recognise that it codifies approaches which they, and their industry, have been using for many years. In other words: it is intuitively right for these businesses. However, as with many areas of business, a clear knowledge of technique and process tends to improve effectiveness still further.

The basis of relationship marketing is the interaction between two people. However, as these people have interaction with other professionals, there are really two interconnecting networks of relationships through which information flows in two directions. These networks reach in and out of the supplier firm, embracing competitors, industry commentators and professional associations.

In Figure 8.2, for instance, a partner in a professional services firm has a business relationship with a representative in a client firm, who also has

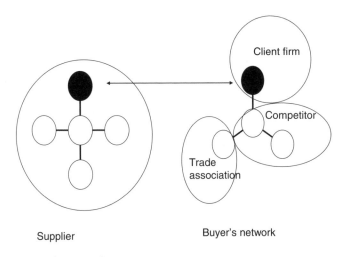

Figure 8.2 *Relationship networks.*

links to both a competitor and the trade association. The supplier can strengthen the messages and input to the contact by developing a link through the trade association. However, they need to be aware that any innovative ideas and proposals are likely to be communicated to a competitor.

These networks of relationships have 'nodes' where suppliers can bring great influence to bear (similar to technical networks). The websites of industry commentators, influential conferences and industry-specific research groups are examples of these. They should be identified and influenced.

Mapping the networks is fundamental to the success of the approach. Academics have proposed three levels of categorisation: 'activity links', essentially normal business transactions; 'resource ties', exchanging and sharing resources; and 'actor bonds', which are created between people who influence each other. These concepts can be used to map and categorise communities and networks which are valuable to the professional services firm.

For example, non-executive directors are very influential in the purchase of some professional services. Some suppliers therefore buy databases of board representatives and then map those who influence their key clients. Proactive marketing programmes are then created to reach and influence these people.

The relationship marketer uses specific techniques to communicate through the mapped networks. For instance, 'word of mouth' is one of the most powerful determinants of reputation within professional networks. The relationship marketer sets out to influence this through "eminence programmes", viral marketing and publicity (see Chapter 11).

Client account management

The concept of client account management is based on the knowledge that certain clients will give a stream of business to a supplier whereas others will not. It developed when product companies began to recognise that benefits arose from a different approach to existing buyers than those used in 'new business sales'. The skills of a sales person focused on getting new business were found to be different to those of a 'representative' dedicated to managing the orders from existing buyers. The latter is focused on creating longer-term relationships and gets involved in many issues, other than direct sales, which could threaten the business between the two sides.

This concept moved into the young computer industry and, with its emphasis upon businesses with a company's installed base of products, led to the progressive codification of major account management as a management discipline – particularly by the likes of global market leader IBM. This has since moved into other industries and has been adopted, to a greater or lesser extent, by the professional services industry. Many leading professional services companies now have partners or senior relationship managers who focus on the needs of one major client account. Others are in the process of setting up such a programme.

There are a number of aspects to this approach. First, the firm must identify and define the major accounts from which business will flow. This can be as crude as listing them by volume of business and ranking accordingly. Some focus on their 'top one hundred', or some version of it, while others have tiered layers of prioritised accounts, with each receiving different levels of attention according to the volume of business.

However, this does not encompass all of the firm's objectives in its market. For instance, it certainly does not recognise that the firm may only be receiving a small share of these clients' spend. Thus the firm may, as a first strategy, want to build on these bridgeheads by identifying clients with the highest potential and penetrating those further. Or it may have more generic strategies such as wanting to penetrate a sector of the market or to take business from a competitor. Some firms set objectives to have certain types of high quality clients in order to meet their own aspiration of being recognised as a high quality supplier. If these 'targets' have low business volumes, they may be labelled as a 'strategic account' and receive the same attention as major clients with a larger business volume.

Second, senior people need to dedicate time to managing the relationship with the client. This is not as straightforward as it sounds. It can be difficult to get agreement for senior people to dedicate time, which could be billable, to developing relationships. This is an investment in the future which can be in conflict with the need to earn cash in the short term.

The success of this strategy depends on how convinced leaders are of the value which comes from long-term relationship management. Some set about the approach convinced by the concept and argue for it based on belief. This is particularly the case in corporately owned professional services, where delegated authority from shareholders leads to clear policy and decision-making. A policy decision to manage large clients with lead managers is costed and implemented. Others, particularly partnerships, take progressive steps. They might gradually release a greater percentage of a partner's billable time to client management or start with a small number of accounts as a test of the total concept.

Another complication is the need to determine the key skills that the firm wants in its relationship managers. These are much more than purely technical skills. For instance, it may be that the firm will need someone with a broad vision of their discipline's relevance to business issues so that they can become a generic advisor to the client's senior management team. They will certainly have to have the capability to understand and present the whole range of skills and services their firm offers. (A surprising number of seasoned professionals know their own field well but cannot talk to clients in any depth about the other skills in their own firm)

At a minimum, this calls for excellent communications skills and a recognised ability to generate work. Successful individuals in this role are also frequently creative, able to spot opportunities and harness their own firm's abilities, forming teams to suggest ideas.

In addition to these soft skills, deep knowledge of the industry in which the client operates may also be essential. Part of the value to buyers of outside advisors is the perspective they develop from handling the problems of several companies in the same sector. Clients are often curious about how they stand when compared to peers and have an open ear to issues or trends that outsiders can spot from such deep engagement. They will even attend confidential discussion sessions and briefing programmes with competitors present if facilitated by a supplier they trust and if there are clear rules for the meeting. Such a powerful position as industry expert is a very rich source of projects and fees for the relationship manager.

There is, however, a greater reason for deep knowledge of the sector in which clients operate. Clients rarely know the full scope of the services offered by a supplier and often have latent needs which they think are issues to be managed rather than resolved. They may not have formulated them into potential projects or requests for proposals (RFPs). A leading practitioner, who understands the major issues in a sector, is likely to spot needs that their firm can meet. They can then create projects, unimagined by the client, to solve problems. The primary skill necessary to succeed at this is industry and client knowledge, while the secondary skill is knowledge of their own firm's resources or technical expertise. This suggests that relationship managers recruited from the industry and taught a firm's skills will have an edge over internal recruits.

The computing and telecommunications suppliers are a good example of this. When many of the telecommunications companies were deregulated or privatised in the 1980s, some put their own staff with the correct soft skills and characteristics into major account management. However, those who hired account managers from companies in their clients' industry, and educated them in their own products, succeeded in taking market share because the account managers could envisage and create propositions from their knowledge and insight. Suppliers in this sector have since put great emphasis on account management. It is those with a deep knowledge of their clients' sectors, however, who tend to take the lead.

Logically there is no reason why legal firms cannot recruit counsel from within an industry or accountancy partnerships cannot recruit chief financial officers (CFOs) from their priority sectors. Yet, apart from leading consultancies, current practice in the professional services industry tends to follow the former route (using their own staff) rather than the latter. Partnerships in particular tend to move their existing people into these roles, hoping they will gain insight from exposure to the industry. Industry specialisation in many quarters therefore lacks the depth and drive that it might otherwise have.

Third, best practice normally involves an account planning process, usually undertaken on an annual basis. Account planning adds discipline to relationship management. It normally involves an internal meeting of employees who have an interest in the account, led by the relationship manager. At this meeting, the team should cover a number of issues, including:

- Account objectives. These might be financial, relationship building or strategic.
- Environmental awareness. A review of the client's market and challenges, used to understand issues and to identify potential opportunities.
- Creation of potential projects and sales.

Table 8.2 *Marketing tip: typical account plan.*

1. Objectives for the year (financial, strategic, relationship).
2. Summary of account's situation (strategic issues the client faces). Also, account profile (decision-makers, their staff changes, competitive incursion, etc.).
3. Prime opportunities (prioritised list of what propositions are being taken to whom, when).
4. Budgets (cost, revenues and billing profile).
5. Strategic or relationship activities, designed to deepen the closeness of the two forms (e.g. hospitality, social events, etc.).
6. Resource plan. How many people are needed, with what skills and when? What new people need to be introduced into the account?
7. Client service plan.

- Prioritisation of marketing programmes and other events.
- Annual investment in the account.
- Relationship building programmes.

Sometimes, account leaders will involve members of the client firm in the planning session to add perspective and depth to the debate. The output, often in the form of an account plan as shown in Table 8.2, is shared with relevant people in the firm.

Finally, the firm needs to consider what support staff it intends to dedicate to its major accounts. Experienced product companies create teams which include: project managers, sales support staff, client service managers and even telephone sales staff (to handle large volumes of small items for large international buyers). Practice in professional services firms vary. Many dedicate administrative staff to key accounts and some client service staff.

The phenomenon of post-purchase distress

If the purchase of any item is emotionally challenging, or if it is expensive, buyers experience post-purchase distress. This is worry or anxiety caused by the purchase. It is allayed by the buyer's admiration of the purchased product or sales materials. However, as services are intangible, there is nothing to offset this anxiety and worry is therefore more intense. So much so, in fact, that it can lead to the cancellation of the project and client dissatisfaction.

As a result, methods of summarising the emotional relief of a well-executed project have evolved in some markets. The 'tombstones' routinely created after merger and acquisition (M&A) deals, for example, epitomise the achievement of a well-completed, worrisome project. They are a tangible embodiment of the project and a symbol of post-purchase distress.

Clients may be concerned about the effect on their budgets, the effort to sell the project internally, damage to their credibility or risk to their political capital. Anxiety is also increased if the supplier is operating in unfamiliar territory. The client who buys consulting from an accountancy firm may be anxious due more to the risk of using a familiar supplier in unfamiliar circumstances than to normal post-purchase distress. If this anxiety is not managed, then problems occur. Professionals should think through the moments of anxiety that their client might experience and create physical devices to allay this discomfort. A good relationship manager anticipates and obviates such concern.

Sales closing techniques

In all exchanges between sellers and buyers, there comes a moment when buyers need to make up their minds. Very often, success can be improved if that moment occurs with the seller present. In fact, the marketing and sales professions have created tools to help focus on this moment. Called 'closing techniques', they include:

- **Asking for the business:** it is obvious, and therefore often forgotten, simply to ask buyers if they want to go ahead. A surprising number of sophisticated and experienced professionals do not do this.
- **Overcoming objections:** this is based on asking buyers whether there are any reasons why they can't proceed and then handling each and every objection as they arise.
- **Open-ended questions:** this really is an extension of 'overcoming objections'. A series of questions are asked to get further and further into the buyer's needs and to match the offer closely to them. As professionals frequently have to start working with a client by diagnosing need, the consultative approach required closely resembles this technique. This is probably the most practised closing technique in the professional services industry.

- **Exaggeration to the absurd:** here, the seller may take one of the objections buyers present and exaggerate it to the point of the ridiculous in order to overcome it as a barrier to purchase.
- **The 'assumed close':** here a client's body language signifies that they are happy with the suggestions and want to buy. The supplier moves to talking about next steps and assumes the sale is agreed. However, the seller may be concerned that, if the client is asked for the business or asked whether they want to go ahead, barriers will be raised in their mind.
- **The 'go-away':** in this context a seller is convinced that the offer matches the needs a buyer has. If the buyer tries to negotiate on price, or cut corners, the seller can suggest that they don't go ahead. This causes the buyer to recommit to doing the work.

Health warning: closing techniques developed in product selling have made their way into the professional services industry and are taught in sales courses throughout the world. However, as professional services are intangible offers, and the client is therefore vulnerable, if the seller is too overwhelming and uses closing techniques too forcefully, once the buyer has a moment to think, he or she is likely to feel cheated and the deal might unravel. These approaches need to be handled with real care in a professional services context.

Sales or business generation issues specific to the professional services industry

The demand-pull context

This concept was outlined in the Introduction and represented in Figure I.1. The fundamental way in which nearly all professional services businesses grow is through the generation of repeat business or referrals that come from a good reputation for excellent work. If the professional has such a reputation, clients talk about it and word of mouth causes them either to refer the professional to others in their network of contacts, or to buy again. As a result future clients come to the professional when they have a need which, in turn, keeps cost of sales down and prices high.

Any consideration of business generation and sales for professionals needs to be done in this context. The leaders need to think through how they institutionalise and enhance the process of reputation enhancement in order to bring in business. If their marketing is working properly, then the professional needs to participate in the demand-pull process, making sure his or her reputation is understood by the market and responding to any request for work.

> **Health warning:** if, while under pressure to increase revenues, the practice goes out 'to sell' or tries 'to get meetings', the professional is pushing expertise at the clients. The power in any negotiation is then with the client who will tend to be sceptical about relevance and price sensitive. Introducing sales processes outside the context of demand-pull can lead to an increase in sales costs and price pressure.

The phenomenon of the rainmaker

Rainmakers are individuals who have above-average capacity to generate a book of business and a healthy revenue stream. While many professionals generate income and revenue, these people sometimes generate two or three times the industry average revenue figures. They exist in all professional services, from architecture through engineering consultancy and marketing services to accountancy and management consultancy.

The skills and attributes of rainmakers include:

- **A driven individual:** these people have drive. They need to achieve and put this energy into business success.
- **Market focus:** they know the market they operate in very well and understand both developing issues and key individuals within it. They focus their team's skills and expertise on the market and apply their knowledge.
- **Reputation management:** they create 'thought leadership' to enhance reputation and understand the use of public relations (PR) and the media. They write books and articles; and speak at conferences.
- **Client targeting:** they identify high probability projects which would yield high returns and seek out buyers with needs.

- **Networking:** they put enormous effort into building and energising networks of professionals. They have frequent contact with clients; building trust and relationships. They ask questions and listen carefully, identifying projects to meet needs. They close deals and then sell on other projects.
- **Delivery is reliable:** they manage expectations and deliver high quality work. They ensure a good team works on their projects.
- **Measurement:** they ask for feedback, adapt and develop. Over time, they build a track record.

The leadership of the professional services firm who are focused on revenue enhancement should consider the strategies and processes by which they recruit and manage rainmakers. The practice in many professional services firms is to promote lively and successful fee generators into management. The gravity of the firm is therefore towards taking successful rainmakers away from clients. This is risky. Very often rainmakers are adverse to systems, processes and administration. They may not be particularly good at management and after a while, might either cause poor performance or leave the firm altogether.

A professional services firm should therefore have clear human resources policies to identify rainmakers, either in new graduate recruits or in experienced client service staff. They should be managed appropriately and given the correct support with increasing responsibility for either markets and revenue streams or major accounts as they progress through the firm. The culture of the firm ought to be friendly to such difficult human beings. It also needs to explain their importance and their behaviour to other members of the firm.

A particular area of difficulty is rainmaker development. It is surprising how often experienced professionals will have difficulty generating income in a large firm but, once on their own, and more focused, are able to generate quite large sums for themselves. Facing the winds of the market often helps a rainmaker to really develop.

The development of rainmakers within a large firm is best managed with some form of apprenticeship. An experienced rainmaker should be given one or two potential revenue generators to introduce into accounts. These junior professionals, perhaps on a partner promotion track, need to be told that they are to work with the experienced rainmaker and adopt the successful techniques of that rainmaker in their own style.

> **Health warning**: rainmakers consistently say that they do not know how they generate business and, because of their driven nature, rugged character and lack of fondness for administration will tend to be uninspiring teachers. This needs to be explained to the junior professionals so they understand the context in which they are operating.

'Business developers'

Many professional services firms employ specialists who assist with account management or sales. (In a product company these people would be called sales support.) Their backgrounds, role and tasks vary enormously but they seem to have one overriding objective: to maintain focus on client development and marketing issues while client service staff execute projects.

They may assist with account planning (preparing, attending and participating in account planning sessions) or they may manage the production of proposals. Some participate in account development, creating relationships and opening doors for client service staff. Some even come from a sales background and are briefed to sell into client accounts. However, they have to rely on the partner to finalise any deal, because the partner is also the deliverer of the service. Many firms report success in deploying sales people in this way, particularly in cultures that are receptive to sales calls such as that of the US.

The 'trusted advisor'

This concept was introduced by leading industry specialist David Maister and his colleagues (Maister *et al.*, 2001). Their work seeks to put structure into the development of a professional's relationship with their client and, particularly, the need to earn trust. They argue that a professional's relationship can develop from a basic service offer to trust based through various states. This is represented in Figure 8.3.

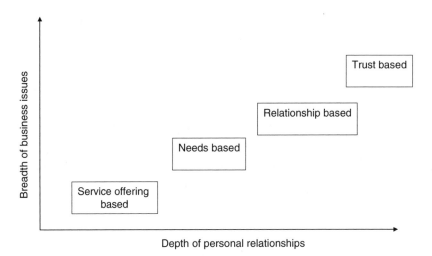

Figure 8.3 *Four types of relationships.*
Source: Maister *et al.* (2001). Reprinted with the permission of The Free Press, a Division of Simon & Schuster Adult Publishing Group, from THE TRUSTED ADVISOR by David H. Maister, Charles H. Green, Robert M. Galford. Copyright © 2000 by David H. Maister, Charles H. Green, Robert M. Galford. All rights reserved.

Their work is a sophisticated development of relationship marketing theory as it is applied to professional services practice. They illustrate the differences and benefits of a trust-based engagement when compared to other forms. They also propose economic arguments to calculate the benefits arising from this approach.

Academics have also researched the role of trust in professional services. While they have produced no accepted definition, their research has underlined the importance of trust in different parts of the professional services industry and its relationship to employee response and behaviour. They have also developed some useful concepts.

Sue Halliday, for example, used research (Halliday, 2004) into health services to distinguish between 'placed trust' (placed by the client at the initiation of service) and 'trust as a response' to trust building behaviours. Both are valuable to building profitable revenue streams and can be the subject of different strategies.

Client buying behaviour

It is difficult to generate business without understanding how, why and when people buy. This is not, however, as straightforward as it sounds. Human beings are erratic, unpredictable creatures driven by both the rational and the emotional in their decision-making, whether buying for work or for personal life.

Generally, there are a number of key decision-making criteria clients have in mind when looking for suppliers of professional services. The first is that the potential suppliers have listened carefully to what the client has said and hence really understand their needs. The second is the willingness of the professional to challenge and not be subservient.

Frequently, though, buyers don't know what they want and cannot articulate their needs. They will often have an intuitive, confused mix of ideas and look for the proposition that best fits their perceived needs. Often there is little structure to their buying processes, even when buying for business. More often than people are prepared to admit, their decisions are driven by emotion rather than logic.

Sometimes they approach decisions carefully, collecting as much data as possible, sometimes they return to trusted suppliers and sometimes they buy on impulse. Considerable research and experimentation have been undertaken over decades to understand buying processes. Much of this is useful in giving pointers to practical approaches or market opportunities. Any professional looking to create a stream of business must actively seek new insights into the way their buyers are thinking or behaving and what information sources they use in reaching a decision.

It is dangerously easy for a firm to institutionalise its former view of buyer needs or to ignore them because it has succeeded by creating and pushing products or services in the past. Professionals can get a distorted view from their close proximity to one client or by their perspective from a certain type or seniority of buyer.

For instance, partners in leading firms are used to dealing with senior business leaders. At the time of writing, many still ignore the internet as an influence on these buyers' thinking and neglect investment in their own website or internet marketing strategy. Yet these buyers do access the internet. Some chief executive officers (CEOs) search the internet themselves, often when they have time at home but, more commonly, their employees use search engines when researching proposals to put to them. Those professionals who don't understand this shift in buyer behaviour risk damaging their business.

There are three types of buyer that the professional services industry needs to understand:

The consumer

Consumer purchases range from a wealthy individual buying investment advice through a myriad of people by directly accessing advice for significant life events (such as realtor/estate agent assistance in house purchase) down to the huge variety of retail purchases (such as dentistry and optical assistance).

The organisational buying unit

Although there has been detailed work, research and models developed in relation to organisational buying behaviour (OBB), research into the organisational buying of services was a relatively neglected area until the 1990s as with much of service marketing. That decade saw the rise of outsourcing, facilities management companies, call centres and an explosion in professional services, particularly in management consultancy projects built around huge systems and change management initiatives. These firms needed to understand the buying criteria of their clients, so demand for research and concepts applicable to this field grew.

Suppliers need to understand the roles of different people in the organisational buying process, the weight given to different purchase criteria and the sources of information used to come to a decision. For professional services the situation is complicated by the network of relationships between firms and by the influence of the formal purchasing process, particularly in government or public work. It is also complicated by the interactive nature of many professional services. The consultative or diagnostic stage of a project frequently forms part of the project scoping, pricing and contractual process.

There are clear differences in the way different organisational buying groups behave in different sizes of company. For instance, the influence of the CEO is likely to be more dominant in smaller companies and, because they have limited expertise, they are likely to filter information through trusted advisors or business networks, such as chambers of commerce. In large firms there are normally a group of people involved, called the 'buying centre' by academics. The buying of professional services, however, can still be very personal, with little involvement from purchasing specialists.

The sources that buyers refer to in collecting information about a supplier are: representatives of the firm, word of mouth, industry networks (e.g. contacts in other firms or industry associations), directories, press releases, brochures and internet searches. Each of these has different influence in different markets. For instance, research has shown that, in business-to-business markets, personal contacts with colleagues, including peers in other companies, is the most influential source of information whereas direct mail has virtually no effect.

This is exacerbated with business-to-business services because they are difficult to evaluate in advance. Reputation in the market, or the view formed by fellow professionals from the practitioners and from the firm's brand, is likely to be more powerful an influence. This is not to say that non-personal information sources (directories, advertising, professional registers) can be neglected. Buyers use them early in the process to create a short list or to generate alternatives suppliers or to gain a perspective on favoured suppliers.

The individual business buyer

Different people react differently when buying business services. They might be selecting and buying alone or they might be buying as part of an industrial buying group. However, their motivations and needs have to be understood. Some, for example, have a hunger for learning and personal growth. They will seek to bring expertise into their organisation so that it might learn. Others want reflected recognition from using a famous name and others emotional reassurance. Their individual motivations can be the deciding factor in the buying process.

Crafting the client's need: the consultative approach

Whether dealing with an organisational buyer or a consumer, ultimately the supplier has to create a proposition which meets the client's perceived needs. The methods to create scalable propositions are dealt with in Chapter 10. However, it is the lead client service practitioner who has to determine the cluster of needs and adapt the firm's skills to meet them. They must therefore take a diagnostic, consultative approach.

Table 8.3 *Typical issues in buyers' minds.*

- Understanding of their needs.
- Technical ability to handle the project.
- Willingness to challenge assumptions.
- Relating to their issues, empathy.
- Quality of ideas.
- Quality of pitch presentation.
- Strength of the team and senior involvement.
- Fee.

In some circumstances the buyer has a clear idea of the service they are buying. In others, they are aware of a problem and need help to clarify the issue before identifying an approach. The practitioner must diagnose those needs, bringing them into greater relief in the client's mind. The effect is for the client to recognise a cluster of needs that they didn't realise they had, and thus to be able to agree the shape of the issue.

Table 8.3 is a generalisation drawn from various research projects into the issues clients claim are in their mind when they evaluate services. A skilled practitioner will learn which is most important, ranking and scaling their clients' priorities. This is then crafted into a value proposition or proposal.

Note that 'fee' is not the highest consideration. Nobody, in any market in any part of the world buys anything on price alone. If professionals report that price is the prime consideration of their clients, either they are not diagnosing need properly or their offer has been allowed, by their industry, to become a commodity. In other words, the offers of all suppliers are so similar that the client can only find difference in price.

Figure 8.4 contains research from the 2004 Brand Tracking Study carried out by the Information Technology Services Marketing Association (ITSMA). It shows the attitudes of clients of IT professional services firms. It ranks the various issues they are searching for in a supplier and is typical of those sought by clients in many sectors.

General principles at different phases in the sales cycle

The following general principles are a distillation of experience and research which will seem elementary to many experienced professionals. However,

When you and your company are selecting a professional services consultant or solution provider, how important is it that this vendor ___?

Follows through on promises and commitments	4.9
Is driven by customer satisfaction	4.6
Employs experienced people	4.5
Recommends practical solutions	4.5
Has industry expertise	4.5
Transfers knowledge to customers	4.4
Works collaboratively with customers	4.4
Has a strong reputation built on trust	4.3
Helps you reduce cost	4.3
Demonstrates measurable business value	4.3
Is a trusted business advisor	4.2
Aligns business and technology priorities	4.1
Delivers fast results	4.1
Helps you manage risk	3.9
Demonstrates thought leadership	3.8
Has effective alliance partners	3.5
Is the low-cost services provider	3.4

Mean Rating (N=400)

Figure 8.4 *Importance ratings of IT professional services firm's attributes.*
Source: ITSMA

the neglect of these principles is often shown by the many mistakes and obvious lack of attention even among premier professionals.

'Targeting'

Professionals tend to use the term targeting for either the process of selecting potential clients or the act of approaching them. Some, of which merchant banking is an example, tend to create ideas which they suggest to the target client. Others analyse clients in anticipation of a general discussion. Still others look to develop a vague, friendly relationship which, they hope, will develop into mutual work. Some create elaborate diagnostic tools or benchmarking data with the aim of stimulating client interest. Others employ specialist telephone sales or marketing groups to 'open the door'.

The success of such initiatives vary enormously. As a general principle, though, it takes time to develop a profitable relationship with a new client and all such programmes need to be seen as investments.

'Pre-sales'

At this stage it is important to adopt a consultative style. In other words: to listen and diagnose. This is much more than cursory attention to words. The professional must listen actively. They must demonstrate understanding and check back with the potential client. With a serious problem it may be wise to ask for time to consider the issues and book a further meeting to suggest potential approaches.

With an unfamiliar client, they must look for non-verbal signals. This starts with the environment for the chosen meeting. If the approach is by telephone, it may be that the issue is seen as relatively non-critical, or worse, that there is already a favoured supplier. If in a restaurant or bar, this may be a signal that the client is open to a range of ideas and approaches. (Or that they have a preference to be entertained.) If in the office, their work space will give clues. An uncluttered environment speaks of focus on issues, whereas pictures of family (which should always be commented upon) demonstrate values outside work. Tokens of previous success (team photos, client mementos) speak of a need to demonstrate achievement and worth; which may be a hidden objective of the current project.

Body language, which has been the subject of many research projects and learned publications, is a powerful indication of underlying thoughts. Someone demonstrating power displays needs to be handled in a certain way; whereas someone moving from a 'closed' to an 'open' posture is ready to listen to proposed approaches.

At this phase in the discussion it should be an objective to avoid a formal proposal. This is more common than many who have to suffer 'beauty parades' assume. In the European M&A market, for instance, up to 30% of lead advisor roles can be carried out without a competitive tender. The ability to move straight to work is an indication of the strength of relationship, the respect of the client and the skill of the practitioner.

It is common to suggest different methods of solving the problem and ask which the client most favours. Many then arrange to return with a 'draft' programme. As the client comments on this at a further meeting, they feel in control of the process and able to express concerns about their own, unique environment. Very often the project proceeds from there.

Sometimes, pre-sales work includes getting on to approved supplier lists from which employees in a client organisation can choose. There will be no substantial progress without this. This may, therefore, become an objective of an account or 'targeting' plan.

The proposal or sales meeting

A response to a formal request for a proposal must be carefully managed. At the very least deadlines, formats and specified areas of information must be met accurately. This is particularly important in government or public sector proposals where non-compliance can mean that suppliers are automatically excluded.

The proposal document, the pre-proposal process and the proposal presentation should all be treated as communications exercises. It is an opportunity to listen and respond, not to bore, pontificate or show off. If the client has specified meetings or people to consult with before submission deadline, they should be used. In these, as much detail as possible should be asked about technical issues, the problem, budget and those involved in the decision-making process. Some clients take a lack of questioning as a sign of lack of real interest. The team formed to manage the proposal process must plan the approach to warm up the client who needs to be influenced.

The proposal itself must first be written as a clear communications document. Something which starts with pages of description on the supplier's resources and history is unlikely to communicate effectively. It should outline need, suggest an approach, articulate the benefits of the approach, say why the supplier is unique and give indicative pricing. The production of the document should be managed as a project, leaving enough time for proof reading and rehearsal.

The team presenting the proposal needs to be chosen carefully. First, they need the right technical skills and experience. They also need the right level of commitment. Clients are irritated if a senior person presents the proposal and is never seen again. (In fact some suppliers make a virtue of the fact that the team presenting will deliver the work.) However, the team needs the right communication skills and chemistry with the client. In fact, one reason for fielding a team is to lower the risk of rejection of the whole firm because the client does not take to one person.

If possible, the presentation should be interactive, checking understanding and asking questions. A key objective of the proposal meeting should be to leave with a mutually agreed course of action and, if possible, a suggestion on how to sell the work into the organisation. The subsequent legal contract should be an extension of the pitch, not the firm's document.

Post-sales

This is primarily about excellent delivery of the work. But it is also about reassurance. If something goes wrong it is important to sort it out quickly. It is better to admit that the supplier is not perfect and remedy problems, than to ignore them. If possible, find tangible expressions of progress for the client such as weekly progress reports and 'contact' reports, summarising each meeting.

Useful tools and techniques

The loyalty ladder

The loyalty ladder in Figure 8.5 seeks to classify buyers according to their disposition toward the supplier. It recognises that the lowest level is not buyers who are uninformed but antagonists. These are people who are negative about the firm. They are important to professional services firms because they create negative word of mouth and damage reputation.

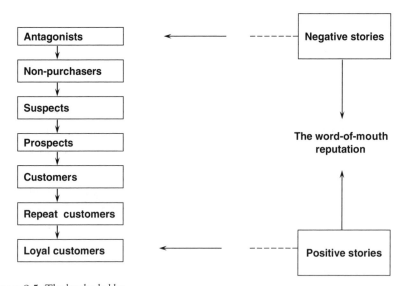

Figure 8.5 *The loyalty ladder.*

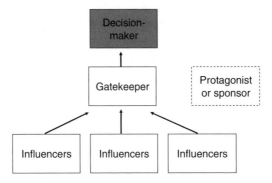

Figure 8.6 *The decision-making unit.*

Non-purchasers might be unaware of the offer, whereas suspects are considering purchase. Buyers and repeat buyers are clients. Loyal buyers, or protagonists, are a valuable asset because they create positive word of mouth and build the reputation of the firm. Research can identify the clients that are in each group. Policies and marketing programmes can then be directed at each one as appropriate.

The decision-making unit

The decision-making unit (DMU) seen in Figure 8.6 categorises the different roles in the organisational buying group. Influencers are generally junior employees who research or contribute to the evaluation of the proposed purchase. The 'gatekeeper' is normally reasonably senior and presents the project to the decision-maker. A sponsor is an employee who is particularly well disposed to the supplier.

Suppliers can use the tool to categorise different people in the account. Different approaches to each one can then be designed according to the role each one plays.

Summary

This chapter has outlined the range of marketing and sales concepts which professionals can employ to be successful at generating business. They include managing the pipeline of business to create a smoother flow of work, building on client relationships, and account management. In addition, professionals also have to devise processes to gain a better understanding of their clients, including how and why they buy. Integral to this is a clear grasp of the rhythm of each sales cycle, from targeting through to pre- and post-sales activities.

9

Creating or relaunching services

Overview

Professional services firms are rightly proud of the expertise they offer their clients. But some are unaware that well-established tools and techniques exist which can turn their expertise into services which can significantly enhance revenues. Services can be developed, improved and marketed like products. This approach can also help revive services which are in danger of becoming undifferentiated commodities. This chapter discusses those marketing concepts relevant to new service design and offers a comprehensive and practical guide to the service design process.

The role of service design and development

It is sometimes difficult for professionals to think of their practice as a business which needs to be nurtured and marketed. It is perhaps even more difficult for them to think of their expertise as a competitive service which can be researched, designed and translated into a market-based value proposition.

To many professionals, it feels as though they are simply experts, recipients of years of training and experience, who are offering the benefits of their technical knowledge to people and organisations which need them. But when their offer is wrapped in a brand, presented in conjunction with other expertise and is accessible through a client process, it becomes a competitive service offer. These offers can be changed, improved, marketed and withdrawn just like physical products.

In fact, many of the techniques of new product design can be adapted and adjusted to the service sector in order to improve the likelihood of success. This is called new service development (NSD), after new product development (NPD) from the product sector. NSD is a powerful way to generate funds. It can be applied to the creation of new, refreshed or 'added value' services.

As the service sector has grown, so has the work by a myriad of firms to generate revenue by enhancing their core service or creating new services. There is therefore a growing understanding of the importance of NSD to continuing success and growth. Firms in the service sector, largely outside the professional services industry, have experimented with NSD and explored related techniques. At the same time, theorists and researchers have confirmed many of the success factors. The experience of these specialists should, at least, be considered by professional services firm leaders who are assessing their firm's market capabilities and seeking to introduce new offers to their clients. It is likely that, if they do so, the chances of success with new offers will be increased and costs will be saved.

Attitudes to NSD in the professional services industry vary. Some professionals regard themselves as individual advisors, working on unique issues and 'above' the techniques of NSD. Whereas others, particularly in bigger firms, talk of their offers as 'products', often grouped under 'line of service' management structures.

In practice, NSD is a common, if unstructured, phenomenon in the professional services industry. For example, the executive search industry created new services such as 'executive selection' and 'management audit' during the last recession. Accounting firms have created 'internal audit', 'shareholder value reporting' and various forms of tax advice, while management consultancy has devised new managerial concepts, such as 'process re-engineering' or 'total quality management'. This has all supplemented their income and helped them to thrive or, in some cases, survive.

Traditionally, the way to grow extra services has been to recruit a new partner with a new skill or expertise. By finding a senior person with relevant expertise in a new revenue stream, in effect a new service can be created. But some professionals are unaware that it is possible to create new services and manage a structured process to identify and develop them in a logical way. They rarely use the processes and techniques of NSD.

Most have not heard of 'features analysis' or 'molecular modelling', let alone deployed them in their business. Their staff, when faced with the need to create a new service offer or adjust a weary one, simply make up their approach, often damaging their project en route. They don't realise that developed processes and recognised techniques already exist to create potential propositions in a logical, rational and professional way; or that income generation through new service launch need not be such a 'hit and miss' affair.

Common mistakes in service design

In the same way that some new products do not sell, there are many services which do not generate revenue or profit for the businesses that created them. Common mistakes include:

A lack of differentiation

Due to inadequate marketing, many services look the same as competitor offers and, therefore, the only basis of choice is price.

Allowing the service to become a commodity

A commodity is a product or service which is not valued by potential buyers. They see it as a necessity and are not prepared to pay what they consider to be a high price for the offer. Offers only become commodities because suppliers allow them to. It is quite possible to turn commodities like financial audit, conveyancing, house valuation or tax advice into value propositions with the right approach.

A poor understanding of buyer needs

Often people do not know what they need or want. They can be unaware of technical possibilities or be unable to express some of these needs, and will therefore rarely be a source of valuable new ideas for propositions unless specialised research techniques are used. A product example of this would be Coca-Cola. If researchers at the turn of the last century had asked people if they required 'a black drink, full of caffeine and sugar' they would have received a negative reaction. But once the proposition was placed in front of potential buyers in a way that was attractive, the most successful marketing proposition of the twentieth century was born. Research which can uncover such possibilities needs to be explorative or observational.

One disservice that the gurus of after-care and service quality have done is to imply that, by simply asking buyers what they want and meeting or exceeding those desires, firms will engender loyalty and create profit. Yet, if people generally do not know what they want and cannot envisage new propositions, their vision will be limited to improvements on an existing proposition. They may ask for it to be provided faster or cheaper (a course which will drive a supplier progressively out of business) but it is very rare that they will suggest creative new insights.

If suppliers take a technical, superficial approach to the analysis of their clients' needs they will therefore be misled. However, there are a range of needs beyond the purely technical. Suppliers must use research techniques to understand the true benefits sought by clients, the underlying emotions and their unarticulated needs. An insight into these might open up a totally new approach.

Overreliance on industry reports

Another common mistake is to rely too much on industry-produced reports as a means of gaining market perspective. In many service industries there are specialist research companies who dedicate themselves to tracking buyer and supplier behaviour in those industries. But sometimes these research companies are staffed by technical specialists from the industry rather than marketing researchers and, in order to maintain their own margin, conduct trend analysis based on previous interviews and analyses. There is a huge danger that these industry research reports can be used by internal management and sales people to justify a preconceived notion, so that industry mediocrity becomes a self-fulfilling prophecy.

The 'one-off' service

This is a phenomenon seen in many service organisations in many different business sectors. The one-off service seems to arise from a need expressed by a client to which the supplier takes a consultative approach. A project team is drawn together of various functional experts from across the organisation that creates a unique answer to the client's needs. As it is an individual answer to a specific need, there is much effort involved and costs are high.

Once successful, they are presented as a potential for the future portfolio and seen as a 'future direction for the company'. However, this relies on the company's ability to replicate or industrialise services. As service companies rarely have established processes to turn ideas into replicable services, the costs of turning customised projects into firm-wide offers are often prohibitive and the attempt fails.

'Overclaim'

The sales literature of many professional services firms claims that their service is 'leading edge', 'world class' or 'the best'. Yet there is rarely any objective measure or justification for this claim. In fact, the service is often the same as that of peers. Whereas it is accepted that product companies can be niche or least-cost suppliers, producing different products and encouraging choice, this is more rare among professional services companies. Many exaggerate the benefit of their service and thus create cynicism among their clients.

The lack of a proposition

A good number of service offers, particularly in business-to-business industries, are unclear and complex. In many instances the supplier fails to create a simple value proposition, a failing which has been exacerbated by the trend to focus on ill-defined 'solutions'. Suppliers should present their offers to clients in a way that stimulates their imagination and helps them to clarify their needs with the benefits of that proposition. A mistake that is often made is to suggest that the firm is a 'full service provider', or that it can do anything. To the client this appears as a lazy lack of clarity which implies no particular skill or emphasis worth paying for.

A 'product-led' approach

Most industries have evolved through a sales boom. This a period of powerful natural demand when it is only necessary for the suppliers to keep improving on the features of established offers, customising them more and more to untapped segments of buyers. During this phase the industry is supply driven and 'product led'. This successful behaviour can lead to mistakes. Markets and needs change. Firms which are primarily production machines are exposed to huge costly errors if they have no NSD management process after such a fundamental shift in their market.

Servility rather than service

Client orientation and service values are vital to the success of professionals. However, years of client service creates something akin to servility in some. This undervalues themselves, their firm and their offer. It leads to discounting and, eventually, declining revenues. Professionals with a servile attitude should be constrained from pricing work.

Clearly, for companies to create real value out of the services that they are designing, they must introduce techniques, skills and practices to minimise the mistakes listed above.

A reprise of relevant marketing concepts

Lessons from new product development

The proactive creation of new products (NPD) has been established practice for many years in a number of different businesses selling physical products. Leading organisations in markets where new product innovation is a critical success factor have highly sophisticated processes which are managed at a senior level in the firm. They aim to present many innovations to a fast changing market, knowing that some will be successful.

The processes and concepts behind new product development are well established and known to provide demonstrable value. Research has shown, for example, that a new product design process in manufacturing reduces risk of failure. A further finding is that innovation is costly and that a new product development process reduces those costs.

The factors which contribute to the success of new product design include:

- Senior management involvement and control.
- A clear and managed new product design process.
- Superiority over existing products.
- Investment in understanding the market.
- The proficiency of marketing operations.
- Degree of business/project fit.
- Effective interaction between R&D and marketing.
- A supportive management environment.
- Effective project management.

These factors are now widely recognised. As a result, many companies in many sectors have in place clear and formalised new product creation processes, portfolio management techniques and dedicated product managers.

In 1991 Canada's Ulrike de Brentani conducted research designed to apply the 'conceptual and research paradigms that have evolved from studies of new manufactured goods to services'. Based on his analysis, it was suggested that the strategic issues facing service organisations were similar to those for product companies. While the technology of new product development, and the steps included in the process, vary, the underlying notions behind their use does not. The main steps involve creating as many good ideas as possible and then reducing the number of ideas by careful screening to ensure that only those with the best chances of success get into the market place.

Reasons for new service design

There are several reasons for the development of new services:

- **Obsolescence of old services:** the need to create new services to replace old ones which no longer appeal to buyers.

- **Revenue creation:** service ideas are launched as new revenue streams.
- **Commoditisation of services:** if buyers have lost a sense of value due to bad pricing practices by the suppliers, services can be repositioned and relaunched with a new pricing regime and greater margins.
- **The desire to take advantage of new opportunities:** clearly, if a company spots a gap in the market, it will seek to take advantage of the opportunity.
- **Increased competition:** services may be created or revamped to stay ahead of competitors' offers.
- **Spare capacity:** services may be launched to use up spare capacity due to troughs in demand.
- **Seasonal effects:** some services, like financial audit, are subject to seasonal changes in demand. New services might be created to compensate.
- **Risk reduction:** new services are launched to balance a portfolio reliant on one service.

The concept of integrated service

Research into quality of service has shown that the provision of any given service must be 'holistic'. This means it is not only important to manage all the components of service, but to ensure that they work together in such a way as to create an integrated experience which meets all the buyer's expectations without interruption or aberration.

Integrated service is a little like a theatrical performance. In a ballet the components of the production are prepared and rehearsed so exactly that, at a particular beat in the bar, of a particular piece of music, the point of a ballerina's toe will come down at a particular point on the stage which will be lit by a particular light. Each component of the ballet, whether music, stance, dress, gesture or set, is integrated to give a seamless (and wondrous) experience for the viewing public. In the same way, the components of service need to be completely identified and integrated so as to make the service experience enjoyable and complete.

The key components of service, which need to be integrated in this way, are:

- Brand and image.
- The service concept.

- Environmental design.
- Access to the service environment.
- Access into the service process.
- The behaviour of the people who deliver the service.
- The process through which the client moves.
- The technology used to support the service.
- The product or physical components which are part of the offer.
- The means of measurement of the service.

When constructing a service it is important that service designers decide the means of delivery of each of these items. But, more importantly, they must plan how they will all be integrated. Focusing on these features and their integration means that excellent services can be planned from the start. The concept of service component integration ensures that a service planner can create unique offerings which give buyers choice and enable suppliers to make a profit.

The concept of component design

Products and services comprise components which can be identified, adjusted and mixed to appeal to different groups of buyers. These components might be physical, technical, artistic, human or emotional. Product designers use design and planning systems to adjust physical product features because manufacturing or packaging processes need detailed specifications if they are to change. Some volume services have large system or process components and therefore need equally detailed specifications if they are to change. The techniques and processes of NPD design have therefore been tested in this end of the service sector.

Unfortunately, some suppliers of services with less system or process constraints launch an ill-defined or poorly designed idea because of a lack of internal competence and often use the excuse of market urgency. Such poorly planned initiatives rarely succeed. Experience shows that suppliers need to think through the components of the service and ensure that all relevant processes are in place before launch. Service companies need to engage in proper component design.

The concept of value propositions

A value proposition is an offer to buyers which meets most of their buying criteria at a price which they regard, however unfairly they form that judgement, as value for money. Contrary to popular belief in many industries, price or, more accurately, cheapness is not a buyer's prime consideration. Sometimes they are willing to pay more for a particular item and sometimes they deliberately choose an 'expensive' offer. It depends on the value of the offer to them.

Some new services fail to make money, not through poor planning of the service concept or its components, but because it is misrepresented in the market place. The marketing and sales literature is merely a description of the various components and features of the service. To succeed, it is essential that the raw elements of the service are turned into a proposition to which buyers can relate.

It would be ridiculous, for example, to describe a fast food outlet as follows: 'Our service contains people in a carefully designed uniform who prepare food very quickly using the latest technology to cook a limited range of food so that it is both hot and ready to eat very quickly.' Buyers would be bored by the time they reached the end. Yet this is exactly what many service firms do, particularly in the business-to-business sector. As a result, they waste many forests of expensively produced brochures. Instead, an attractive proposition, which summarises the offer in clear terms, must be put to the market.

The creation of a value proposition is frequently fragmented. A project team will create the components of the service, a leader will agree pricing, account managers will work out benefits to clients and an advertising agency, if used, will create the one sentence proposition. Instead, this crucially important process should be managed as one, integrated project within the firm. A dynamic model is needed to turn the raw components of the service into a unique proposition. This is represented in Figure 9.1. The leadership should ensure that their firm is responsible for creating all these elements.

There are several elements to the creation of a true value proposition:

- A clear understanding of the buyers it is aimed at, their rational and emotional needs.

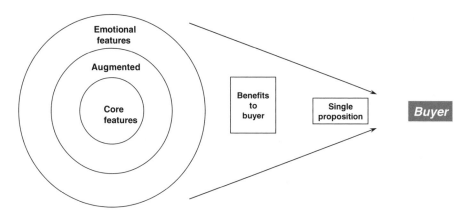

Figure 9.1 *Developing a value proposition.*

- An integrated view of the practical, design and emotional components of the offer, and their value to the buyers.
- A clear view of the benefits of the proposition.
- A short market-based description of the offer.

The concept of portfolio management

Product portfolio management is a much discussed aspect of marketing theory. It is argued that, in order to stay competitive, a business must continue to offer an up-to-date and broad range of products in a relevant way to a particular market. If a company is offering a range of products which are, for example, all reaching the end of their life, then its survival is threatened. Strategists argue that new offers should be created before this dangerous situation is reached.

Logic would imply that such a strategy is relevant to service businesses and that a regular competitive review of the range of offers would benefit the firm. However, few service developers seem to have tried to apply portfolio planning to services, or to build balanced portfolios of service offerings.

The management of creativity and innovation

There are well-researched projects and many anecdotal stories about the need to bring innovation to new product development. Creativity and innovation are vital to a firm which needs to bring new products and services to market. In fact, some researchers have suggested that the ability to innovate new products and services is the key to survival for some companies operating in a number of fast changing markets.

The management of innovation in those product companies is often a clearly defined discipline, whose principles are well understood. Some companies manage innovation and creativity by keeping the organisation small and by ensuring the management team stays focused on the creation of new opportunities. This has generally been the strategy followed, for example, by Virgin Group. As its founder and head, Sir Richard Branson, said at a conference of the UK's prestigious Institute of Directors in the early 1990s, as soon as a business unit gets to a certain size, he breaks it down to retain the benefit of small company innovation inside a large brand.

Other companies have turned from large bureaucratic organisations to smaller, innovative cells in response to a near disaster which meant missing an opportunity. This is reported to be the experience of the company 3M after its initial lack of response to the original idea of 'Post it' notes.

Some other product companies have managed creativity by using an external agency. These agencies, which came to prominence in the 1970s, are known as 'new product development companies'. They take a brief from managers in the same way that advertising agencies or research companies take briefs from marketing departments. These briefs contain requirements to produce new products, offering benefits to new markets for whatever reason. These suppliers have specialist processes to explore the target market, to design the offer and to specify manufacturing and packaging. They return to the company a researched concept which can be taken, through a detailed business plan, into manufacture.

Some service companies use similar innovation techniques. Yet it is rare for them to have established idea generation processes and it is relatively rare for them to set about the creation of ideas proactively. Formal schemes, such as they are, generally consist of a method of recording ideas, or an escalation route to a manager or 'ideas' group for assessment of potential. Most service companies encourage their employees to submit ideas, but following up the resultant propositions is often a weak point at which the process can break down. In short, the management of innovation in the service sector appears to be weak and should be improved.

Categorisation and its implications to new service design

Category management is well known in the consumer goods sector as a way of producing and distributing products to buyers. It has been very successful in creating new markets, new products and lines of profit. Producers think of their products and display them in a category that is relevant to buyers such as 'convenience health foods'. The response of buyers leads to further ideas and product innovations.

The same concept exists in the service sector as a guide to spotting opportunities. The method of categorising a service affects service design, guiding the type of service to be created and identifying gaps in the market. It can therefore give competitive advantage and is a key strategic issue which ought to be defined by the leaders of the firm before the start of design work.

There are a number of ways of categorising different services. These include:

(i) Customised services (sometimes called 'solutions') versus industrialised services. When most people think about professional services they tend to think in terms of high end customised services such as law, strategy consultancy and merchant banking. Elsewhere in the service sector, services have been the subject of intensive efforts over years to streamline them and make the process of delivery to a mass market as efficient as possible (e.g. fast food, hotels and airlines). This has been called the 'industrialisation of services' by Theodore Levitt (Levitt, 1976).

The margins, approach to market, degree of client engagement and personnel used, vary enormously between these offers. In fact, these extremes form a spectrum, represented in Figure 9.2, which was proposed by R. Johnston and G. Clark (Johnston and Clark, 2001).

This can be used to plan the offers of professional services firms. For instance, a consultant might undertake a project and solve a unique client problem. This might involve detailed analysis and highly experienced specialists. It is at the extreme upper left of the diagram. However, if the professional meets this problem several times, the type of engagement will be given a name and a new concept is born in the industry.

If the issue reoccurs, then other suppliers will take up the offer and create processes and tools to handle it. It moves down the 'industrialisation' line,

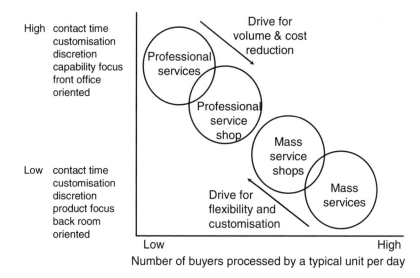

Figure 9.2 *Customised/industrialised service spectrum.*
Source: Johnston and Clark (2001). Services Operations Management, Johnston and Clark, Copyright © 2001 with permission from Pearson Education Limited.

picking up volume but losing margin. Eventually the approach becomes commonplace, is captured in software tools, is trained in professional academies and undertaken by clients themselves. It becomes, usually over years, a professional services commodity. Offers as diverse as double entry bookkeeping, portfolio planning and process re-engineering have all followed this course. Yet, different offers suit different firms at different stages in their evolution. A high end strategy firm like McKinsey might specialise in unique customised approaches, whereas one of the IT-based management consultancies, such as Accenture, might be more suited to more volume, process-based offers. For both these firms, however, offers which are so commonplace that they can be automated are unlikely to yield good margins.

Firms can therefore use this tool to agree their position, based on the type of offer to which their firm is best suited. They can then launch new offers as concepts move into their area of competence and hand them off as the margin falls out of them. Trying to cover all types of offer is likely to result in depressed margins and lower profits.

(ii) Infrastructure-based services. Some services are based on an infrastructure, a technology or a network. This might be a water supply, a computer platform in a major company, a telecommunications network, an

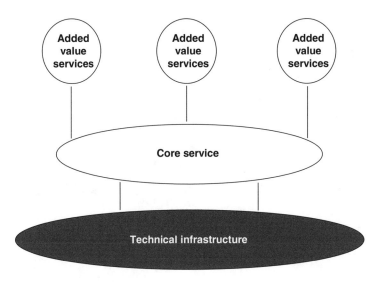

Figure 9.3 *Technological/infrastructure service.*

airline or a set of maintenance contacts. The issues, development and degree of reliance on that infrastructure affect the nature and the content of those services. Very often there is a core service (communications in telecom companies, support in computer maintenance companies and power supply) and opportunities for added value services, as illustrated in Figure 9.3.

The dynamics in this category of services are similar and can be an opportunity for professional services. For instance, the first notable privatisation was that of British Telecom (BT) by the UK (Margaret Thatcher) government in the mid-1980s. Yet many of the dynamics of this technological network industry were relevant to other sectors. They created nearly two decades of work around the world for merchant bankers, brokers and consultants as they applied it to other industries.

(iii) Product-based services versus pure services. Some services are adjuncts to product propositions and are therefore intimately tied to the value, development and pricing of that product. Other services are unique propositions in their own right which will stand alone in the market place. This was described by Lynn Shostack in her groundbreaking article (Shostack, 1977) and is illustrated in Figure 9.4.

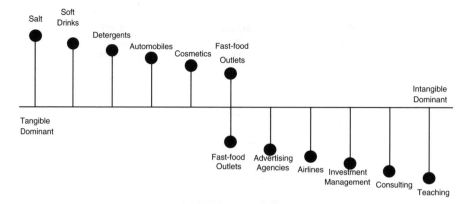

Figure 9.4 *The Shostack continuum.*
Source: Shostack (1977). Reproduced from the Journal of Marketing by permission of the American Marketing Association.

A service supplier can use this tool as a way to develop new services and manage its offer. For instance, in the early 1990s the IT industry was comprised mainly of product companies with associated technical support skills. Their advice and repair services were built around products, represented by the left-hand side of the diagram. While many industries make enormous efforts to simplify their propositions to buyers, the IT industry at the time was complex and tended to pass this complexity on to its buyers. A myriad of suppliers were therefore able to create healthy businesses by moving to the right-hand side of the diagram and providing independent service offers, based on advice and assistance.

(iv) Technology-based services versus people-based services (high tech versus high touch). Some services (extranets for clients, for example) comprise technology through which clients are served. Other services are reliant on the skills of people. In some cases, the difference is based simply on the buyers' preferences. In others it is linked to market evolution. A supplier in a market where service by people is the norm might introduce a technological innovation whereby clients can undertake some work themselves. In doing so, the supplier needs to plan the use of the technology, the impact upon the service process, how clients will be trained to use the technology and how this training will be spread to the total client community afterward.

The latter two points are very important. Clients need to be shown how to use the technology. People have a reluctance to change and to adopt new technology and this reluctance needs to be managed. Simple brochures or unattended demonstration equipment will not work. This needs to be non-intrusive, led by people who are competent and, above all, preserves the dignity of the client.

The introduction of technology in this way will reduce costs but will also increase perceived quality, because clients will be in more control of their service experience. However, the converse strategy is also effective on some, rare, occasions. In a market where suppliers have become remote or the service automated and commoditised, a premium supplier can gain advantage by introducing people into the service. To be successful, the supplier's brand must be high quality and aspirational, and, in addition, the service must be high priced.

(v) Self-service versus performed service. Some services are performed on behalf of a buyer, whereas others provide an infrastructure whereby the buyer can perform the service themselves.

(vi) The purpose of the service. Services may be directed at people's bodies (health care), belongings (laundry), minds (education/information) and financial assets (securities, banking).

(vii) Transaction versus annuity services. Some services are one-off transactions or project-based services. With these, it is difficult to create an ongoing relationship with a client other than by ensuring that each transaction is satisfactory. Annuity, or what Christian Gronroos (Gronroos, 2003) calls 'continually rendered services' have some form of contractual relationship which repeats the service. This allows a strong relationship to develop and the opportunity for the sale of other services. (Although it can mean that the loss of the client has a devastating effect on the finances of the business.)

Some suppliers encourage a warm relationship with clients by creating a membership structure. Membership may range from formal paid-for inclusion in a club to an emotional attachment to the grouping or community at whom the service is targeted (see ITSMA case study in the Introduction).

QinetiQ creates science-based services

QinetiQ is a defence research business, formerly backed by the UK government, which positions itself as a global advisor on defence and security technology. Previously called the Defence Evaluation and Research Agency (DERA), it became QinetiQ in 2001 when the UK government decided to put its defence laboratories on a commercial footing (see case study in Chapter 4 on building its brand).

Exploiting expertise

In February 2003 a 32% stake was sold to the Carlyle Group, a US private equity firm, to capitalise on QinetiQ's research and development expertise, with the British Ministry of Defence (MOD) retaining the principal shareholding. (A public flotation is intended when market conditions allow.)

The company, which employs over 8000 leading scientists and engineers in the UK and USA, provides services essentially of two kinds: major managed services, principally to the UK MOD running its ranges programmes, and solutions businesses, creating new inventions and intellectual property for exploitation in defence, security and other civil markets. Examples of these have been liquid crystal displays, flat panel speakers, carbon fibre, and nano material production.

There is also a growing business in the US in homeland security and defence, with clients such as the US Departments of Defense and Homeland Security and private contractors like Lockheed Martin and Boeing.

The organisational structure is designed to exploit the firm's scientific and technical expertise within a commercial context. First, there are the service line divisions, where the scientists and engineers are based, which have profit and loss responsibility.

Second, as with many other professional services firms, there is an industry emphasis: a number of teams, called market channels, deal directly with particular industries, such as healthcare or energy. These are charged with developing detailed client understanding and market definition in order to help the firm to develop relevant propositions.

Finally, there is another layer called 'Macro Asset Capability' (MAC), concentrating on the firm's integrated propositions. This consists of senior scientists with a good grasp of all the capabilities the company can muster in any particular area across divisions and who can act as interpreters between the scientific and market sides of the equation.

Defining client need

One of the key challenges is helping clients define their problems in what are often very complex areas of operation and then figuring out the right scientific or technological approach. There are two ways this occurs. One is for the market channel teams to bring a potential problem faced by a client to the experts to refine the issues and find the answers.

The other route is to hold a number of innovation sessions. These bring together the market experts with the appropriate scientists who then bounce ideas off each other. These are then sifted through to see not only if the possible solution is feasible, but also whether it is affordable.

It has been a learning experience for both the company's scientists and their clients, according to Simon Hardaker, group head of internal relations. For example, early on in its new commercial existence one oil company approached the firm because it was having a problem finding a way to lay pipelines in very deep water. The former approach worked well in shallow water but not at greater depths.

At first the oil client asked if it could borrow QinetiQ's facilities to test other solutions. The old-style organisation would have merely said yes. But the company was keen to develop stronger relationships with the oil business so it began to discuss alternative solutions, one of which turned out to be the right answer. So what started as a question of borrowing facilities became instead a consultancy project about how the firm could help the oil industry by understanding its problems and finding solutions.

There was a further benefit which has helped lay the groundwork for closer client relationships and hence more business. Rather than produce a report to be sent to the client, which used to be normal procedure, the company offered to send its scientists along to the oil company to speak about their findings and what ought to happen next. The meeting was a watershed: for the company, in engaging with such experts, and for the scientists, who, to their surprise, thoroughly enjoyed the experience.

The focus of new service development

NSD can be focused on either the firm's core service, added value services or brand new offers.

The 'core' service offer

Many service companies claim that they have been 'creating service for years'. By this they mean that they have invested resources, processes, training and skilled people into the systematic improvement of the core service that they offer to the market. They are moving down the 'experience curve' so that, over time, costs systematically decrease and enhancements are made to the service. This is a natural evolution which can be helped by NSD approaches. It is now widely accepted that the systematic and careful improvement in the processes of the core service is an important aspect of service design.

An NSD approach is particularly important if a company's core service is a commodity and it needs to turn its offer into a value proposition to stop the erosion of profits. It needs to create a new perception of value for the core service. First, the supplier must create different versions of the core service for different segments of buyers. If the core service has been reduced to a basic commodity, differentiation can be achieved if the service is positioned differently in different markets. Second, NSD techniques can be used to create ideas which enhance the existing service, and improve its perceived value over time. This is illustrated in Figure 9.5.

Through an innovation process the supplier identifies improvements to the core service which will appeal to buyers. These are launched as a 'premium' service for which an extra price is charged. Eventually, as client perceptions change, these fall into the core service and replace the basic offer.

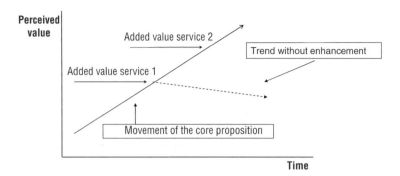

Figure 9.5 *Maintaining the value of the core service.*

A product analogy illustrates the value of this evolution. The basic car offered by a manufacturer establishes value expectations in the market. By putting a basic model into the market, the manufacturer is able to set a benchmark that defines the features for which specific groups of buyers will pay extra. This becomes the 'GTI' or 'Supra' model. (Note: in order to make the package aspirational, the supplier puts one feature that buyers of the basic package would probably want, such as video games on the back seat, into the elite version. This can cause growing dissatisfaction with the basic version over time.)

Over time, car buyers begin to expect a different package of features which they think should be included 'as standard' with the prime offer of a car. The enhanced features become the standard offer and a new benchmark becomes the norm. To the modern car buyer the bundle of features offered by the car industry some 20 years ago (i.e. a low performance engine with no sun roof and manual windows) would be unacceptable. Over time the core offer has increased in value through the introduction of added value features. This management of features is highly sophisticated and requires an institutionalised approach to NPD or NSD, which normally develops as a result of market trauma.

Through the application of creativity to the core service it is quite possible, then, to turn a commodity into a value proposition. Services offered by utilities, banks and high technology companies have been rescued from crisis and commoditisation in this way and the same techniques can be applied to professional services. This is the role and purpose of service design for the single service company.

The application of service design to 'added value' services

In many industries, added value services have been created to increase revenue and profit from product propositions, where no service content has existed before. These include services such as maintenance contracts or warranty programmes. They have also been created in professional services markets, particularly where one core service has dominated the relationship with buyers.

The benefits of added value services are:

- They maintain the value of the proposition in a mature market.
- They increase profit.
- They enhance the relationship to buyers.
- They create a knowledge of future needs through more regular contact with customers.

Service designers can apply NSD techniques to added value services, whether the added value proposition is:

- An annuity service, such as a benchmark service or annual audit.
- A service or complaints department.
- A maintenance or support service.
- A proposition wrapped around a product sale.
- A service component of a product sale which now needs independent value.

The creation of new services

This is the focus of much of the research, theory and writing on NSD. It demonstrates that it is possible to create new service propositions that have their own value and succeed in the market. They may be delivered electronically, through people or via physical channels. Either way, it is clear that the proactive creation of service and techniques to make this effective are an important competence that service companies need to foster.

Pricing professional services

A very important part of a professional service, which every professional has to deal with at some stage of their career, is the price to charge the client. Important though this is, it is still only one aspect of service design and only one of the features which clients will consider. No buyer in any part of the world ever bought any offer on price alone. Buyers look for a cluster or mix of features which serve their needs and aspirations best. Price only becomes a determining factor if all the elements of the various offers are exactly the same.

In practice, there are various approaches to pricing in the professional services sector.

Cost-plus pricing

This involves estimating the time to be taken on each element of the project by each type of skill deployed by the firm. In reality, the cost of that time can be based on either a percentage mark-up on the cost of employment (the market for human capital thus setting value) or the firm's judgement about value.

Commission

The supplier charges a commission as a percentage of the deal for the work they undertake. This approach is employed by professionals as diverse as advertising agencies and merchant bankers.

Value realised

The professional only charges if certain criteria, agreed with the client, are met. The 'no win no fee' practice of some lawyers is an example of this, but some consultants who are focused on achieving efficiency and cost saving have also used this to good effect.

Competitive approaches

Some price on the basis of what they think their competitor will charge. The drawbacks to this are serious. First, they are unlikely to know exactly what others will charge and risk cutting prices too far. Second, the offer is unlikely to meet the client's view of value and their service is therefore in danger of becoming a commodity over time.

The service design process

The Canadian researcher de Brentani (de Brentani, 1991) demonstrated that the existence of a new service design process was a good indicator of a firm's proficiency in service design and marketing – and ultimately of its competitive success. The research indicates that, by using a rational design process, it is possible to create new service-based propositions proactively.

The NPD process is applicable to service design, although in many cases certain elements are added or heavily modified. As a general rule, those services that are high volume, low margin and easily reproducible can more easily be developed using a rigorous development plan than those that are highly customised like high end professional services. The world's leading software companies have found, for instance, that they have been able to apply their rigorous software development processes to their support services.

The process suggested in Table 9.1 contains the tasks necessary to develop services. It contains the recognised steps needed to create services and works well inside professional services firms.

The process starts with the creation of ideas. Many service firms develop an attractive idea without first stopping to consider if there is an alternative which will have greater appeal to the market. This tendency is exacerbated if there is pressure to generate funds. It is sensible, however, to stimulate ideas from partners and clients before putting effort into new service creation.

Once a list of potential ideas has been created they need to be prioritised. A variety of criteria can be created which might be related to the objectives of the firm, the need to generate more funds from existing clients or the

Table 9.1 *Marketing tip: a service design process.*

Step 1 Analysis: business backdrop and buyer analysis
Step 2 Idea generation
Step 3 Prioritisation against firm's criteria
Step 4 Detailed component design
Step 5 Creating the value proposition

Quality check: are the unique considerations of services thought through?

Step 6 Create the concept representation
Step 7 Research: focus groups with clients to test the concept
Step 8 Write the business plan
Step 9 Trials

need to develop a new area of expertise. The criteria must be specific to the firm and practical.

The process then moves on to the design of the detailed components of the new service and the translation of those into a value proposition. Finally, each aspect of the service, including marketing materials, sales process and service delivery, are summarised into a detailed business plan, which will test the viability of the service, through financial rigour and research.

The techniques of component design

Detailed and recognised techniques can be used to design the components of a service. There are three main techniques, detailed in Part III, which are:

Features analysis

Every proposition offered to a market has three levels of features which are represented in Figure 9.6.

The 'core' feature is the heart of the proposition which buyers are seeking. It is often difficult to define. One cosmetics firm, for instance, decided that it was in the business of selling 'hope' rather than make-up. In a similar way, one management consultancy decided that it was in the business of 'problem solving'.

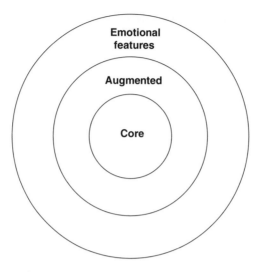

Figure 9.6 *Features analysis.*

'Augmented' features are those items (such as materials or processes) which are the methods by which the service is delivered into the market through that supplier. Finally, and most importantly, are the emotional issues, which need to be built into the proposition. These are often a major factor in the client's view of quality and value, and should not be neglected by service designers.

Blueprinting

Another well-developed technique is called 'blueprinting'. Every service that is offered to a market contains a process through which buyers move. This can be mapped and designed. It is an important step in producing effective services and a blueprint for a simple shoeshine service is represented in Figure 9.7.

The service process must direct and encourage clients to receive the benefits they are seeking. It must be designed to help clients and to allay any fears they have. Any hiccup in the process or lack of forethought will cause them to become disaffected.

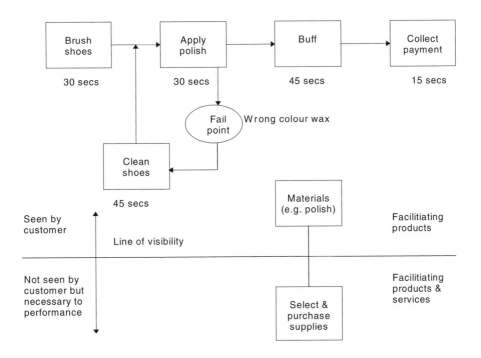

N.B.   Standard execution time = 2 minutes
Total acceptable execution time = 5 minutes

Figure 9.7 *Blueprinting.*
Source: Shostack (1982). Republished with permission, Emerald Group Publishing Limited.

Molecular modelling

The final technique is called molecular modelling and is represented in Figure 9.8. This recognises the mix, in some propositions, between physical and service content. It is undertaken in a similar way to features analysis.

Portfolio management tools

The 'Boston matrix'

The 'Boston matrix' (shown in Figure 9.9 and detailed in Part III) plots relative market share against relative growth. It was developed in an attempt to give corporate strategic planners a way of evaluating different business units in different markets.

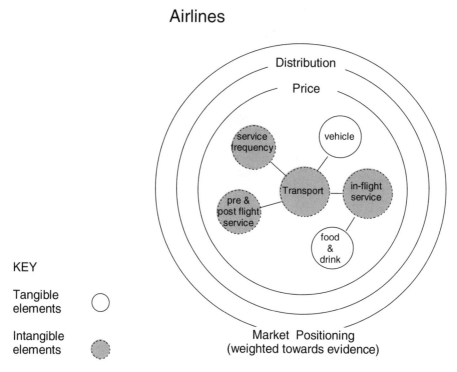

Figure 9.8 *Molecular modelling.*
Source: Shostack (1977). Reproduced from the Journal of Marketing by permission of the American Marketing Association.

A business which has just started operations would be a 'question mark' because the skills of the management to improve on its competence would be unproven. A company that had established itself in the market place and was beginning to thrive could be considered to be a 'rising star'. More established companies are 'cash cows' because they are producing profit but unlikely to achieve dramatic growth. Companies in decline are labelled as 'dogs' and candidates for withdrawal.

There are four steps to compiling the matrix. First, the annual growth rate of each business unit, in each market, is calculated and plotted on the matrix. Similarly, the relative market share of each unit is calculated and plotted. The turnover of each unit is represented by circles. The portfolio of business units is then categorised by the matrix into four groups and gives indications as to the strategy that can be adopted for each business, as shown in the diagram.

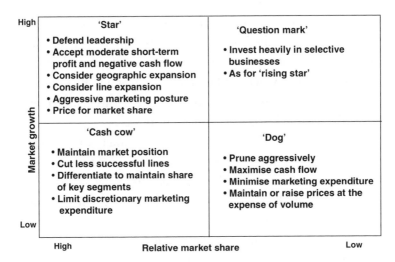

Figure 9.9 *The Boston matrix.*
Source: Boston Consulting Group (1968). Reproduced by permission of The Boston Consulting Group.

The matrix can be used to determine strategy for firms with a number of businesses. Theorists suggest that such firms require a balanced portfolio of businesses which use money from the cash cows to invest in other development areas.

> **Health warning:** some companies have tried to use this model to understand the behaviour of individual products or services rather than business units. Managers can be heard to talk of their products as either being a 'cash cow' or a 'dog'. This misuse of the concept is dangerous, because the phenomenon on which the tool is based does not always reflect the volume sales history of individual products or services.

At face value, the Boston matrix would appear useful to the leadership of service firms which have a range of businesses each of which focuses on a single service or market. The varying core competencies of these different businesses in their different markets may allow them to be managed as if they were product businesses specialising around their centre of expertise.

However, its applicability is not clear-cut. For example, one of the fundamental assumptions of the Boston matrix is that market share is a measure of success. This is based on the experience of consumer product industries, where the likes of Coca-Cola and Pepsi, or Unilever and Procter & Gamble may fight over tiny percentage increases in share. However, market share is not necessarily a critical issue for service businesses.

An example of this is the executive search market, where high quality suppliers operate an 'off limits' rule. This means that, if they are contracted to find senior executives on behalf of a client, they agree not to approach their employees as candidates for other searches. Clearly if they had a high share of one business sector this would restrict the number of companies available in which they could search for candidates, and thus limit their ability to deliver the service. Market share is not, therefore, a measure of success in this market.

The directional policy matrix

Another well-known product portfolio technique is the directional policy matrix illustrated in Figure 9.10. This was developed by McKinsey for its client General Electric at the same time as the Boston matrix. It is a way of categorising products against markets and is designed to be more flexible than the Boston matrix, using criteria created by the management team

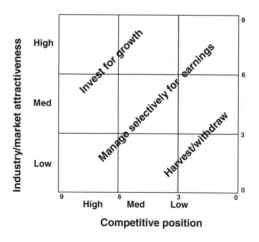

Figure 9.10 *The directional policy matrix.*

themselves to rank the portfolio. It can therefore be made more relevant to the individual firm and its leaders. The tool plots 'market attractiveness' against 'business strength' and allows management to prioritise resources accordingly.

There are six basic steps to compiling a directional policy matrix. They are:

- Identify the strategic business unit (SBU).
- Determine the factors contributing to market attractiveness.
- Determine factors contributing to the business position.
- Rank and rate the features determining market attractiveness and business position.
- Rank each SBU.
- Plot SBUs on the matrix.

Strategy can be deduced from the matrix and the options are detailed in Part III. This tool has been used with various service organisations to help them prioritise resources and to approach new markets. In each case it has proved to be a useful tool for creating viable, practical service strategies. It is particularly powerful at creating a consensus among professionals during the ranking of criteria and the rating of individual practices.

Line extension

A further method of developing a product portfolio is 'product line extension'. This categorises products according to a 'range' or a 'line'. Designers look for applications based around the competence that produces them, and then try to apply them to new markets or different segments within a market. Theorists argue that the range should have 'width and depth'. 'Width' refers to the number of different lines offered, while 'depth' refers to the assortment of offers.

The goods/services spectrum

A drawback of recognised portfolio planning techniques is they do not help managers to think through the product/service mix of their propositions to market. However, the model created by Lynn Shostack and modified by

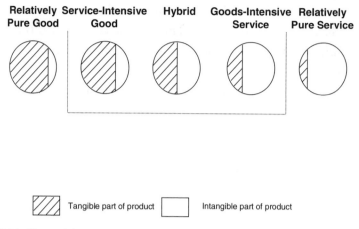

Figure 9.11 *The goods/services spectrum.*
Source: Berry and Parasuraman (1991). Reprinted with the permission of The Free Press, a Division of Simon & Schuster Adult Publishing Group, from MARKETING SERVICE: Competing Through Quality by Leonard L. Berry and A. Parasuraman. Copyright © 1991 by The Free Press. All rights reserved.

Leonard Berry (Berry and Parasuraman, 1991) in Figure 9.11 can be a particularly useful and practical method of planning the strategic direction of a portfolio.

Changes in the strategic direction and positioning of the company, or changes in demand, can be incorporated into this diagram and used to plan the structure of the company's 'proposition portfolio' (i.e. the mix of products and services).

Management issues

The creation of 'product managers' for services

Chapter Seven outlined one of the most important management issues for successful NSD: the creation of service managers. Its suggested that, if the creation of new services is important to organisations, they should consider creating dedicated 'service managers' who have equal weight and responsibility. In larger professional services firms, very senior leaders often have responsibility for a 'product' or 'skill set'. They will be responsible for the resources to deliver projects to clients, managing partners, staff, development, resourcing, recruitment and secondment. They are frequently the heart of the business, yet their NSD techniques and approaches are often rudimentary.

The role of a 'new service development manager', modelled on the product approach, would be:

- To create new services.
- To adjust the features mix of existing services.
- To withdraw old services.
- To prepare and manage the business plan for a particular service.
- To be responsible for the profit of the service being brought to market.
- The establishment of all processes necessary to launch the service successfully and generate revenue from it.

Senior champions

One of the criteria for success in NPD is senior management sponsorship, often from a board committee. In the service sector, the 1990s saw the emergence of 'service champions', or senior individuals responsible for the spread of a new service concept through the organisation. These tend to be senior managers with weight in the organisation who take on the role of 'political champions' for the concept of that service.

This role became necessary because of the difficulty of selling new service concepts inside an organisation. The need to get buy-in from so many different functions and individuals to support a new service concept means that internal marketing is critical to the success of that service. A service champion needs the skill to encourage the members of a project team to perform at their optimum level and achieve the NSD objectives. They have to lead the team and smooth over disagreements and, particularly, give support to the new service concept at all levels in the organisation.

One difficulty in NSD is how to achieve the necessary level of integration between headquarters functions and field groups, particularly if the latter are virtually independent partnerships in different nations. Ideas generated in the field need to be drawn together and coordinated by an individual with an international perspective. They should draw together teams of individuals to take each idea and establish it as part of the common service range. Service champions have to overcome any difficulties between the local and global perspective.

Table 9.2 *Marketing tip: issues to think about for NSD measures.*

- Does the new service meet its objectives (whether revenue, account penetration or market share)?
- Is the service creation team able to produce services quickly that are accepted by the market?
- Do clients accept the new service?
- What is the return on investment?

Investment controls – 'development gates'

Experienced product manufacturers build control points into their NPD process (often called gates), which manage the rate of investment in a new idea. Product managers are given a budget to complete initial feasibility and research. They are then, at the first 'gate', required to return to the management group for authorisation for further funds to go to the next phase. Some service companies are as disciplined in this as manufacturers and build as many as eight gates into their NSD process. Controls of this kind would save many professional service firms from wasting investment.

Measurement of NSD

Leaders ought to establish criteria by which the new services that are created are considered to be successful. The measurements put in place by top management give signals to the organisation as to what is important and what gets priority (Table 9.2). If the creation of new services is important to a company appropriate success measures must be created. De Brentani's research (de Brentani, 1991) identified a number that are used in American and Canadian firms:

- Sales performance.
- Competitive performance.
- Cost performance.
- 'Other booster' (i.e. how it affects other costs).

Table 9.3 *A checklist of service design considerations.*

1. What is the categorisation of the service?	The service should be examined against the nature of the market to which it will be offered. An appropriate category of service must be decided. This is a profound strategic decision which will affect all other design considerations.
2. What is the process through which the client will move? Is it thought through and clearly described in client friendly terms?	This must be designed to be efficient, enjoyable and fluid. The process must be robust and allow for the client's individual needs. It must blend the interrelationship of client, service staff and technology in the environment in which the service will be experienced, be it on-line or physical. The process must also be designed to allow for known eventualities and for the growth of clients' understanding.
3. What will be the expertise, role and behaviour of the people who will be engaged in the client's project?	If people are part of the offer it is critical that their language, dress and behaviour reflect the brand position of the service.
4. How will any technology models or tools be deployed as part of the delivery to the client?	The role of technology has expanded dramatically with the advent of online services where the degree of human interaction may be non-existent and/or irrelevant to the buyer. In general, the role and nature of all technology must be blended into the mix of delivery process and people behaviour.
5. How will the service be designed in order to allow the client to learn the service process?	As clients use the service and gain experience they will want to improve upon it. There must be flexibility and possible short-cuts built into the process which allows the client to get more directly to what they want and customise the service to their own requirements.
6. Have the clients' emotional needs and expectations been explicitly designed into the service?	The use and enjoyment of services raises emotions that the use and enjoyment of products often does not. All these emotional needs must be researched and understood, and the service must be designed to meet them. In particular the prior expectations of the target group must be considered in the design.

Table 9.3 *Continued*

7. How will the corporate brand be manifested at all points of interface to overcome the issue of intangibility?	During or after consumption the client is unlikely to be left with anything tangible. The corporate brand must be represented at all points of interface and there must also be an explicit strategy to manage 'post-purchase distress' (see Chapter 8).
8. How will the clients' need to retain dignity and control be managed if naive clients are using the service for the first time?	The people involved in the service must be able to accommodate all eventualities, giving clear, flexible and understanding client service. There must also be a robust and effective service recovery mechanism.
9. Will the mix of process, people behaviour and brand reassure the novice and generate a climate of trust?	The use of brand, people and process must be clear, simple and reassuring.
10. Are there clear interfaces with the field to ensure that their views on the actual delivery and performance of the service, once established, are taken into account?	The intimacy of contact between front line staff and clients means that front line people will have powerful contributions in service performance.
11. What is the value proposition?	The mix of features needs to be designed to appeal to a client more than competitor offers and summarised into relevant communications.
12. How different is the service from competitor offers? Really? Have you checked?	The service must be different, really different from other offers.

A checklist of issues for service designers

Table 9.3 contains a checklist of key questions to be asked by leaders responsible for designing a service. It draws on theorists' views of the differences between services and products and experience of working with senior managers in this field. It covers the key issues which must be addressed as a result of the unique characteristics of service dominated propositions.

Summary

There are recognised and well-developed processes and techniques by which professional services firms can create effective new services. The future success of professions hinges on their ability to generate funds and to create viable propositions based around their skills. Professionals should become as adept at creating new propositions for their clients as they are at using their technical skills. Service design should be part of professional practice management.

10

Communicating with markets

Overview

Professional services firms should take advantage of the range of communications tools available to build their businesses. While many of the most commonly used techniques, such as advertising, public relations, direct marketing, can be adapted for services marketing, firms can also usefully employ approaches specific to the sector such as reputation enhancement, creating stars, relationship marketing, viral marketing and thought leadership. However, any programme should be built on the resolution of a number of strategic marketing communications issues, such as understanding the target market and designing meaningful messages. This chapter sets out how to address effective communication with markets. It includes a guide to managing and implementing marketing communications.

Managing the messages

Individual professionals must put great emphasis on communicating with their clients if they are to succeed. They must listen, diagnose, propose answers, advise and listen again. However, once the professional service becomes a business of any size, its leaders must consider how effectively it communicates with the market as a whole and with individual markets within the broad economy. This might entail messages targeted at potential clients about the firm's capability, focused campaigns to existing clients about the firm's approach or broadcast messages to the wider community about its values and brand.

All have their place and, managed properly, can contribute to improved margins through enhanced revenue and successful cost control. This is a different method of communication than the one-to-one relationship of normal client involvement. It requires processes and methods which communicate effectively across different media in concert with other messages in order to influence the thinking, behaviour and actions of a group of people.

Properly done, it is a highly sophisticated and subtle two-way communication with buyers and potential buyers. It can influence thinking, steering potential clients towards a firm's skills and thus helping to keep the cost of sales down. The function requires experienced, specialist individuals working in a well-managed team to be effective over time. It is poor leadership to allow inexperienced or unqualified people to run this function, since it results in both wasted expenditure and ineffective communication.

A reprise of relevant marketing communications concepts

Promotion

In the past marketers have described mass communication to a market as 'promotion'. This form of marketing communication has a long history and has unquestionably worked for product companies. It fits with the view that there is a need to 'push' a product or concept; that ideas can influence and manipulate people; that promotion is one way. A product marketer will promote products through advertising, sales promotion, direct marketing and merchandising. There is a degree of sophistication behind this, of course, because the communications need to be targeted at a particular group of people, be benefit based and be crafted to appeal both to the rational and emotional needs of buyers. Yet it is promotion nevertheless.

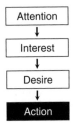

Figure 10.1 *AIDA response model.*
Source: Strong (1925)

Response models

In the latter half of the twentieth century, marketing academics and practitioners developed various response models which are designed to understand how buyers respond to broadcast promotion. For instance, the AIDA model in Figure 10.1 (and detailed in Part III) describes a learning process, whereby targeted buyers move from 'attention' to 'action' (i.e. buying) through the influence of marketing messages. The aim of different communication activities is to influence the thinking of buyers to cause them to buy. While measurement of marketing effectiveness is erratic and varies in sophistication, there is evidence that marketers in various markets have achieved this.

The habit of many in the professional services industry is not to employ mass communication or to do it badly. However, these models show that it can be used to influence opinion toward a supplier and to prepare the ground for purchase. It can be much more cost-effective than allowing each practitioner to generate their own work alone. Unfamiliarity or lack of competence is not, therefore, a rational explanation for dismissing an approach which has proved cost-effective and profitable in many markets.

Integrated marketing communications (IMC)

Integrated marketing communications is a new concept. It goes beyond the relatively unsophisticated practice of broadcast marketing promotion in that it plans, from the start, a process of two-way communications between the firm and the buyers. It examines all the channels through which people receive messages about the offer and uses models to plan the frequency of communications through different media. The practitioner plans both the message and the mechanism of response from the targeted buyer.

Above all it looks for a response from the buyer. A response, through a database or a response-driven promotional campaign, can give the company an idea of the effectiveness of the communication. It can also point to improvements the buyer needs from the company in the form of either quality of service or adjustment to the proposition. The company can then improve its profits by responding to these messages.

At the same time, IMC improves the cost-effectiveness of marketing communications. To date marketing promotion has tended to be a supplier-driven industry. External specialist agencies have been hired by companies to carry out one of a wide range of promotional techniques. Developing an integrated approach has been made difficult by the focus these agencies have of their own area of expertise.

Most advertising agencies want to do advertising, most direct marketing and public relations (PR) consultancies want to do direct marketing or PR, and so on. They all tend to stay in their own silos. (For a time there was a move in the industry toward a 'full service agency', or the one-stop shop, but that concept has not really taken hold.) Even the big networks, which own a range of different marketing specialists, have difficulty in combining them effectively to produce the best balance of communications vehicles for clients. However, a firm that adopts IMC can itself manage the balance of different agencies, saving costs.

Integrated marketing communications stress the need to plan the media through which the message goes, the message itself and the mechanisms by which the response from buyers can be measured. This must be done by the firm itself to achieve a good balance of effective communication and spend. Normally a marketing communications director will manage a group of different agencies throughout one campaign to achieve this.

The effort is worthwhile, however. By planning an integrated approach and managing various agencies to deliver it, a concerted approach can be made to communicate an idea to a client. The client might receive an invitation to an event one day, see a newspaper article the next, notice an advertisement after that and, finally, talk to an employee of the firm. These communications approaches therefore prepare the way for direct conversation, optimising time with the client.

Brand communications

As outlined in Chapter 4, a firm's brand is one of its most precious intangible assets, affecting both the price and quality of every job done throughout the world. Part of the strategy to enhance the value of the brand is likely to involve programmes to communicate the brand specifically to the general market place in order to make it famous. Such programmes need to be designed to broadcast to the entire market, through the right media, to enhance the brand values. These needn't be through expensive advertising programmes though. Some very successful brands have been built through targeted PR alone.

Communications aspects of relationship marketing (RM)

As described in Chapter 8, relationship marketing is a different paradigm to more established marketing theory. It is also very relevant to professional services.

The communications processes of RM start with database marketing, often based on 'customer relationship management (CRM)' systems. These systems hold details of clients and have a facility (called 'campaign management') which controls communication with them. They register clients' interests and preferences. They also often allow relationship managers or client service partners the chance to edit out communications from their firm which are unwanted or irrelevant.

This solves a very common client service problem: erratic and uncoordinated mailings to clients. Marketers planning any communications to clients (from hospitality invitations, through thought leadership pieces to the annual report) must then target their communications and iron out any conflicts with other communications at the planning stage. Relationship marketing therefore introduces a discipline into the communications processes of the firm which removes potential client dissatisfaction.

RM also seeks to use the identified networks of client contacts to enhance reputation. Buyers use their professional networks to gain information on professional services providers. In fact, these networks are often the most influential source used prior to purchase. A strong reputation and positive word of mouth will therefore yield work. Marketers can use reputation enhancement and 'viral' marketing techniques (see below) to increase word of mouth about the professional or the firm. This will increase the propensity to buy.

Data-driven marketing communication

If there is one major difference between industries which value marketing and those which don't it is the willingness to invest in data to aid marketing decisions. Whereas some industries use weekly market research to aid their decisions, the professional services industry is more cautious in its use of research or good quality data to guide strategy or marketing. Yet good marketing communication is also grounded on data. Many broadcast advertisers know how many shoppers they are aiming at and their attitudes to the product through systematic investment in research data.

There is no reason why professionals should not have data on: their clients' attitudes, their competitive reputation, the propensity of clients to refer them to others and the play of their brand in the purchase process. All can be obtained through careful, systematic research and all will increase the effectiveness of communications. There is no excuse for the arrogance of 'gut feel' based on the experience of a few direct clients and internal dialogue.

The applicability of different communication methods to professional services

Advertising

Advertising is the practice of buying space in various public media in order to communicate a message. The media used includes broadcast media (television, radio and cinema), print media and outdoor media (poster sites) to make an impact on the intended audience. Advertising campaigns are calculated on the basis of the likelihood of the intended audience seeing or hearing the message a given number of times over a sustained period.

Advertising is attractive in that it communicates a message to a large audience very effectively. It is particularly good at communicating messages that require impact, like the launch of a new business, or those that need fame, like a tired or new brand. It does, however, have a number of drawbacks. First, it can be expensive, requiring large spends to reach audiences of television or radio networks. However, the ability to target messages very finely has improved considerably over recent decades and the proliferation of media has reduced costs. A business-to-business campaign, for example, if it uses radio, business- or news-oriented TV channels and specialist publications (such as inflight magazines and trade papers) can be cost-effective.

Second, there is such a deluge of messages aimed at modern buyers that it is hard to make a message stand out. Campaigns therefore need to be creative and sustained. A well-planned and eye-catching campaign running for, say, two years will eventually affect the intended audience and influence its thinking.

Finally, the impact of advertising can be hard to measure. It is difficult to measure precisely the effect that a campaign is making, even if it is well remembered or wins industry awards. Firms tend, therefore, to create their own measures over time. One common practice, for instance, is to have one geography reserved as a quiet area which does not receive the campaign. Differences in the effect on sales is then measured.

The professional services industry, despite the belief of many in it, does advertise extensively. Practice ranges from the placement of advertisements in directories to the large, sophisticated campaigns of leading firms like IBM Global Services and the larger chains of retail professional services. Some professions, like law, accountancy and medicine, have only been allowed to advertise relatively recently. There is therefore still debate within them about whether and how to advertise.

However, the use of advertising in large partnerships can be erratic and ineffective. For instance, individual partners might place advertisements in what they believe to be influential publications. This leads to inconsistent representation of the firm and expensive media buying. For such firms it would often be cheaper to have one centrally developed advertising strategy which produces advertisements for local use.

An example of ineffective communications with a market is the use by many professional services firms of what is called the contract publishing industry. This involves the appearance of articles in targeted journals or publications produced by publishers for their clients. A worthy organisation might sponsor a report on a significant issue to which partners are invited to write an article. They are then informed that a full-page space is reserved for an advertisement next to the article.

Table 10.1 *Advertising principles.*

- A clear communications strategy.
- A clear idea of the target market.
- A compelling message.
- Excellent creative, normally produced by a specialist agency.
- Good media choice, relevant to the target market.
- A sustained period of communication to allow the market to assimilate the message.
- Some form of measurement, even if judgemental.

But this form of advertising, called an advertorial, is both expensive and wasteful. It can even harm a firm's credibility since it is usually plain that the editorial stance is driven by the type of advertisement, the number of which can frequently cheapen the magazine. In major firms it is cheaper to use a media buying company to position a few pre-designed advertisements in media that the firm knows its target clients will read.

In approaching its market, the leadership of professional services firms should not dismiss advertising out of hand. Many need to communicate the essence of their brand promise to broad markets and suffer from not considering this medium. They should, however, ensure that this is approached using proper advertising principles, summarised in Table 10.1.

Direct marketing

Direct marketing is the practice of communicating to buyers through written or virtual messages. The communication can range from a letter with printed insert, through elaborate creative campaigns (such as London-based River Publishing, which launched its business by employing an actor to deliver chocolates to its potential clients by hand) to internet-based newsletters. It requires an accurate and up-to-date database of contacts (something harder to achieve than might be imagined), a relevant offer, clear written technique and a concise message.

Direct communication is most effective when part of a relationship with clients or when the client has given permission to mail. This is an act of trust. Most modern buyers are adversely affected by direct mail, whether physical or email. It irritates and frustrates them to receive unwanted mailers, however attractive. By giving a supplier permission to mail to them, the client is acting on trust that the firm will take the trouble to filter out unwanted communications and make their written offers relevant. This is not always achieved, even by leading firms, due to inadequate attention given to systems and planning.

Again, direct communication is used extensively in the professional services industry. Firms invite clients to hospitality events and to seminars on technical subjects. They also send research reports or other material. Some use internet-based communication. More than one merchant bank, for example, sends an internet-based newsletter on mergers and acquisition (M&A) activity in their clients' industries. These are widely appreciated by people at all levels in their clients' organisation, even chief executives, because they are timely, relevant and give valuable insight.

Any professional services firm which engages in these activities should ensure that they are effective and well planned. If not, erratic and ill-planned communication can be very costly in terms of print, design and management time. Worse, it can undermine the prestige of the firm in the minds of client and cause dissatisfaction. Even leading firms have sent out poorly written communication or have inundated their clients with so much communication that they became annoyed.

It is sensible, then, for the leadership to ensure that there is a direct communication strategy. This should include:

- **Accuracy of data:** most leading firms now invest in a client database with a campaign management facility. The data in this system should be seen as an asset of the firm. It needs to be kept up to date by internal disciplines (ensuring that client service staff keep records up to date) and by a, perhaps annual, check with clients. It also needs to comply with local data protection laws.
- **Planning of message and campaigns:** all invitations, announcements, reports and mailings should be planned in advance. This gives the firm the chance to ensure that they have a clear, consistent message. It also gives the opportunity to eliminate any conflicts or to even out communications.
- **Response management:** how the clients respond to any material should be made clear. Simple invitations can be returned to the event manger, but more strategic communications should be handled through the relationship manager.

Public relations

'PR' is a generic term for a range of specialist and sophisticated skills. Media relations, for example, is the process of managing a firm's relationship with the broadcast media. This might involve regular contact with journalists and their representatives, fielding a range of enquiries from new business ventures, through to the chief executive's press programme and on to handling embarrassing aberrations or professional errors. It is rare to find a professional services firm that does not have at least a 'press officer' dealing with these enquires. As specialists, they develop their own skills and their own networks to handle press enquiries. In fact, their expertise is often better judged by what they keep out of the media than what appears in it.

It is in the field of proactive media relations that many professional services firms fall down. Some press officers, particularly in smaller firms, find it difficult to get time away from the demands of ad hoc events and enquiries to take any initiative. When they do, it is often to issue press releases that go out to general circulation lists. Unfortunately, journalists receive so many press releases that they rarely give these much attention. It is best practice to create a proactive media relations plan. This will identify which messages will be emphasised by the firm and which media it will focus on. The aim of the plan is to develop good relationships between principals in the firm and the editors of key media. In fact, some take an approach similar to client account management with important publications.

Events and hospitality

Different industries have habits which are customary approaches used by all suppliers, some of which continue long after they are effective. Client hospitality is definitely a habit of the professional services industry. Paid hospitality ranges from large customised events, through packages bought at large public events (such as the Ryder Cup or Wimbledon) to individual meals with clients. The philosophy behind client hospitality is that the informal situation will help to create a relationship with the client which will encourage further work.

A well-managed and targeted event can certainly contribute to closer relations, especially if seen as part of a wider communications programme.

There can be, however, a lot of waste and personal indulgence which is irrelevant to business success.

Events need to be well planned, with the objectives, suitability and target audience carefully thought through. It is easy, for instance, for attendees to end up as client contacts with little influence, or worse, as predominantly internal people, because of poor planning or choice of event. In addition, some clients, particularly public sector organisations, are reluctant to accept hospitality. A relevant seminar can be just as effective.

Employee interaction and networks

One of the main communication channels to clients is the employees of the firm. If a professional services firm has 10000 employees talking to three clients a day on average, there are 30000 opportunities to communicate with clients every day. Communications planning should therefore take into account the views of employees when preparing any external communications. At the very least, people should be told about any campaign before it is released to clients. However, effectiveness is dramatically improved if employees are drawn into the campaign and enthused to talk to clients about it.

Collateral

Collateral is a term which covers the manifestation of marketing messages in brochures, case studies and other physical handouts. It also includes virtual collateral such as websites. These need to be carefully designed and crafted to communicate benefits clearly. It is good practice to create a 'collateral strategy' for the whole firm covering: intended use, design structure, renewal and reprinting methods, plus the types favoured for particular clients.

Viral marketing or 'word-of-mouth' communication

Service marketing academics have demonstrated that 'word of mouth' plays an important role in building services revenue. This is particularly important for professional services firms because it is a major contribution to reputation enhancement. Techniques to enhance word of mouth have come to the fore with the internet and have been called 'viral marketing' (viral because the aim is to spread an idea among a target community in much the same way as a virus spreads in a body). The technique exploits social communications and gossip.

Internet users have demonstrated the propensity of human beings to chat and gossip. They copy emails and jokes to each other. For example, there have been several famous instances of sexual indiscretions being discussed in emails with friends and then being copied to so many people that, within days, they are reported in national newspapers. Some companies have exploited this phenomenon by creating short, humorous video clips that are for the internet alone. As the technique involves the transportation of an idea from person to person, it is a powerful way of judging popularity.

However, the internet version of viral marketing has distracted attention from an effective use of the technique exploited by consultants and IT companies for several decades: the marketing of business ideas. A new idea will emerge from a business thinker or a consultancy in the form of a 'white paper' or book. It will be presented at a few leading conferences. (It has most impact if it gets a hearing at a chief executive-level conference such as the World Economic Forum held each year at Davos.)

Product managers in conference companies then spot the idea, allowing time on agendas for it to be presented. Soon whole conferences are dedicated to it, articles published and books authored. Leading consultancies dedicate partners and staff to practise in the area. They adjust case studies from past projects and present briefs to their clients. At this stage, academics get funding for reputable research into the idea and add to its visibility. The new idea is 'viral', carried and reinforced by debate in the business community.

Interestingly, certain, generally large, corporations are nearly always the same 'early adopters' of a new idea. If it moves into the next phase of adoption it becomes, for a time, unchallenged. Many management concepts, both credible and not-so-credible, such as process re-engineering, CRM, total quality management (TQM), globalisation and shareholder value, have grown in this way. After a while, however, the ideas are challenged ('Has process re-engineering damaged corporate America?', 'Does TQM pay back?'). Some of these management fads then fail. Others become established concepts, validated by academic research. (The 'Boston matrix' as a strategic planning tool, process management and quality management are but a few.)

Professional services firms can exploit this phenomenon to gain revenue and competitive advantage. They can pioneer ideas (the most costly approach), validate new ideas (an approach open to leading brands), join the wave as a sales tool (most powerful when professional services, IT and City firms all join in) or play the sceptic. Each is a viral marketing strategy which can enhance the reputation and position of the firm if properly resourced and managed.

Online marketing communication

Marketing communications have, as with many things, been dramatically affected by the advent of the internet. At its most basic, no firm can now ignore the need to create an impressive and representative website. Moreover, while many of the absurd claims of the dot.com bubble have proven ill-advised, human behaviour on the internet demands that all firms address it as a serious medium.

Currently, many buyers (whether at home or at work) search for information on services and products on the internet. It is quite common for top management to commission junior employees to research a subject and often the medium of that research is the internet. Firms must, therefore, ensure that they have a web presence and produce materials with key words that will be found by search engines. They should, however, consider an 'online' marketing strategy as part of their communications programme. Properly managed, email electronic newsletters and internet communications can be extremely effective mechanisms to communicate with clients.

Marketing communications issues specifically for professional services firms

Reputation enhancement

As the Introduction to this book showed, the momentum for growth of revenues in professional services firms is the creation of 'demand-pull' based on a reputation for excellent work. Any marketing approach should therefore begin with mechanisms to enhance this natural reputation. This will increase repeat business and referrals. The first step, as shown in Figure I.1 in the Introduction, is to undertake objective research to understand the quality of the firm's competitive reputation.

The issue here is the competitive reputation in the minds of clients. When buying professional services how does the firm rate in their buying criteria? Every professional takes pride in the quality of their work. None sets out to do a bad job. However, clients may use different criteria to assess a firm's performance, based on more than technical expertise. Any marketer beginning marketing communications for a professional services firm ought to start with an audit of competitive reputation. Having understood that, the second step is to put in place mechanisms to amplify that natural reputation. The sort of mechanisms likely to do this are PR-based initiatives that make visible the expertise and accomplishments of both the firm and individuals.

Interbrand thrives through reputation enhancement

Interbrand was founded in 1974 as a specialist brand consultancy and now has offices in 35 countries around the world. Over the years it has developed expertise in a diverse range of brand skills, including brand development and management, naming, design, corporate identity, communications and brand valuation, a discipline which it pioneered. For instance, Interbrand was the first company to put a value on a brand publicly, a project which helped give it global recognition.

One of the main techniques the company has used to differentiate itself from competitors and be seen as a leader in all aspects of branding has been a continuous and consistent programme of reputation-enhancing materials. For example, its professionals publish up to two books every year, write numerous articles for publication in different countries, speak at conferences and are quoted regularly in the media.

The firm also runs themed evenings for clients and the media in some of its main offices. In addition, the firm set up brandchannel.com, which publishes papers on a wide range of branding topics, as well as acting as the conduit for a worldwide exchange of views on brands and branding.

What has really secured Interbrand's place as an authority on brands is the annual survey of the world's 100 most valuable global brands, a survey it has been carrying out since 1998 (Figure 10.2). For the first two years it was done in conjunction with the *Financial Times*. In 2000 it

Figure 10.2 *Examples of Interbrand's thought leadership.*
Source: INTERBRAND

formed an association with *Business Week* to get more of a global scope and wider exposure.

In the survey, Interbrand uses its now well-established brand valuation process to determine as closely as possible the true economic value of what it describes as the complex array of forces that make up a brand. There are also a number of local league tables done with local publications in countries such as France, Brazil, Mexico, Spain, Australia, Singapore and Taiwan. Additional regional surveys are used to help introduce the firm to new markets.

As a result, one of Interbrand's key advantages is that, when people think about brands, they will often think about the company's valuation league table. This can not only be used as a calling card to attract new clients, but it also gives Interbrand credibility in the boardroom of those target clients. This is in line with the company's objective of creating more in-depth relationships with clients, traditionally the preserve of management consultancies, as branding becomes more integrated into overall business strategy. Evidence of the success of this strategy came from a US survey of chief executive officers at the end of 2003, which found that it was the third most valued league table.

Creating stars and gurus

The reputation of a senior professional for excellent work is behind the success of most professional services firms. It is at the very heart of single practitioner firms and small boutiques. It is also the main plank of the single practitioner 'guru' strategy (see Chapter 1) which has been so successful in management consulting, architecture and hairdressing. However, the dynamic can be distorted in large firms with strong brands. Individuals who join these firms can get lost in the size and reputation of the firm.

Nevertheless, without successful leaders, firms cannot grow. So one strategy is to readdress the balance. A communication dynamic that can therefore be used by professional services is to create a 'star' in an area of practice which the firm wants to emphasise. Partners with expertise may speak at conferences, write books and publish articles to gain attention in that field of expertise.

Thought leadership

Thought leadership is a term used commonly within the professional services industry for the publication and dissemination of ideas for commercial advantage. The assumption behind it is that reputation can be enhanced (by the publicity gained from such publications) and work gained (by demonstrating expertise in a technical area). In practice, it can range from an article in a magazine to a major, sponsored programme or a complete book. Wherever, it can also be pernicious, adding to the momentum of management tools which, in the long term, turn out to be dubious or damaging. Firms too closely associated with questionable trends to make short-term cash can damage their reputation. Thought leadership can also be enormously expensive in terms of both cash and time costs. It is sensible, therefore, to create a discipline to manage thought leadership investment across the firm. This might include:

- **Proper cost management:** cash costs include research, printing, promotion and publication. Time costs include the opportunity cost of staff taken away from chargeable work and support staff.
- **Criteria for approval:** these might involve: payback, commercial opportunity, quality, reputation enhancement.
- **Anticipated revenue or leads stimulated.**
- **Timetable of all projects.**

A leadership team should be responsible for the firm's thought leadership programme. It should manage, using peer review, proposals for thought leadership investment, balancing the potential for short-term gain against long-term, sustainable reputation.

Joel Kurtzman: developing thought leadership programmes

Developing a thought leadership programme in a professional services firm can absorb a lot of time, effort and resources. But when it is done well, the impact on the firm's reputation can be substantial, according to Joel Kurtzman, who has overseen two thought leadership programmes.

The first was for the consultancy Booz-Allen Hamilton and the second for PricewaterhouseCoopers (PwC).

Kurtzman was editor of the *Harvard Business Review* in the early 1990s. Then, in 1995, he was asked by Booz-Allen to set up a framework for thought leadership, a term he coined when he launched consultancy's highly regarded monthly publication, *Strategy + Business*. He created this as an independent brand so that it could be used to 'authenticate' the content that Booz-Allen produced, which meant that the magazine's editors had the right to reject articles.

The idea was to create content that could be leveraged in a number of different ways. He saw this as a process with several stages. First, there would be a short article. Publishing several articles on the same topic could then lead to a book, which in turn then offered the opportunity to launch a conference.

In 1999 he was approached by PricewaterhouseCoopers (PwC) to become a senior partner and mount a similar programme of cutting-edge thought leadership which would encompass both the consulting and accountancy areas of the firm. When he arrived, he found that there were no defined areas of responsibility in terms of who originated what, which meant there was little coordination of the firm's various publishing efforts. So his big challenge was to bring alignment and find the right vehicle to produce high quality and consistent thought leadership to raise its profile in its markets.

A champion is essential to success. At PwC Kurtzman had the backing of the senior leadership of the time, who, he says, understood the value of ideas. They were looking for some sort of vehicle related to 'transparency', which was seen as the heart of the firm's business. Kurtzman thus put together a group of economists from around the world, and talked to key figures involved in this kind of research. These included former US President Jimmy Carter, now of the Carter Center, who had always taken a great interest in this area, and Peter Eigen, chairman of Transparency International. The result, after a lot of effort and discussion, was the 'Opacity Index'.

The thinking behind the project was that global companies face two types of risks: large-scale, low-frequency risks and small-scale, high-frequency risks. Although the large-scale risks, such as earthquakes and major acts of terrorism, receive so much attention, the small-scale risks, such as fraudulent transaction, bribery, legal and regulatory complexity and unenforceable contracts, represent the real costs to business. These risks interfere with commerce, add to costs, slow growth and make the future even more difficult to predict (Kurtzman *et al.*, 2004).

So a methodology was developed to project what aspects of a country's economy carry the greatest risk. By assessing and comparing the costs of those risks on a country-by-country basis, an overall Opacity Index was created, in which higher levels of opacity strongly correlate with slower growth and less foreign direct investment in most markets.

The first Index was produced to much acclaim and attention in 2001, with another one the following year. That was followed by a period of re-evaluation and reworking to improve it further. However, by 2003 the PwC leadership had changed, following the sale of the consulting arm to IBM. The new leaders weren't keen to back the project, so the rights were sold to Kurtzman's strategic consultancy, the Kurtzman Group, which produced the latest version in 2004 (Kurtzman is now a part-time senior advisor to PwC).

Kurtzman has identified several possible stages in the evolution of a thought leader programme:

- Recognise the germ of an idea which could develop into something significant and test it out in a short article or research brief.
- If it lives up to its potential, take it further with a more substantial publication, such as a white paper.
- Put it at the nucleus of a new management idea, possibly with a book, that is seen as pertinent to a current business problem faced by companies.
- Finally, find a powerful vehicle to disseminate this knowledge, whether a regular publication, a summit or conference. In the case of *Strategy + Business*, the firm's reputation was greatly enhanced when material from the publication was adopted for use by a number of leading business schools.

This approach leads to new and measurable avenues of work in a number of ways, Kurtzman found. The first, where someone contacts the firm after reading an article type, is immediately identifiable. The second, when the firm starts to become associated with a strong concept, is more indirect. The final one is the impact on the brand of becoming generically known for expertise in particular areas. Recruitment also benefits, since a successful programme can widen the pool of excellent people for hiring.

Use of collateral in professional services firms

In the world of retail professional services, collateral is generally 'point of sale' which, properly devised and presented, helps a client to choose and reassure themselves about the purchase. It is frequently provided by manufacturers, but in large chains is self-generated. It needs to reflect the brand of the firm and the objectives of the campaign. It should also be easy to assemble, durable and have high impact. The chain needs to control the number of point-of-sale (POS) campaigns and their effect on shop space, to ensure there are no adverse consequences.

Collateral is also important in the business-to-business context, particularly for those buying for the first time. It may be that a client is in emotionally distressing circumstances, such as a significant medical or a complex critical business problem, or it may be that the service seems expensive. Collateral plays an important role for the professional services firm in these circumstances.

For example, if the firm is presenting its credentials during a 'beauty parade', those involved should leave behind a bound copy of the presentation in a format acceptable to the client, so that they can leaf through it and consider it after the meeting. Also, at the point where the client is about to make a decision but hasn't yet signed a contract, it makes sense to send a case study of a company which has purchased a similar service from the firm, so the client has something physical to refer to.

Finally, after signing the contract, it is sensible to leave behind a directory of the key people involved in the project, their experience and contact numbers in a format the client can use internally to show others. At the very least send a thank-you note to the client for their business and consider delivering regular progress reports.

Brochures in particular can be an exorbitant waste of money in professional services firms. Many produce expensive annual reports with photos of their own people, sometimes with clients. There are several problems with this approach.

First, there are frequently few differences between competitive brochures. They are often filled with the same pictures of people and descriptions of dubious, irrelevant 'values'. Second, these brochures are frequently written to extol the virtues of the firm and its leaders, rather than focusing on client needs and the benefits the firm's staff provide. Third, they are fixed in time, printed and bound using expensive, high quality printing and design techniques. (A more effective strategy is to create a 'gate folder', a designed jacket which positions the firm, its values and benefits. Individual partners can then insert descriptions of expertise, case studies and CVs.)

More important, though, is whether the firm's practitioners understand how to use collateral and the moments in the client relationship when it is most effective. For instance, it can be used to overcome post-purchase distress (described in Chapter 8). A piece of material, delivered at the right time, can allay client concerns and safeguard the value of a project.

Collateral is not just printed material. The internet can be used as very effective collateral. Currently, the most common online behaviour is for people to research products, services and suppliers before purchase, so the website can act as the 'welcome' mat of the firm. Also, when clients meet a professional services provider for the first time, it is very likely they will look up the firm on the internet, when back at the office, to read about its offer and its experience. Some firms, therefore, create individual microsites on each of their professionals' (and sometimes referred to as their business cards) which, when the client looks the firm up, contains the biographies of the key contacts, articles and examples of expertise.

All of these communications, from the written material through to the web microsite on the business card, are techniques to make the intangible tangible and to manage the emotional discomfort of potential clients. It is all too common for professionals in firms of all types and sizes to get on with the work immediately after the contract is signed without communicating with the client using these considered techniques. The client is therefore confronted with days and even weeks of silence in which their anxiety about the project can grow.

Strategic marketing communications issues

Marketing specialists have found that, to communicate effectively with a group of buyers so that they influence their purchasing behaviour, a number of strategic issues need to be managed carefully. These strategic issues need debate and resolution at senior levels in the firm before planning and implementation, because they have financial implications. These include:

- Creating a deep understanding of the target market.
- Designing a message which is meaningful to the target market.
- The choice of media through which the company communicates.

Any firm attempting to communicate with a market should put in place skills and management processes that ensure these issues are properly handled. All too often inept management teams will launch a marketing or brand communications piece without these being properly worked through, using phrases such as a 'soft launch' to hide the fact that insufficient funds are available. Such firms are often inexperienced at market communications and are able to obviate this because benign market conditions have allowed them to prosper.

However, some in the professional services sector (such as Accenture) are bringing first-rate communications disciplines to their firm-wide marketing communications. This will eventually give them a competitive edge which others will have to mimic if they are not to fall behind.

The target market

Even firms conducting large broadcast programmes, aimed at a wide audience, have to have a clear understanding of the people they are targeting. Whether it is a consumer or business-to-business group, the supplier is aiming to reach and influence people who will make a decision to buy the services on offer.

Before starting, it is important to understand who the target group is and how many are in the group. Moreover, the supplier should know several detailed things about them: what they read, what they listen to, which conferences they attend, which voices of authority, individuals or organisations, they respect, and what professional associations they belong to. By understanding this level of detail, targeting of communications will be far more effective and hence the investment will be well directed. Media planning specialists in advertising companies can determine which media has the most impact upon a target group whereas good quality research will give insight into their attitudes and needs.

Designing the message

Experienced marketers have learned that effective communications often comprise one simple and relevant message. It has to be relevant to the target group to ensure response and simple enough to be taken in by people in a brief moment of time. It needs to contain a definite proposition which should be unique and strong enough to persuade. The message might be:

- **Rational:** giving the reasons why the service should be bought.
- **Testimonial based:** using examples of others who have bought.
- **Dramatic:** using a story to convey meaning.
- **Humorous:** using laughter to appeal.
- **Focused on fear:** raising concern about consequences.

It takes enormous effort to achieve the elegant simplicity of an effective message. The firm needs to work with communications specialists in order to frame what it says to the market place appropriately. In corporate firms this is managed by senior communications specialists responsible for crafting the message with clearly delegated authority. However, in partnership-based professional services firms, not only is there rarely the appropriate investment in communications specialists but, because of the tendency to operate through consensus, there is also a danger that each partner will add their own level of complexity to the message, diluting impact.

The timing of the message also needs to be considered. At the lowest level this involves timing in relation to client needs or in terms of other messages. In Europe, for instance, the culture of many countries is to take long holidays in August. Many business people return in September ready to start new initiatives and this is a good time to start campaigns. However, suppliers should also think about the timing in terms of the clients' phase of thinking. Messages can be tailored to clients who are at the early phase in their thinking. This would introduce the concept, whereas messages aimed at those near purchase will emphasise benefit and include a call to action. This will contrast with messages aimed at those who have purchased, which may be about service, process and reassurance.

PricewaterhouseCoopers targets technology companies

The merger in 1998 of Price Waterhouse (PW) and Coopers & Lybrand (C&L) to form PricewaterhouseCoopers (PwC) presented PwC's Technology Industry Group in Europe with a big challenge. Although it acted as advisers to many of the world's leading technology companies, it was not necessarily seen as active in the smaller, fast-growth company sector.

Between them, PW and C&L were advisors to such leading technology stalwarts as IBM, Nokia, Ericsson, Sony, Dell and Cisco. But it was not generally known in Europe that the firms were equally active with fast growing technology start-up and medium-sized companies. In fact, PW and C&L had been advisors to several of today's multinational technology companies from their earliest days.

In order to place itself firmly on the map, PwC in Europe developed an extensive marketing, communications and public relations (PR) programme to operate from the first day of the merger for its combined technology practice. This involved the appointment of a lead partner in each country in Europe to champion the technology programme in the fast-growth company and venture capital (VC) community. This was supplemented by a series of thought leadership materials for the fast-growth company and VC market place. A specialised technology PR agency was appointed to support the launch of the group in the UK, supplementing the in-house technology PR teams across Europe.

Developing relationships with the European Private Equity and Venture Capital Association (EVCA) and the British Venture Capital Association (BVCA) was a key part of the programme. PwC was appointed to carry out the annual surveys of private equity and VC investment activity for both professional organisations. In the case of EVCA, this resulted in PwC sending out questionnaires to over 1500 private equity organisations in Europe, analysing the results and preparing the European and country reports to be included in the EVCA Yearbook which is distributed to all EVCA members.

Additionally, PwC presented the summary results of the survey at the annual EVCA symposium in front of around 900 senior representatives from the private equity and VC firms. This helped to raise PwC's profile considerably among the venture capital community in Europe. The survey covered the entire industry across all stages of investment and all industries.

On the back of the EVCA survey, PwC now prepares an annual report, 'Money for Growth', on investments in the technology industry by private equity and VC firms in Europe (Figure 10.3). This report covers the computer hardware and software, communications, semiconductor, biotechnology and medical equipment sectors. It provides a forum for PwC's experts in these areas to comment on past and future trends in their sectors, while acting as the basis of seminars for fast-growth companies on the status of the VC industry and the opportunity to profile PwC's services to these companies.

PwC has also prepared the 'Guide to Private Equity' for the BVCA, which explains to entrepreneurs and middle-market management teams how the entire private equity process works. The Guide is now used extensively by the VC industry to help early-stage companies to understand the VC process and has further helped to raise PwC's profile in this market place. Both 'Money for Growth' and the 'Guide to Private Equity' are used throughout Europe and, in fact, translated versions appear in Finland and Russia.

Limited sponsorship has also formed part of the programme, including PwC's sponsorship of the European Tech Tours Association and the UK Technology Partnering and Investment Forum. With the Tech Tours, PwC co-sponsors up to four visits to different countries in Europe each year by selected international and local VCs to meet with up to 25 promising early-stage technology companies from the host country. The UK Technology Forum includes a glittering awards dinner, hosted by PwC, at which awards for 'Hottest Prospect of the Year', 'VC of the Year' and other categories are presented.

The profile-raising, thought-leadership and business development initiatives referred to above have helped to strengthen PwC's reputation

Figure 10.3 *Example of PricewaterhouseCoopers sector marketing.*
Source: PricewaterhouseCoopers

both with the fast-growth technology companies and with their VC investors. This has, in turn, helped the market realise that PwC not only serves many of Europe's and the world's leading technology companies but also the promising young companies, destined to be the future ARMs, Dells and Ciscos.

Competition, share of voice and other influences

Suppliers need to consider the weight of communications needed in the light of communications from direct competition or competing concepts. Both can influence the clients' attention to the message. Too little communication will mean that the message will not reach the threshold necessary to command attention, in the light of other demands. On the other hand, too much will lead to saturation, undermining the impact as buyers become bored.

The choice of media

There is a variety of media which influence the target market, from broadcast communications through to the firm's partners and employees plus referrals and recommendations from people they respect. The impact of all these needs to be understood. The frequency and style of the message being communicated needs to be planned carefully. In an ideal world a target client will receive the same message, whether it is from the professional association to which they belong, an article they read, an informal discussion with a colleague or a presentation from the supplier. Well-crafted messages will get through to the market place, with a subtlety that hides the calculated planning of appearance in relevant media.

Managing and implementing marketing communications

The marketing communications plan

Larger firms have such a complexity of media, market and messages that they employ communications specialists and dedicate resources to communications planning. Some create a dedicated communications plan. Others include communications in their marketing plan. However it is done, in order not to waste resources in this area, it is sensible to plan communications activities alongside other business tasks. An idealised format is in Table 10.2.

The value of campaigns and campaign planning

A communications campaign is a set of interrelated actions, coordinated over a period of time to convey one message. A firm might have one or

Table 10.2 *Marketing tip: format for a communications plan.*

1. Business and marketing objectives.
2. Related communications objectives.
3. Key messages and prime target markets.
4. Media.
5. Key campaigns and programmes.
6. PR plan.
7. Collateral strategy.
8. Agencies.
9. Budget.
10. Outline of campaign timetable.
11. Success measures.

many campaigns running at any one time. They need to be properly planned and coordinated with each other.

Managing the creative execution

Professional services firms invest heavily in the creative execution of their communications needs. They use graphics designers for client proposals or brochures, web designers for internet-based work, video teams for both staff and client communications and advertising agencies to design advertisements. The variety and range of work is as wide as the methods, or lack of methods, used to manage this resource. For instance, some accounting firms have spent large sums to design computer-based games to educate clients about a complex issue whereas some consultancy firms have used elaborate design techniques for individual client proposals. Many have large in-house design teams, often supplemented by ad hoc design consultancies.

In an ideal world, creative work ought to be selected using competitive processes and an agency brief. While many firms work well over many years with small agencies which learn their culture, a new, complex or significant project should be subject to competitive tender. The process of agency selection and a generalised agency brief are both detailed in Tables 10.3 and 10.4.

Communications during a crisis

An important aspect of marketing communications which professional services firms have to deal with is when a serious problem attracts significant

Table 10.3 *Agency selection process.*

Step 1: Write agency brief
This document is to be sent to agencies as a basis for their proposals. However, it is also useful as a mechanism to summarise the firm's view of the project. It should contain the issues listed in Table 10.4.

Step 2: Create a short list of agencies
Create a list of potential agencies from recommendations, contacts and directories.

Step 3: Contact agencies to see if they will compete
Make a telephone call or write an email to the new business director. Not all agencies will be able to pitch because some will have a potential conflict of interest.

Step 4: Send brief to agencies

Step 5: Create selection criteria
Define the pitch process by creating a set of criteria on which to rate agencies. This will help ensure objectivity on the day. Criteria might include: previous experience, understanding of the brief, etc.

Step 6: Agencies present to team
Invite agencies to a day of presentations to a team of leaders.

Step 7: Select final agency and engage
A contract should be negotiated using appropriate functions or skills.

Table 10.4 *Agency brief format.*

Step 1: Communications objectives
Step 2: Other enterprise or business objectives
Step 3: Description of target market
Step 4: Message and desired take-out
Step 5: Agency dynamics
Step 6: Constraints
Step 7: Time scale
Step 8: Budget
Step 9: Internal clients and resources

press attention. This might be when a client takes legal action, or a regulator is publicly critical, or a significant individual in the firm receives adverse attention.

The first step is to plan to avoid this happening. Communications plans should be put in place alongside regulatory or policy guidelines. These should include:

- **Editorial relationships:** when a negative story appears it is the editors who decide how to treat it. The firm should set up mechanisms to develop relationships between key individuals in the firm and editors of print and broadcast media in the major world centres. Such relationships (apart from helping to raise the profile of the firm) will not stop a negative story running altogether but it will minimise damage and enable the firm to put its perspective.
- **Rehearse the leadership:** experience suggests that it is the one word ('shredding' in the case of Andersen) spoken by a leading figure which can cause final catastrophic damage at the end of a period of difficulty. Leaders should be well rehearsed in media management and publicists should have control over how to respond to media interest.
- **Preventive management of sensitive issues:** meetings should be established between the firm's media team and the firm's leadership to discuss how to handle potential issues. Press management is as much about what to keep out of the press as what you get in it.

Once a crisis occurs, however, a multidisciplinary team needs to be formed which has authority to act. It is likely to comprise: line management, media specialists, legal and regulatory managers. It should become the focal point for all media comment and questions, deciding which to respond to and how. It should determine the degree of revelations on the issue and strategies to take momentum out of the story.

Summary

All companies must communicate with their markets and the professional services sector is no exception. In an increasingly competitive environment, firms should get to grips with the well-established range of tools and techniques to communicate effectively to buyers and potential buyers in order to build their businesses. In addition, they have to make sure that the wider community understands their values and brand. Firms can now call on an array of concepts tailored to their specific needs, from advertising and PR through to understanding how best to use collateral. Even more importantly, they must make sure that this vital function is overseen by qualified and experienced teams to see a return on their investment.

11

Client service

Overview

The concept of service quality and client care has become one of the key factors contributing to how well or badly a business does in its market. This is particularly acute for the professional services sector, where understanding not just what clients expect from a service, and what is actually delivered, but also the gap between the two, has strategic implications for competitive advantage and business performance. There are a number of issues that need to be understood and acted upon, including the type of service being offered and how it resonates with clients, the determinants of client expectations, and all the different aspects that make up the client relationship. Developing strategies and processes which result in the design of appropriate services, excellent after care and regular reviews of progress is essential. This chapter provides a detailed examination of all these areas.

The critical role of client service

First class professionals take pride in the way they engage with their clients and can be affronted when asked to consider how their style of client service might affect the health of their business. Yet it is important for several reasons. First, clients may judge the service they receive on different criteria from that of the provider. Whereas the professional might focus on technical expertise or speed of execution, the client may value 'bedside manner', the way they are treated and the perceived attitude of the professional just as highly. In fact, the latter can cause clients to question the former if unsatisfactory. One research study (Venetis, 1996), for example, found that, counter-intuitively, the interaction with medical staff can be more important to clients than competence.

Second, if the supplier does not respond to their needs for good service, clients will form unfavourable impressions of the whole firm. Referrals or repeat business will then decrease, damaging revenues. If this poor client care is the result of a senior figure in the firm or is representative of the firm's approach, then its long-term survival might even be threatened. By contrast, a firm with very good client service is likely to grow in both revenue and reputation.

Most difficulties with client service begin to occur when an individual's practice grows into a business or an organisation of any size. As business volume increases and staff are added, mistakes can occur in business processes which, while unintended, cause offence and harm reputation, cutting off repeat business. For instance, the principal of a single partner business can become so entangled with growing the business and supporting the infrastructure that insufficient time and attention is paid to individual clients, causing long-term damage. Alternatively, larger firms can cause affront through simple administrative processes such as people being unavailable and clients being referred to voicemail.

Professional services firms need to determine which issues influence client views sufficiently to enhance or degrade reputation. They have to understand the components of the service which lead to repeat business and referrals (and thus future revenues) and which processes or techniques should be employed to improve them. This is as much about setting policy and installing processes as any other aspect of sensible business. It is a marketing issue because it affects the growth of the firm.

IBM Business Consulting Services: ensuring excellent quality of service

IBM Business Consulting Services is the world's largest consulting services organisation and part of IBM Global Services, the world's largest business and technology services provider. It was formed in mid-2002 by combining IBM's existing Business Innovation Services division with the $3.9 billion acquisition of PwC Consulting, the biggest in IBM's history. By the end of 2004 there were 60000 consultants and staff in more than 160 countries in the $13 billion-a-year business.

Determining the moments of truth

In creating IBM Business Consulting Services, IBM had to ensure that it maintained its reputation for excellent quality of service. Reputation within the services field is built significantly from the personal relationships that clients have with their providers. Hence, in such a people business, deepening the understanding of anything which affects the customer experience is a critical role. That is why Kevin Bishop, BCS Strategy and Marketing Leader for Europe, the Middle East and Africa, and his team in Europe carried out an analysis of the 80–100 different 'touchpoints' clients have when they experience an IBM service engagement and prioritised the nine 'moments of truth' considered most critical for focus. These varied from proposals, to the way references are presented, to hiring the right people from the outset.

Throughout their career, the objective is to give the consultants a workable frame of reference and to influence behaviour so that the core proposition comes across clearly and consistently. Towards the end of 2004, for example, Bishop oversaw a 'university' educational session in Germany for 3000 consultants drawn from central Europe. In the past, marketing's role would have been confined to producing a video and sound, making sure the facilities were what was required and giving all the participants a common template.

This time Bishop not only briefed the presenters in advance, but he also spent the day before the meeting with 150 senior partners to take them through the positioning and how to reinforce what they heard at the session when they returned to their teams in order to have an impact on behaviour.

Account management

International account management has been affected as well. Until the acquisition, IBM client managers were in overall charge of anything to do with their clients. With the formation of IBM Business Consulting Services, client managers work alongside what are being called relationship partners. These relationship partners are consultants with detailed and deep client knowledge and a range of board-level contacts. The idea is that together they form a powerful combination of industry insight and knowledge on the one hand and an understanding of the wealth of products, services and the asset base available throughout IBM on the other. It is the combination of deep industry and process expertise, extensive IT deliver capability and the ability for shared use with clients of selected world class assets that IBM uses to run its own business.

Service quality and 'customer care': a recent history

Although articles and debates about quality of service and 'customer care' have been in circulation for many decades, it really became a focus of management attention in the late 1970s and early 1980s as a result of a number of significant forces:

(i) The then-steady decline in the performance of much of Western manufacturing in the light of the success of certain Asian, particularly Japanese, companies.

(ii) Emphasis on after care and service in some sectors, particularly retail and computing.

(iii) The then-powerful quality movement in manufacturing and its emphasis on 'just in time' processes and the 'zero defects' policy of 'total quality management'.

(iv) The publicity gained by several writers and speakers, particularly Tom Peters, who in his book, *In Search of Excellence* (Peters and Waterman,

1988), modelled the dynamics of successful businesses, creating general principles out of case studies. His primary emphasis was on quality of service and customer care. He thought that much Western business had moved away from an emphasis on serving their buyers and had lost world leadership as a result.

(iv) Certain well-publicised, dramatic improvements in service which affected the share price of the firms involved. Two, for example, were in the European airline industry. In 1983 the then-chairman of British Airways (BA), Lord King, and his chief executive, Colin Marshall, created a radical improvement in the market position of the newly privatised airline by engaging front line staff in a massive improvement prioritisation programme across the whole firm.

Called 'putting people first', the programme engaged many thousands of staff in workshops where the importance of excellent service to passengers was stressed and barriers to such service were removed from the employees. This was one aspect of a broader marketing programme which encompassed a new brand initiative and new quality measures to drive the organisation, based on extensive market research.

At the same time the new chief executive of the Scandinavian airline SAS, Jan Carlzon, introduced a similar programme under the banner 'moments of truth' (see below). Carlzon introduced a company-wide programme to enhance all moments of truth which, again, had a major impact on the company's market position.

(vi) The publication of a number of influential research reports. One was, for example, the oft-quoted research by TARP (Technical Assistance and Research Programmes) conducted in the United States and Canada, for the White House Office of Consumer Affairs. This research, which covered 200 companies, showed that:

- The average business did not hear from 96% of its unhappy customers.
- For every complaint received, there were 26 other people with problems and six with serious problems.
- Most people did not think that it was worth complaining. Some did not know how and where to start. Some did not think it was worth investing the time and effort in doing so. Some were sceptical of being dealt with effectively, because of considerable past experience of poor problem handling.

- People with problems who failed to complain were far less likely to repeat their orders (for the same product or service). They were also far more likely to stop completely their business with the supplier.
- People who complained and whose problems were handled well were much more likely to continue doing business.
- People with bad experiences were twice as likely to tell others about it as those with good experiences.
- The average service business lost 10–15% of its buyers each year through poor service.
- Nearly half of all service problems were caused by failure to read instructions.
- Over half of all telephone calls to companies were to get information.

This combination of factors attracted the attention of management and put a spotlight on quality of service principles. It became the subject of many books, conferences and consultancy projects. At the height of this management fad, a number of reputable academics began to research the issue in depth. A series of good quality academic studies into service quality then established a number of reliable principles and techniques.

They argue for strategy, research, process and measurement. It is indeed the case that, over time, many professional service firms have grown and thrived because their decentralised and flexible partnership structures ensured they were responsive to client needs. However, as professional services markets tighten, firms grow larger and practices harden, these approaches become more and more relevant to the sector and should be incorporated into the business.

Reprise of relevant quality of service concepts

Service strategy

Quality of service is so important to service companies that an explicit service strategy should be developed as part of the normal planning processes of the business. It should be based on market and client insights and address several key issues.

The first is the style and ambience of service, which should reflect the positioning of the firm (see Figure 2.2). For example, the service style of a market leader, like BA, ought to be very different from a niche provider, like Virgin, and a least-cost provider like Ryanair. In professional services, the service that a client experiences from one of the 'Big Four' audit firms or one of the 'magic circle' law firms ought to be substantially different to that of a boutique or single practitioner.

The second issue is strategic impact. There are moments in the evolution of a market when quality of service is strategically significant and can enable a supplier to gain real competitive advantage. By creating a new standard of service for the market, the suppliers can improve their profit and share price dramatically.

There are several examples of this. The airline examples quoted earlier (BA and SAS) are clear cases. In their markets at the time of those programmes general service standards in the industry were very poor. Frequent flyers would move from airline to airline as their dissatisfaction grew. Very often they would circle back to their original supplier after time. Interestingly, both the leaders of the two initiatives were new to the industry and brought with them expectations and standards from other businesses. By creating new service standards, they surprised their buyers and retained them.

Another example is the famous British retail store Marks and Spencer. In the mid twentieth century, a time when consumer spending power in Britain was just beginning to increase, the company met one of the emotional needs of their buyers with a money back guarantee. This meant that consumers were happy to buy and felt a warmth and loyalty to the company which underpinned their profits for many years to come, even if the reality of service didn't always keep up with changing expectations. IBM met a similar emotional need with business buyers in the early computer market by offering leasing deals. This made it easy and low risk for buyers to invest in the new technology, enabling IBM to become global market leader for many decades.

However, all of these companies have since suffered real business difficulty, suggesting that the immense gains from their exploitation of the strategic significance of their service strategy were dissipated by later management teams who failed to institutionalise service improvements.

A current example of strategically significant service gains are those suppliers creating new service offers for experienced buyers using new

Table 11.1 *Idealised format for a service strategy.*

- Strategic context.
- Summary of client and market insights (including client's views of service attributes contrasted to competitor services).
- Service style.
- Improvement or change programmes.
- Marketing communications on service issues.
- Resources.
- Measurement.
- Service recovery policy and practice.

technology. As explained elsewhere in this book, the experienced buyer looks for self-service. Those companies (like airlines introducing self-service check-in or supermarkets introducing self-service bar coding) who do this, capture a new position in the market. They provide better quality at less cost and dominate segments of experienced buyers. Opportunities exist in the worldwide professional services market to do this now.

The third issue is the adjustment of the features of the core service in order to meet changed buyer values. (See features analysis and the core service in Chapter 9, page 244.) The firm should know those values which are important to key clients and how they match its competencies. It should also know client views of competitor services and their service strengths or weaknesses. These should be integrated into a view of how technical and client service features of the service need to be changed, if at all.

The strategy also ought to address resources, measurement and service recovery policy. An idealised format is in Table 11.1.

The concept of loyalty

The concept of 'customer loyalty' relates closely to service quality. It suggests that, if buyers think that they receive good service, they will be loyal to the supplier, returning again and again to buy. Some have asserted that it is the primary determinant of profit and growth because loyal buyers produce greater cash flow, cost less to service and spread positive word of mouth.

Loyalty, a long-term feeling of attachment to a supplier, is thought to occur when buyers are satisfied and have investment in a relationship with a supplier which is too great to sacrifice for a cheaper or lower quality alternative. It has been the thinking behind many discount retail schemes to repeat purchasers and huge investment in customer relationship management (CRM) systems.

There is evidence that people do become loyal at the point of purchase, feeling warmth to a supplier and returning to buy. Yet loyalty is far more than a revamped direct marketing programme or the launch of a consumer magazine. People need something to be loyal to; they need emotional resonance. For instance, by gaining emotional allegiance to some features of a brand, product managers have been able to earn incremental revenue over many years. Their brands have remained high in their category's sales leagues due to repeat purchase.

The phenomenon also occurs with some corporate brands, such as BA, McDonald's or Virgin. Buyers find that these services offer them an experience which is reliably the same. It saves them time and effort, meeting a need in their life time and time again. (This is explained in detail in Chapter 4.)

But some corporate names and some service firms have no brand value or emotional allegiance. There is evidence to suggest, for example, that a number of clients regard the service of some competing accountancy suppliers as technically similar. Their reluctance to change is more apathy than loyalty. Trying to create loyalty schemes in these circumstances, or relying on the assumption that the business is 'all about relationships', is risky. If another supplier were to come along with a better scheme or, more effectively, a better value proposition, it would attract these buyers away. Suppliers need to take a hard-headed view of this issue. They need to understand the level of emotional allegiance of their clients in terms of the relationship and the value of any goodwill in terms of repeat purchase.

There are some difficulties with this concept. For instance, some people actually want anonymity. Not everyone wants to be recognised personally in all situations. There are some circumstances where it is delightful to be known by name and given special treatment, but in others buyers just want to get on with the purchase and not to be interfered with at all. They want some transactions to remain insignificant in their lives and the supplier should recognise that.

Second, there are some buyers that a supplier does not want. Satisfaction is not an end in itself, but ultimately a contribution to shareholder value. It is quite possible to have satisfied buyers who are not at all profitable.

Logically, suppliers should choose which buyers they want and discourage those they don't. This makes segmentation, as explained in Chapter 3, a key strategic issue behind loyalty investment.

The importance of expectation

Researchers have demonstrated that, across a range of industries, buyers' views of quality of service depend on their expectations. If the performance of the service meets their expectations then they regard it as good service. If it does not, it is bad service. Moreover, the degree of negative reaction depends on the degree of difference between the two. Their research has also shown that different degrees of satisfaction occur in different conditions and in different product or service groups. For example, there appear to be different expectation/satisfaction dynamics between products and services and also between 'high involvement' or 'low involvement' products.

Tom Peters (Peters and Waterman, 1988) put great emphasis on exceeding expectations and 'delighting the customer'. Many companies then set out to delight their buyers in this way, with some even claiming they had 'customer delight measures'. The problem with this is twofold. First, it builds cost into the organisation (an alternative would be to use communication and marketing techniques to lower expectations). Second, it introduces an upward spiral of exceeded expectation, with expectations being increased and delivery having thus to be increased even further. This eventually becomes unsustainable, and the momentum of the company to provide excellent service eventually runs out.

In order to engineer the consistent delivery of service quality into a business, it appears that it is necessary to construct processes to understand clients' expectations. Professor Valarie Zeithaml, as part of her work with her colleagues on 'gap analysis' and 'zones of tolerance', undertook research to understand the influences on expectation. Her model, shown in Figure 11.1, is an excellent guide for research agencies or employees trying to understand this issue in different markets.

Dimensions of service quality

When trying to plan service improvements, particularly in a large firm, it is necessary to break the offer into recognisable components, or 'features',

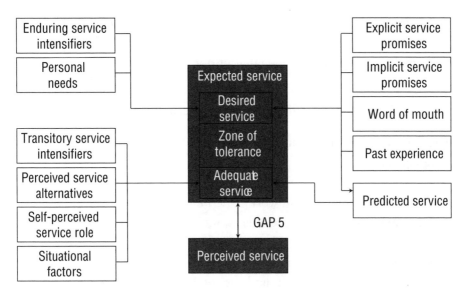

Figure 11.1 *Determinants of expectation.*
Source: Zeithaml *et al.* (1993)

which can be individually improved. By doing so, suppliers can understand which aspect of their service is deficient when compared to clients' expectations or competitor performance. They can then rank these in importance and calculate the real cost of any improvement. Service improvement then becomes a practical and manageable programme and not a vague wish list.

Service marketing academics have made a very valuable contribution in this field. For example, Professor Christian Gronroos suggests (Gronroos, 2003) that services have both a 'technical or outcome' dimension and a 'functional or process outcome'. Both affect client perception of value and need to be studied.

On the other hand, Professor Leonard Berry and his colleague (Berry and Parasuraman, 1991) have demonstrated in their research that there are five general criteria by which buyers judge service quality. These appear to be largely constant across any sector and can form the basis of discussions with clients on service quality. They are:

- **Reliability:** the ability to perform the promised service dependably and accurately. This is reported to be the most important of all.
- **Tangibles:** the appearance of physical manifestations of the service.
- **Responsiveness:** the willingness to help with prompt attention.

- **Assurance:** the knowledge and courtesy of employees plus their ability to convey trust and confidence.
- **Empathy:** caring and individual attention.

The concept of lifetime value and client profitability

The concept of lifetime value of clients suggests that firms should learn four things about a client:

- The total revenue from all work done in any given year.
- The costs of service to those clients, including proposal and prospecting costs.
- The duration of the relationship of the client to the firm.
- The profit in any given year and the total profit over time.

This analysis provides the total value or equity of clients and can change perspectives. It may be, for example, that the cost of service to major accounts is high, making them relatively unprofitable, and needs to be adjusted. On the other hand, a simple analysis of acquisition costs in comparison to service costs has caused many firms to put more emphasis on quality of service to existing buyers than gaining new ones.

Despite the sensible logic of the lifetime value concept it can be hard to implement in the reality of a professional services firm. Unfortunately, the profit centres of many companies are built around the products or services that they offer to the market. Many large professional services firms have parts of their organisation dedicated to specific technical offers and partners in them are paid from its profit pool. These are the centre of gravity of the firm because they influence the reward and motivation of most people in the firm. The firm is built around products, not clients, and hard to change.

The concept of holistic service: designing the core service

The concept of holistic service, introduced in Chapter 9, argues that all the components of service need to work together in a way that the buyers perceive to be a fluid and uninterrupted experience. It suggests that the core service of the company should be designed, like a product offer, to meet client needs. However, service quality and client care often refer to more than the technical components of the professionals' work. They refer to the way in which the client is handled by the firm.

In product companies this is seen as 'after care' or 'service support'. In professional services firms, however, the interactions with the client are continuous and need to match the technical quality. Professional services suppliers therefore need to ensure that their client care and their technical performance are integrated into one seamless performance which meets client expectations and creates one value proposition. This will have an enormous effect on reputation, and hence on repeat business and referrals. This is why the best marketing of any professional service begins with the work itself and the way it is delivered.

Client service and the propensity to repurchase

Researchers have explored the effect of quality of service initiatives on the propensity of people to repurchase from the same supplier. Their particular initial area of interest was in transactional measures such as satisfaction surveys which are often sent to buyers asking for an opinion of the way the supplier performed and about their experience. They found that these can be poorly designed research questionnaires, asking the wrong questions about the wrong issues and giving no manageable data which the supplier could use to improve service still further. Worse, they found that it cannot be assumed that satisfied buyers will return to buy again.

They found that there was very little evidence that good quality of service increased the propensity of people to buy again. It was quite possible for a buyer to be entirely satisfied with service and yet, next time, buy from an alternative supplier because there is a better value proposition. Many now argue that quality of service feedback mechanisms must therefore look at underlying motivations and tease out the rational and emotional needs that buyers want satisfied. Suppliers should therefore concentrate on managing quality of service as part of the overall value proposition.

The perceived transaction period

The perceived transaction period is the time that the buyer thinks they are engaged with the supplier. Service issues arise if the client thinks that their engagement with the supplier is longer or shorter than the supplier does.

Moments of truth

A moment of truth is any moment of interface between a buyer and the firm. These range from interfaces with clients and service staff, reception and support staff through to administrative processes like invoicing or contracts. All can positively or negatively affect their impression of the service, enhancing or damaging reputation. It is sensible to conduct a periodic review of all moments of truth to ensure that all contribute to the health of the firm.

Client satisfaction issues specific to professional services firms

Specific selection criteria for professional services

Academics have undertaken research into the service dimensions used when choosing professional services firms. Harte and Dale, for example, (Harte and Dale, 1995) produced a table based on six pieces of research in accounting, architectural, engineering, management consulting and general services firms. The attributes required by most clients were:

- **Timeliness:** the service is provided promptly.
- **Empathy:** the organisation understands the clients' needs.
- **Assurance:** technical correctness of the work.
- **Fees:** providing value for money.
- **Tangibles:** providing evidence that the work is performed correctly.
- **Reliability:** the firm does what it says it will.

They found that these criteria were consistent across all these industries with only a few minor variations.

Ethical and legal conflicts

Sometimes clients are wrong; completely wrong. They may have wrong expectations of a simple requirements issue. Perhaps a consumer wants a hair style that is not right for them or a business leader wants endorsement for a dangerous strategy. In these circumstances the practitioner is faced with a dilemma. Do they give the client their view of the dangers of the path they wish to take? If so, how forcibly should they put these views? If the client wants to continue, should they decline the work?

Some take a short-term view. Like the mergers and acquisitions (M&A) specialist who was heard to say that he would do any deal the client wanted, even if he thought it was wrong for their business. Good client service is not pandering to every whim. It includes giving sound or best advice, even if unwelcome. In fact, experience suggests that those who take the harder path and advise against dangerous courses of action build a more secure reputation and eventually command higher fees.

The practitioner is faced with a real issue, however, when the client wants something which is against legal or regulatory principles. Assuming that the practitioner operates legally and ethically, they must, in extreme circumstances, explain that the client's needs cannot be met. Yet these issues are not always easy and clear cut.

Auditors, for example, may find small irregularities which need to be discussed with the management team of a client company. Their only ultimate recourse is to qualify the accounts which they may be reluctant to do for minor issues. Maintaining a valuable and continuing professional relationship in these circumstances is difficult. The practitioner needs sensitivity and excellent communication skills while holding to professional principles. As a result of this, many larger firms specifically develop ethical guidelines for their people.

The opportunity cost of client service time

Any programme initiated by a supplier to improve service is costly. It has to be funded alongside other business demands and must compete for resources among other business needs. Ultimately, the leaders of firms have to decide if the cost of an improvement programme gives better business benefit than other projects. As some initiatives involve changes to systems and processes they can be seen as large investments. Most firms are therefore aware of the cost of service.

For a professional services firm, however, there is a much more immediate effect on costs: any demands on the time of client service staff reduce billings. Professionals are therefore immediately aware of a tension in any substantial need to improve service, or the conflict of short-term cash against long-term growth.

If, for example, partners need to put time into developing a relationship with an organisation, they will need to consider how much it will reduce their immediate billable hours. Any reduction needs to be set against a judgement, and it can only be a judgement, of the economic benefit from the relationship-building work. As it may take a number of years to see return from efforts of this kind, professional services firms need to balance the cost to short-term billings against long-term investment in client care and relationship management. Yet, surprisingly, few have clear measures of profit per client and the return against time invested.

Planning service quality

Once a professional services firm becomes an organisation of any size, its leaders have to plan. This planning might be fast, unstructured and intuitive or it might be detailed, complex and written into an elaborate document. Whatever the approach, leaders have to plan growth, resources, and strategies. In the midst of this planning exercise, as argued in Chapter 1 and illustrated in Figure 1.1, service issues also need to be planned and resourced. This is a management process, like any other, which ensures that service improvements are integrated into changes in the whole business. It ensures that the firm's service evolves with changing market needs.

There are different constructs that leaders can use for this. For example, Figure 11.2 is Professor Leonard Berry's 'framework for great service' (Berry, 1995). It is based on analysis of different service companies and allows leaders to think through the logical components of a specific service strategy and how it might be implemented in the fabric of the firm.

Figure 11.3 is an alternative route, covering similar steps (Young and Stone, 1994). It is based on practical programmes worked through with a number of European companies. The main thrust of the process is to link it to a strategic perspective on the market and to make sure it is a cyclical activity. In this way the firm will improve progressively by responding to data on client views and market needs.

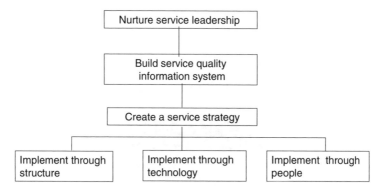

Figure 11.2 *Prof. L. Berry's framework for great service.*
Source: Berry (1995). Reprinted with the permission of The Free Press, a Division of Simon & Schuster Adult Publishing Group, from ON GREAT SERVICE: A Framework for Action by Leonard L. Berry. Copyright © 1995 by Leonard L. Berry. All rights reserved.

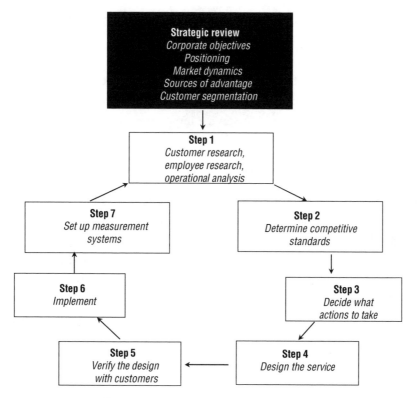

Figure 11.3 *A proposed design process.*
Source: Young and Stone (1994)

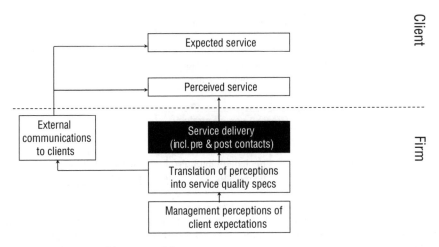

Figure 11.4 *Gap model – service delivery process.*
Source: Zeithaml *et al.* (2000)

Diagnostic techniques available to aid service improvement

There are a number of tools that firms can use to understand quality performance and needs. Each gives different insights into the priorities that leaders ought to place on client service improvements. They include:

The 'gap' model

Professor Berry and his colleagues (Zeithaml *et al.*, 1985) have been responsible for creating one of the most significant diagnostic tools: the well-regarded 'gap model' (Figure 11.4 and Part III). This takes a perspective of a firm in its environment, including in particular the views and expectations of clients in the management process and the effect upon their thinking of messages from the firm. As a result, it identifies five gaps to which management should address attention. This has the effect of focusing the whole firm on implementing the insights from research.

The gaps are:

- **The management perception gap:** this focuses upon any difference between management's views and those of clients or the market.

Type	Frequency	Typical reasons	Average quality	Outcomes
Letters				
Invoices				
Brochures, etc.				
Mailings				
Telephone reception				
Website and email				
Account meetings				
Project management				
Receptions				
Client service staff				
Buildings, security guards, etc.				
Advertising (TV, Press)				
Hospitality events				
Reports				

Figure 11.5 *Contact audit.*

- **The quality specification gap:** this exists when quality standards, strategy or plans do not reflect management objectives or views.
- **The service delivery gap:** this exists if there is a difference between quality strategy or plans and the firm's delivery to clients.
- **The market communications gap:** this tracks any difference between marketing communications and service delivery.
- **The perceived service gap:** this exists if there is a difference between the service delivery perceived or experienced by clients and their expectations.

The model has been tested in a number of research and real business projects. It has held up well and yields useful, practical insights for leadership teams about the client service performance of their firm. It helps managers understand both how and where they need to improve.

The contact audit

The contact audit, illustrated in Figure 11.5 and detailed in Part III, is borrowed from the direct marketing industry. It identifies all the points of contact a client has with a firm and reaches a judgement on the level of influence they have on clients' perception of service quality. The technique allows the leadership to identify all the 'moments of truth'. Those are times when clients have contact with the firm and form judgements of capability which influence reputation and, as a consequence, future work.

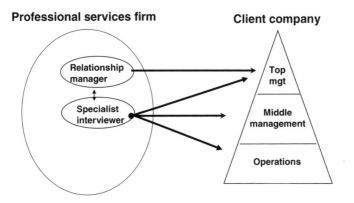

Figure 11.6 *Annual service review.*

'Zones of tolerance'

Another technique proposed by Leonard Berry (Berry and Parasuraman, 1991) is called 'zones of tolerance'. This suggests that people's expectations have two levels: a desired level and an adequate level. If the service delivered falls between these two standards then it is tolerated by the client.

Tolerance levels vary by client and by service attribute. In fact it seems that clients are less flexible on technical outcomes of service than in client service processes. The concept can be used as the basis of research projects that can be designed to understand first, the client's ideal preferences, second, acceptable levels of service and third, unacceptable levels of service (see Part III). This will help management to understand where improvements need to be made.

Annual account benchmarking (business to business)

Suppliers in various sectors have pioneered a method of quality of service improvement in the business-to-business context which is represented in Figure 11.6.

Once a year the supplier asks an independent researcher to conduct a survey of the 'decision-making unit' inside the client. The people to be interviewed and the number of interviews will be agreed with the most senior representative in the client to whom the supplier relates. The interviewer will ask people throughout the decision-making unit about two key issues.

The first is their experience of the service from the supplier in the previous year and the second their needs for future services. The interviewer then draws these into one report which is presented to the senior client representative before going back to the supplier. Best practice is for the supplier to hold a workshop with its client service team in order to respond to service problems during the past year and to plan ways of responding to service needs in the future. For the suppliers who are experienced in this technique, it often becomes the annual account planning process.

Some even invite the senior client representative to attend the last part of the workshop to comment on the team's planning. At the very least, the supplier must present back to the client how they intend to tackle the issues in the report. One supplier found that it moved from being the third to the first preferred supplier in one of their major European accounts as a result of this technique.

Dealing with service breakdown

A number of general principles about managing service aberrations have evolved which are sensible and practical courses of action. These need to be put in place in a firm to avoid long-term damage. Research in several sectors suggests that, if service recovery is properly handled, buyers feel more positive toward a supplier after a difficulty than before.

When things go wrong with client service the first action is to make sure that leaders are informed about it. Both individuals and the culture of a firm can remain in denial about service difficulties. It is possible for the leadership, by their attitude, to suppress the identification of service aberrations inadvertently. If they create an antagonistic climate, client service staff may not be prepared to take the risk of exposing problems and even written complaints will be suppressed.

The analysis and measurement processes described in this chapter should help to ensure that general trends in quality aberrations are identified and rectified. However, a blameless and open culture is much more effective. Although leaders will encourage the very highest standards of technical work and client care, they need to acknowledge that no organisation and no individual are perfect. They need to encourage an honest approach to service aberrations.

If a problem occurs, the supplier should immediately apologise and set about putting the problem straight. They should then find some adequate compensation for the distress and inconvenience caused to the client. (People are often as anxious about making complaints as much as they are distressed by the service aberration itself so they need to feel compensated for making the effort to complain.) Finally, measures should be put in place to ensure that the processes of the business stop any reoccurrence of the problem.

Satisfaction measurement

The experience of managers and academic studies in this field have suggested that there are several types of measures that are important to understand and have in place in a firm in order to manage ongoing client satisfaction. These are:

- **Event-driven feedback:** sometimes called transaction surveys, because they follow a specific transaction between the supplier and its client, this is feedback from the buyer in response to a specific event or project (e.g. a completed consultancy project or a specific visit to a shop). These feedback mechanisms can either be through some form of questionnaire or response to a telephone survey. Their purpose is to capture the clients' views of their specific experience while it is fresh in their mind. It is therefore important to gather the clients' responses as soon after the transactions as possible.

  The surveys need to be carefully designed using experienced researchers. If not, they are likely to reflect the wrong views and mislead the company. They need to be carefully administered and sent to the correct people. (More suppliers than would admit send these to anonymous departments or invoicing addresses.) Finally, the firm should keep careful records and undertake full trend analysis as an input to its strategic direction.

- **Generic perception studies:** these are research projects undertaken on a regular basis in order to understand the general view that different groups of buyers have about a supplier. Frequency of surveys vary according to volume (some might be monthly, some might be annual). Quite often suppliers will carry out a number of surveys each month and then have either a quarterly or annual summary of trends. Techniques for conducting this research vary although many suppliers have used conjoint research (see Part III) because it yields powerful insights into changing client views of different aspects of service.

These are very different in style, purpose and design to event-driven research. They are frequently conducted by independent research companies using independent sampling techniques. The aim is to get a generic view of the firm's service performance which can then be contrasted to the trends in event-driven measures.

- **Internal measures:** firms should establish internal measures of service quality (e.g. percentage of projects completed to predicted time scales). These should be prioritised around client need and the leadership's objectives. They should be communicated to all, set as individual objectives and used as a basis for reward. However, they should also be compared with external measures to identify any gaps. If, for instance, a firm's internal measures show excellent performance in an area that clients criticise there are two possible solutions. Either internal results are distorted and need adjustment or client perception needs to be changed through marketing communication.
- **Explorative research:** many service suppliers have used explorative techniques as a basis for fundamental design of the service. Some, for example, use observational techniques to watch the behaviour of buyers as they interface with the service. Others use conjoint research and change their service in the light of it.

Young and Stone (1994) proposed the method in Figure 11.7 for drawing these elements together as an ongoing management system of satisfaction measurement.

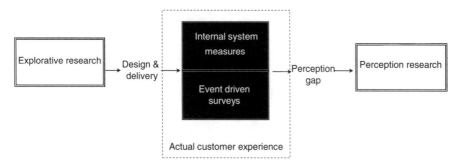

Figure 11.7 *A model of effective measurement types.*
Source: Young and Stone (1994)

Summary

Client service is therefore an aspect of professional service businesses which contributes to growth in revenue and reputation. It has strategic implications to business growth which can, in the right market circumstances, be dramatic. It can be analysed and managed as effectively as any other part of the marketing mix.

It is too important to approach in an ad hoc way. Every element involved in the client service process, from the quality of service offered, to understanding client needs and expectations, has to be carefully planned, implemented and managed. Over the years a number of tools and techniques have emerged which can help firms ensure that client service processes are handled within a much more structured framework. This chapter has summarised those developments and their particular application to professional services.

12

Marketing and human capital

Overview

Managing people successfully is fundamental to the success of a professional services firm. As a firm's brand is one of its key competitive advantages, it is up to the leadership to make sure employee behaviour matches brand promise continuously and consistently. Firms which invest enough of the right resources into this area will see a positive return, not least in the ability to attract and retain the best talent. Marketing can contribute much-needed expertise to many aspects of employee relationships, from initial recruitment through to issues of empowerment and behaviour. This chapter outlines how.

People matter

The success of any professional services firm depends on the people who are part of it. Their skills, experience and motivation are the main driving force of the firm and its main competitive advantage. They are its production line, its sales force, its service support team and, in many ways, the product itself. They are the firm's human capital and, very often, the repository of most of its intellectual capital.

Professional services firms therefore need to attract high calibre people and train them to do good, technical work. They also need to make sure that these people not only execute high quality work but also reflect the values of the firm in that work. In addition to recruitment, the leaders of the firm need to develop and institutionalise strategies to retain good people so that the investment in acquiring and training them is not wasted. For instance, they need to communicate effectively with employees, listening and responding, to ensure that they are supportive of the strategic positioning of the firm as it evolves.

This is so important that it often becomes one of the main focuses of the leaders of professional services firms. They invest heavily in internal communication, reward, development, motivation and recruitment. People management becomes one of the key competences of the firm and one of its critical success factors. They have to focus on what Christian Gronroos (Gronroos, 2003) describes as the two components of internal marketing: attitude management and communications management.

As a result, many of these firms have highly developed human resources (HR) expertise, leading thought and practice in the field and consistently coming at the top of public surveys into the most desirable employers. Some even go on to earn revenues from advising clients about people management issues based on their accumulated experience in the field.

A number of the activities that contribute to success in this area are marketing functions (even if, as with other areas of professional services business, they are not always the responsibility of experienced marketing specialists). For example, these firms compete in a market for talent. There are only so many trained, high quality professionals, or high calibre graduates, in any population. There are even smaller pools of resources with rainmaker, consultancy or broad business skills. With the growth in professional services, and other disciplines, there is a shortage of available talent for which professional services firms must compete. The recruitment market is therefore vital to the success of the industry. Leading firms in particular put enormous emphasis on communicating career opportunities to undergraduates and marketing to potential employees.

While marketing isn't the driving force behind the HR strategy, it should therefore be a key contributor in areas like recruitment, communication and change management. Those responsible for these aspects of the firm's HR policies and programmes should learn and adopt state-of-the-art service marketing processes and techniques, even if they are not marketing specialists themselves. Alternatively, they might seek to engage marketing specialists, from inside or outside their firm, at the appropriate point in their work.

As important, the marketing department itself has to concentrate on the firm's employees if it is to succeed in its role. The firm cannot be successful in its market place or in its marketing programmes if client service staffs are not engaged or supportive. They need to reflect the firm's brand and aspirations. They need to communicate its value proposition to clients and feed back their response to it so that elements may be adjusted. Marketing in a professional services firm cannot be successful unless it fosters good practice and communicates programmes through the firm's people. It should therefore be focused on the behaviour and views of the firm's employees.

Reprise of relevant concepts

The HR function focuses on human capital and is a discipline in itself, with sophisticated tools, techniques, approaches and policies. Large firms normally have their own HR function, while single practitioners ought to have advice from, for example, freelance HR specialists. HR, organisational theory and organisational development are beyond the scope of this book. However, there are a number of concepts that are relevant to the marketing contribution in this field.

People: the 'seventh P'

Chapter 7 outlined the concept of the marketing mix. It suggests that product companies need to get the right balance of four components to appeal properly to a group of buyers. They are: product, price, place and promotion. However, it is rare, even within companies that have very powerful marketing functions, for the specialist marketing department to have exclusive responsibility for all of these items. They must therefore influence other parts of the organisation to ensure that marketing activity has optimum effect.

In service firms the situation is more complex. Marketing theorists have argued for some time that the optimum mix for a service marketing programme has seven major components. They are: proposition, price, place, promotion, physical presence, process and people. While this is rather simplistic (it has already been demonstrated in Chapter 10, for instance, that 'promotion' is actually a simplistic representation of the need for two-way communication with markets), it does suggest that the employees of the service firm are part of the marketing mix. Their talent, behaviour, communication and output are part of the value that clients seek. To quote Professor Leonard Berry: 'Services are performances and people are the performers. From the customers' perspective, the people performing the service are the company. An incompetent insurance agent is an incompetent insurance company' (Berry, 1995).

One of the differences between product and service marketing, then, is the fact that, in the latter, part of the offer to buyers comprises the people who deliver the service. A mass service such as an airline, a fast-food chain or a hotel group will make enormous efforts to ensure that staff are presentable, properly trained and able to take initiative within the scope of their jobs. In fact, in recent years, many suppliers of services have enjoyed notable gains in competitive advantage by training staff to be a key component in the quality of service, improving client care and, as a result, repeat purchase. Employees who understand and identify with the culture and objectives of their employer are more likely to give good service and satisfaction to buyers.

This is made more complex in a professional services firm, however, because they are not offering a mass service. The service is being carried out by people who are highly trained and also highly individualistic in their approach to life. They are self-motivated and committed to the technical areas of their work. They are extremely unlikely to wear uniforms or respond well to highly engineered processes. Internal communications programmes to motivate such sophisticated employees to give appropriate service need to be carefully constructed.

Demand-pull and reputation management (again)

As with the external market for clients, the most effective marketing a professional services firm can use to potential employees is the creation of demand-pull, through reputation management (see Chapter 10). The best way to attract talent is to offer attractive work, good employment conditions and a promising future. Employees past and present then talk about this through their own networks and the firm's reputation spreads. It will become an employer of choice. (Conversely, if the reality of the firm's behaviour to employees is poor, then a poor reputation will grow, whatever its public claims, and this will ultimately affect its ability to recruit good people.) Good firms succeed by gaining a reputation as a good place to work and attracting the best people. This enables it to pick the best and, incidentally, to put less effort and cost into recruitment marketing.

As with client marketing, the point to start with recruitment marketing is to gather an objective knowledge of the firm's reputation in this market and to seek to amplify that reputation. The most successful long-term way to do this might be to highlight to the firm's leaders' any shortcomings in management or employment practice which are damaging reputation.

The special significance of boundary roles

Boundary roles are jobs in an organisation that link it with its external environment. In other words, it is the people employed by the firm who deal with the outside world. Theorists have suggested that there are a range of these jobs from 'subordinate service roles' to those based on 'service or professional experience' (Shamir, 1980). Both of these exist in professional services firms and both need to be managed carefully but differently. Professionals, for example, have different status to subordinate service workers because of their qualifications and the nature of their relationship to clients.

Research shows that people in boundary roles need particular attributes and there are particular managerial approaches that need to be applied in order to manage them properly. If these people are recruited and managed successfully, they will communicate positively the values and aspirations of the firm to their clients, overtly and subtly through the contacts they have every day. If not, difficulties with client service may occur.

At the time of writing, for example, dramatic changes in the accounting and consulting markets are causing firms to ask world class technical experts to become relationship managers for the accounts they have served. Some, however, do not have the advanced social skills to succeed in that role because their career to date has been based on natural demand for their technical expertise. Using such people as boundary workers is likely to lead to difficulty.

Stress resulting from role conflict

Researchers have found that people in boundary roles can experience a particular type of stress and therefore underperform in their role. Shamir suggests that these include:

- **Inequity dilemmas:** feeling belittled or demeaned by putting clients first.
- **Feelings versus behaviour:** the need to be professional and represent the firm means that they cannot always be honest in client situations.
- **Territorial conflict:** clients intrude into personal work space or privacy.
- **Organisation versus client:** where firm policies conflict with client views or needs.
- **Interclient conflict:** where two clients have opposing needs.
- **The fight for control,** suggested by John Bateson (Bateson, 1999): this resulted from his research into the implications of the clients' need for control when buying services (see Introduction). He argues that professionals try to take control of the service encounter, making clients dependent on their expertise. The tussle for control is, in fact, threefold: the client, the practitioner and the firm (through its processes and policies).

Boundary workers experience this stress more acutely if their firm is out of step with the needs and demands of its clients and they find themselves more in sympathy with their clients. Therefore, if the leadership of a professional services firm is out of touch with the market, and the service offered is out of touch with clients' needs, clients will express this to people at the interface, and these front line employees will suffer stress and discontinuity.

It is therefore sensible to listen to boundary workers and adjust the direction of the firm in the light of their feedback from clients. In fact, this ought to be one of the prime marketing functions in a professional services firm: diagnosing stress and poor client service resulting from issues such as these and resolving them through internal or external programmes.

The concept of empowerment

The concept of empowerment represents the discretion given to employees to respond to individual client needs. It has arisen in response to a need for organisations to respond to client service needs and evidence that inflexibility of employees damages reputation. John Bateson (Bateson, 1999) suggests that there are three levels of empowerment:

- Routine discretion, where employees are given a list of alternative actions to choose from.
- Creative discretion, which requires an employee to create a list of alternatives as well as choosing between them.
- Deviant discretion, which expects people to do things which are not part of their job description or management expectation. The latter are normally most appreciated by buyers.

Marketing and the recruitment market

Professional services firms need to recruit people with a variety of skills and talents. Yet, since there has been a boom in professional services, alongside other businesses, and there are limited people with the right skills, the market for talent is intensely competitive. Firms thus recruit at all levels. They pick graduates from leading universities, poach experienced hires from other firms and even acquire small firms to enrich their talent pool.

At the most basic, they need people who are technically competent in their professional field. Leading firms, in particular, need to ensure that they have high quality technical skills in order to provide excellent client work. There is therefore normally a process of ensuring that people pass certain technical benchmarks and standards.

Some leading professional services firms recruit the cream of the graduate crop and run their own apprenticeships in order to ensure that they have an ongoing supply of talent in their professional field. They therefore put great emphasis on marketing to graduates. Many have teams of people dedicated to liaison with leading universities. These people visit universities, exhibit at job fairs and supply literature about the firm in order to attract high quality technical talent.

However, there are also other skills that are needed such as excellent client management skills, consultancy skills, communications skills and rainmaker expertise. For example, someone might be an excellent technical expert but is unable to communicate their expertise effectively to either colleagues or clients. Another highly qualified professional might have a long career of delivering good client projects but be unable to generate work themselves. Professional services firms therefore need to understand these different skills at the recruitment stage in order to lead people into their business.

Marketing skills have a part to play in this competitive market. First, and foremost, the firm needs to position its brand in the recruitment market. It is no coincidence that some of the leading professional services firms (such as McKinsey, IBM Global Services and the 'Big Four' accountancy firms) are among the first choice of firms that graduates want to join when leaving university. Much of the concentration on brand (in collateral, recruitment advertising, and in the communication of employee benefits) is aimed at competing effectively in this elite but early market for talent. The reputation of these firms allows them to pick from the best and they track closely their place in the minds of this young target audience.

Second, collateral is often produced for students to support this brand positioning. This can take the form of brochures, web pages dedicated to careers with the firm and even case studies which include an example of the firm's work in university courses. (In some leading firms the pages of their websites with the highest hits can be the career pages.) This collateral will outline the types of career that graduates might expect with the firm and also the employee benefits on offer.

Finally, there are often specific marketing communication programmes aimed at the recruitment market. Recruitment advertising might be placed in national and local newspapers or specialist publications to attract talent for specific jobs.

This activity can be enhanced by many of the techniques outlined in Chapter 10. Firms should consider, for instance, a properly designed and measured marketing communications plan aimed at this market which links closely with the client communications of the firm. Any representations of the brand, advertising or collateral should work within the firm's general communication and design guidelines. Campaigns using viral marketing and reputation management should also be considered.

Marketing also has a part to play in understanding the dynamics of this market. The analytical and research techniques of routine marketing planning can reveal useful insights into changes in the market for talent. These, in turn, should lead to changes in approach and can, at times, highlight an issue which is of strategic significance to the firm.

For instance, there is evidence that, in the UK, the attitudes of the current group of graduates are changing from previous generations. Whereas the previous generation tended to be career and business focused, these seem to be adopting what appears to be the reverse of Maslow's hierarchy of needs. As they can take for granted the satisfaction of their physical needs, and the relatively rich markets of the West enable them to postpone a traditional career, they want work which first satisfies their values and aspirations. These young people are less likely to buy into the philosophy of some partnerships (very hard work for 20 years leading to a profit-sharing partnership).

The wider marketing profession already understands this generation quite well because they have been researching them in order to target brands and other propositions at them. If this knowledge and insight were applied to the HR and recruitment strategy of professional services firms, it would round out their approach and bring home the implications for long-term HR policy, as well as to graduate recruitment.

It is sensible, then, to ensure that the recruitment and HR teams include marketing skills to ensure an effective focus on the recruitment market, to maintain a perspective on changing attitudes and to respond appropriately.

Human capital as the embodiment of the firm's brand

As human beings are an integral and important part of the offer of a professional services firm, their skills and behaviour influence clients' views. Their character and style help to inform clients about the firm's approach and its value proposition. In many ways they are the face of the firm and the embodiment of its brand.

If the firm is to thrive, leaders need to ensure that the brand equity and brand promise are delivered through its people. The health and future success of the firm's brand depend on the concept of brand integrity which is explored in Chapter 4. A brand is only successful if its functional promise is delivered every time the client experiences it. The firm's people must therefore reflect it. If the brand promises technical excellence, or elite heritage, or 'guru'-style insight, or humour, then the people that clients interact with must have these characteristics. If not, the brand will be devalued over time, affecting the earnings and margins of the firm.

The people of the firm therefore need to be chosen and trained to reinforce its brand characteristics. Recruiters should be briefed to find certain behavioural and attitudinal characteristics, in addition to technical skills, which clearly reflect the brand values. These values also need to be reinforced through training, communication and leadership.

Marketing specialists often face a real difficulty in specifying and influencing human behaviour when embarking on a brand change or refresh. This is often the hardest part of a brand programme. It is particularly challenging if the firm needs to find a new position and new approach. Brand managers first need to understand the attitude of the firm's people to their work and to the firm itself. They also need to understand how clients view their behaviour and values. The brand position and values then need to be translated into specific human behaviours. If, for instance, one of the values is 'integrity', what does that mean in terms of day-to-day behaviours? A gap analysis (see Part III) will then show the degree of change needed to achieve the desired position from current attitudes.

Marketing skills in internal communication

Internal communication with employees of the firm, particularly with intelligent and self-motivated people such as those found in professional services firms, is an important tool in achieving the firm's success. It helps to keep employees informed of important issues, while it can also create a common sense of purpose and can contribute toward positive motivation. However, ill-conceived, poorly planned or erratic communication can have a detrimental effect.

If the leadership of the firm doesn't ensure that there is good internal communication management, the leaders and the people responsible for various activities will copy emails, send out erratic messages and pass on ad hoc technical changes. The firm will suffer from overcommunication, which can be damaging because employees can be overwhelmed by a discordant cascade which conflicts and confuses. If there is no discipline, there will be a multitude of conflicting, disparate messages which will become a deluge that employees are unable to comprehend.

An effective internal marketing programme is likely to be led by a cross-functional group of leaders, involving line partners and functions like HR. However, it must involve communications experts.

There are several components to this:

- **Communications strategy:** just as with external communications, the firm needs an internal communications strategy. What is it communicating, to whom, and why? What are the objectives of the leadership in communicating with its own people? What are the core messages and what are the outputs and behavioural changes that they want to achieve through the investment in communication?

- **Message planning and management:** this involves crafting the message to employees and prioritising against the many other internal business communications. Since putting out multiple messages can give rise to conflicting communication, it is not only important to make sure the messages are simple and straightforward, but also that they do not conflict with other internal messages. As with external communication, they need to be sustained, simple and relevant.

    Yet, with internal communications, one of the prime considerations is credibility. Employees must be able to give some credence to the thrust of senior management claims. The ideas and actions of leaders of the firm, therefore, need to be properly aligned so that, either overtly or subtly, they don't undermine the professed direction. If they do, there is a danger of lowering morale which, in turn, can have a detrimental effect on client service.

- **Managing the media through which employees receive the message:** the prime and best media, through which to communicate with employees, is their own line management. The second best is gossip. Both need to be valued and influenced by communications planners.

    Others include:
    (i) Team meetings and briefings from immediate managers and leaders. This is often the most effective form of communication.
    (ii) Town hall meetings between leaders and different groupings of employees.
    (iii) Published communications such as employee magazines.
    (iv) Intranets containing technical information, policy and changes in the direction of the firm.

Interestingly, many professional services firms which stopped publishing physical magazines and publications when intranets were introduced have gone back to them. Evidence is that employees like to receive at least one written publication. Many read these on the way home and pass them to friends or family. It is an example of making the intangible tangible. Having a credible internal magazine reflects their membership of the firm they work for.

Some professional services firms design their external advertising with an eye to motivating their own people. This was a consideration, for example, in Accenture's choice of advertising in airline departure halls. Many of their staff fly regularly and gain encouragement from being part of a large firm, able to communicate on this scale.

- **Relationship marketing as an internal communications tool:** this approach applies the thinking and processes of relationship marketing to internal communications (see Chapter 10). When initiating internal relationship marketing, the firm again communicates through networks of people but this time they are primarily internal, particularly in a large firm which will be dominated by different networks of people. These might be people who may have been in the same firm for a decade or more, who have learnt to trust each other by working on client projects or in managerial teams. They are circles within circles and networks of trust. There might be, for example, a network of specialists around the world concentrating on the telecommunications market. Or there might be another network concentrating on the financial services market.

  The people involved rely on their internal network to receive information: their leaders and their immediate group of contacts with whom they work daily are much more relevant to them than other messages. So 'gossip' can potentially become more effective than the deluge of emails, magazines and other publications received officially, which are not valued as much.

  Once again, as with external approaches to relationship marketing, the internal approach enables the identification of network nodes, or points at which the networks interconnect. These might be conferences of different partners who focus on industry marketing or an informal meeting of all partners interested in one professional area. All are opportunities for the firm's leaders to target communications more effectively.

Also, all of these networks will interconnect with client networks, and therefore communications from the leadership through these networks will also influence client thinking. Marketing specialists can map these networks and target communications through them. This is a form of viral marketing, where word of mouth is used to influence the behaviour and motivation of the people.

Making a member of the internal communications team responsible for viral and relationship marketing techniques thus makes sense. They need to understand the key internal networks, how those networks communicate, what the word of mouth (gossip) is and how to influence it.

- **Creating campaigns:** as with external marketing, internal marketing is improved by the use of communications campaigns. A campaign is a group of activities coordinated through the available media over a period of time in order to reinforce one message with the target audience. As with external communications, an internal campaign needs to be planned carefully. The communications manager needs to have a clear idea of who the target audience is, what the key objectives are, and what the available budget is.

  They need to refine and agree the message and concentrate on the media to be used over whatever period of time. A firm adopting a campaign approach to internal marketing will ensure that its key campaigns are known to the communications manager and there is no conflict when received by the internal audiences.

- **How the message will be managed over a period of time:** as with external messaging, it takes time for internal audiences to accept and internalise messages. Core messages about the firm's values and priorities should be unchanging or, at least, slow to evolve.

- **The development of response mechanisms:** these need to be open and reliable methods through which the response to messages can be measured. Many firms carry out internal staff surveys to get objective measures of staff reaction to messages and direction. These frequently have to be anonymous, in order to encourage honest feedback.

Table 12.1 summarises the key internal marketing issues.

Table 12.1 *Marketing tip: summary of internal marketing issues.*

- Segment the internal audience.
- Open-minded research of employee attitudes.
- Set communication objectives.
- Set internal brand strategy.
- Plan, create and test internal media.
- Integrate with other influences and manage (e.g. training and reward schemes).
- Plan and design campaigns.
- Manage implementation.
- Measure results through feedback.

Marketing and change management

Organisational change is a fact of business life. Professional services firms need to adjust their talent mix, their service offering, their structure, their leadership and their financial data as the market changes around them. Some are slow to change, resisting the implications for their business until issues become a threat to its health. Others, particularly partnerships, seem to be almost organic, changing shape, priority and structure as the local market changes around them.

The professional services industry is therefore continually introducing change management projects, many of which have quite major implications. They can be strategy projects, organisational change initiatives, and large IT projects. Again, marketing skills have a part to play here. For instance, if changes happen as a result of changed market conditions, understanding that environment and making it the basis of internal communications is an important marketing function.

To make a change project credible the conditions and reasons for change have to be made clear and an effective communications strategy built around it. In major projects this might include unsettling changes to part of what have been considered the established symbols and icons of the firm. For instance, a project aimed at changing a professional services firm from having a geographic orientation to an industry orientation is likely to disenfranchise leaders who have been in charge of geographic offices. It is therefore likely that they will lose their bottom line managerial authority. It will disrupt internal networks and threaten informal relationships. It is insufficient simply to create a communications programme

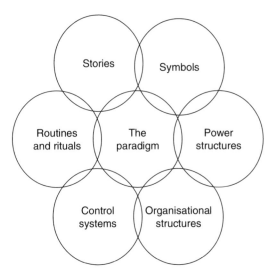

Figure 12.1 *Mapping organisational culture using the cultural web.*
Source: Johnson and Scholes (2004). Exploring Corporate Strategy Text & Cases 7 Edn,
Johnson and Scholes. Copyright © 2004 with permission from Pearson Education Ltd.

with a simple message explaining why this needs to be undertaken. The
firm needs to address fundamental issues and plan each of the areas of
significant change.

The Johnson–Scholes Cultural Web (illustrated in Figure 12.1 and
detailed in Part III) is a corporate strategy tool that identifies the elements
of change needed. For instance, it talks about stories within the firm that
need to be created and changed, and about symbols that need to be
addressed and changed. This tool can be used by communication planners
to ensure that a major change project addresses all of the fundamental issues
that need to be tackled in order to make a major change project successful.

Summary

Developing and managing employees has to be one of the main concerns of
leaders of professional services firms since a key part of the offer to buyers
comprises the people who deliver the service and who have to embody the
brand promise. It encompasses areas such as employee empowerment,
recruitment, internal communication and change management. This
chapter has shown how the use of appropriate marketing tools and techniques can significantly improve the effectiveness of people management.

PART III

The Marketer's Tool Kit

Like other professionals, marketing specialists use a range of concepts, models and tools in their work. This part of the book, therefore, contains descriptions of a number of those that are referred to in the main text. It does not attempt to be an exhaustive review of all the techniques to which marketers can resort, nor does it attempt to provide a detailed description, or critique, of each one. It briefly describes each tool or concept and its use, together with its relevance to professional services. Further reading and details on the use of these tools can be found in the publications listed in the reference section.

Clearly, leaders of firms do not need to be conversant with these tools, just as they need no knowledge of the detailed financial techniques used in parts of their organisation or the analytical approaches used by, say, a surveyor contracted to work on a project. Unfortunately, though, there is a difference. The training of marketing specialists is much less rigorous than other professions and professional development is not enforced. Undergraduate education can be superficial and practitioners can move into marketing roles with very few qualifications of any kind.

It is therefore wise, when employing a marketing specialist or using one as a contractor, to take steps to ensure that they are not only familiar with a number of these tools but have the experience to know when and how they are applicable. Without that, it is unlikely that they have developed the judgement and perspective which can reliably contribute to the creation of value for the firm.

'AIDA' concept

Use: advertising planning

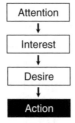

Figure T.1 *AIDA response model.*

1. The tool

Leading marketing thinker Phillip Kotler cites the source for this venerable tool as 'The Psychology of Selling', published by E. K. Strong in 1925. Despite its age, however, it is typical of a number of tools used to design, plan and measure advertising. Although the concepts it is based on vary, they assume that the buyer 'passes through a cognitive, affective and behavioural stage'; according to Kotler (Kotler, 2003).

In other words, buyers move through a number of states in relation to a proposition. This one assumes that they become interested after the proposition has first gained their attention. Properly crafted, it will then cause them to desire it. This, in turn, will spur them on to buy. Advocates of this approach suggest that suppliers break their target market into groups of buyers in these different states and plan their advertising accordingly.

2. Constructing a profile with this tool

The supplier must first understand the total universe it is addressing and the numbers in it in order to gain an empirical understanding of its market. From this, a representative sample can be calculated. Research can then be conducted to understand the numbers of people in the sample who reside in the different states of the model (from attention to action). By multiplying each grouping by the percentage which the sample represents of the total market, the number of buyers in each group can be calculated. If this exercise is repeated after a campaign, the effect of the campaign can be estimated.

3. Use of the tool

The concepts behind this tool are useful in themselves and can help marketers plan sophisticated approaches to communications by reminding them that clients need to move progressively towards a purchase. Communications will then be much more targeted. For example, it may result in a campaign designed with a number of phases. The first might be to raise awareness, while others move the clients towards a direct conversation with client service staff using different techniques.

If, say, a high profile public relations (PR) launch gains attention for a new idea, and is followed by large presentations to generate interest and desire, these will inform the final meetings with client service staff which can result in action. The firm will also be optimising its costs as different approaches are used for different purposes. In this example, client service staff are only closely engaged in the latter part of the programme, thus minimising the effect of marketing on billable time.

The tool can also be used to set communication objectives. If the supplier knows the attitude of its market, then objectives can be set in the light of that knowledge. If the clients are unaware of a skill, for example, then the very first communication objective is to create awareness.

The tool also works quite well in indicating the effect of communications on a large market. If, after a campaign, a number of clients indicate that they have been convinced to engage in the service, then it is likely to have been effective.

Ansoff's matrix

Application: strategy development

	Existing markets	New markets
Existing propositions	A	B
New propositions	C	D

Figure T.2 *The Ansoff matrix.*
Source: Ansoff (1957). Reprinted by permission of *Harvard Business Review*. From 'Strategies for diversification' by I. Ansoff, Sept/Oct 1957. Copyright © 1957 by the Harvard Business School Publishing Corporation; all rights reserved.

1. The tool

The, now, classic representation of Ansoff's matrix is reproduced in Figure T.2. It suggests that firms distil their strategic options by focusing their thinking through a review of existing markets, new markets, existing products and new products. As such it is a useful simplification to help leaders reach consensus during strategy debates.

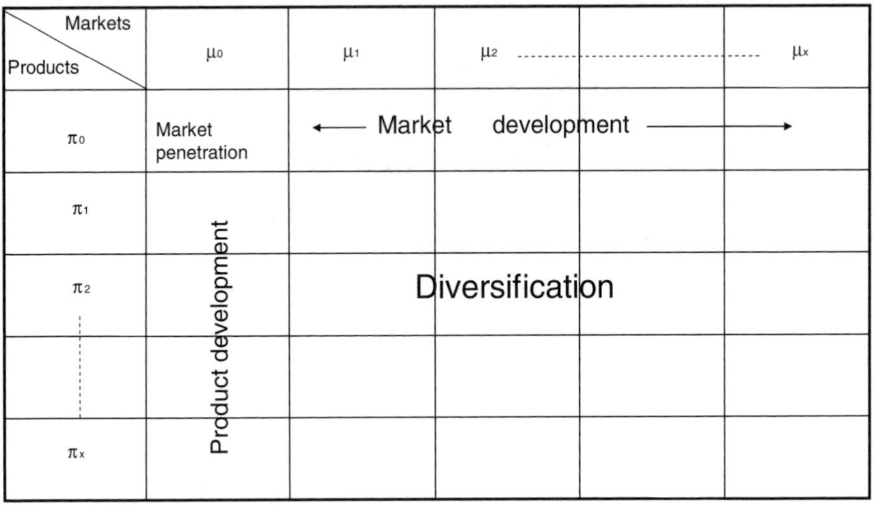

Markets Products	μ_0	μ_1	μ_2 ----------	------------------- -----	μ_x
π_0	Market penetration	◄— Market	development	—►	
π_1					
π_2	Product development		Diversification		
⋮					
π_x					

Figure T.3 *Ansoff's original format.*
Source: Ansoff (1957)

However, Ansoff's original representation of the concept (Ansoff, 1957) was more sophisticated and designed to examine diversification options. His work was based on an analysis of diversification activity by American businesses in the first half of the twentieth century. He suggested that there were two key bases for diversification, which he made the axes of his diagram, shown in Figure T.3. They were:

- **Product lines:** referring to both the physical characteristics of the product and its performance characteristics.
- **Markets:** for the sake of this analysis he referred to markets as 'product missions' rather than buyer segments. By this he meant 'all the different market alternatives' or the various uses for the product and its potential uses.

He proposed his matrix as a way of constructing different 'product/market' strategies: those 'joint statements of a product line and the corresponding set of missions which the products are designed to fulfil'. In his original diagram π represents the product line and μ the 'missions'. Interestingly, this representation of his work puts less stress on market penetration than the popularly used version and details the many strategic options that arise from thinking broadly about the fusion of product and market possibilities.

2. Constructing the tool

The first step in constructing the tool is an analysis of product and market opportunities. This may begin with a simple list of all the existing product/market groups in which the company is established. Then, using market reports, client research and internal brainstorming, it is possible to identify the other opportunity areas.

Once the analysis is available, the options can either be summarised, using judgement, into the simplified version of the tool or crafted into a more thorough analysis by creating a cell for each product/market match with the original version. The opportunities can either be discussed by the leaders at this stage or prioritised using agreed criteria. Ansoff himself recommended that, due to the risk and cost involved, firms conduct risk analysis of the more likely strategies. The most acceptable programmes should then be developed into full product, marketing and business plans.

3. Use of the tool

The matrix helps leaders think through four different growth strategies, which require different marketing and communications approaches. They are presented below in ascending order of risk:

- Strategy A is **market penetration**, or increasing market share with existing propositions to current markets.
- Strategy B is **market extension** or market development, targeting existing propositions at new markets.
- Strategy C is **product development**, or developing new propositions for existing segments.
- Strategy D is **diversification**, or growing new businesses with new propositions for new markets.

The matrix helps to clarify leaders' thinking and to illustrate the very different strategic approaches needed for each of the four strategies. Ideally, an operational marketing plan should be constructed for each strategic option and given final approval.

ARR model

Application: relationship marketing

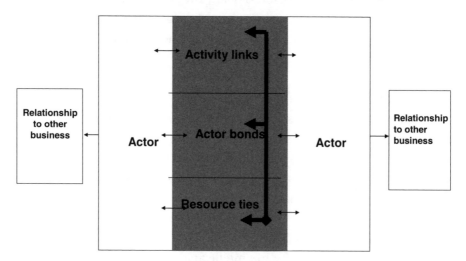

Figure T.4 *The ARR model.*
Source: Hakansson and Snehota (1995)

1. The model

The 'actors–activities–resources' model (Figure T.4) was developed during the early 1980s by researchers and theorists interested in both business-to-business marketing and network marketing. Yet it appears to be a tool that can also be used in practical marketing within a normal business, as well as for pure theoretical research.

The model divides business relationships into three layers:

(i) Actor bonds. These occur when two business people interact through some professional process. Theorists suggest that there are three components necessary for them to develop. The first is reciprocity during the process, ensuring that both sides give something to the interaction, even if one is a client. The second is commitment and the third is trust. As people interact they form perceptions of each other about capability, limitations, commitment and trust. If the relationship develops, these perceptions influence the degree and clarity with which the two communicate and also the degree to which they involve each other in their own professional network.

So, for the client service professionals, the way in which they conduct their work influences the trust their client develops in them and the degree to which they will be invited further into the client organisation, and thus into the possibility of further work.

(ii) Activity links capture the work, or other activity, which is involved in the interaction and business process. These vary with the depth of relationship. They range from simple technical projects through to two firms meshing or adapting their systems and business processes to become more efficient. The latter has created exciting business opportunities for professionals in areas such as outsourcing.

(iii) Resource ties are items used by people during business interactions. Resources might include: software, intellectual capital, skilled staff, knowledge, experience and expertise. People who have resources, or control over them, have greater power in professional networks. This power is the basis of the professional services offer (the client comes to the professional because they lack one or more of these resources) but clearly the immediacy or importance of need and the scarcity of resource influences pricing and quality perceptions.

2. Constructing the model

At its very simplest, the model can be used as a basis of discussion with internal colleagues to map relationships in a network. Professionals can be asked to complete formats of their client relationships using the three levels of the model. Actions arising from discussion (e.g. creating more opportunities for non-task-related exchange or making different resources, such as knowledge, available) to strengthen relationships can be put into account plans.

However, the model can also be used as a basis of detailed analysis and research. A hypothesis of the professional relationships that exist in a market, and the types of interaction, can be created using the terms of the model. The model can then be a guide to designing the research sample and questionnaires. A two-step, qualitative and quantitative research process is likely to reveal powerful insights into the relationships clients have with the firm and its competitors.

3. Use of the model

The thinking behind the model will seem intuitively correct to many professionals. This is its strength, capturing, as it does, the day-to-day experience of many client service staff. It allows a firm to use a common process and terminology in its approach to client relationship management when necessary. However, it also introduces (perhaps for the first time) a reasonably robust mechanism whereby professionals can analyse and understand in detail what many recognise to be their most important approach to market: their relationships with clients.

Blueprinting

Application: service design

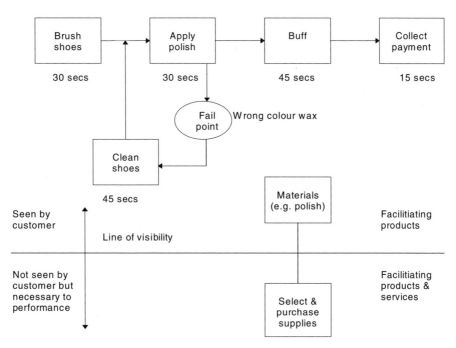

N.B.   Standard execution time = 2 minutes
Total acceptable execution time = 5 minutes

Figure T.5 *Blueprinting.*
Source: Shostack (1982). Republished with permission, Emerald Group Publishing Limited.

1. The tool

As services contain a process through which a client must move, the proactive design of a service through the use of 'organisation and method' (O&M)
techniques has been suggested by several writers. Lynn Shostack, a practising marketer rather than an academic, was first. She pointed out that,
whereas it is relatively easy to design a product through engineering specification, there was no 'service engineering' technique to which service
designers could turn. Services are therefore often poorly presented to clients.

   She suggested that, as a service is a process, it can be 'blueprinted' by
using O&M techniques developed to deal with process improvement. These
included:

- **Time and motion engineering:** Shostack felt that of eight basic charts
  used by methods engineers, those most applicable were the 'operations
  process chart', a 'flow process chart' and the 'flow diagram'.
- **'PERT' charting:** this is an accepted method of planning detailed
  projects.
- **Systems and software design:** she believed that many of the software
  design methodologies could be used to design service processes.

She argued that there needed to be more conceptual work done on the
application of these process design techniques to service blueprinting
because the process needs:

- To show time dimensions in diagrammatic form.
- To identify all the main functions of the service.
- To define tolerances of the model (i.e. the degree of variation from stan-
  dards) precisely.

2. Constructing a blueprint

Shostack offered a 'blueprint for a simple shoeshine service' which is shown
in Figure T.5. She outlined a stepped blueprinting method:

- Identify the client process and map it out.
- Isolate potential failure points and build in subprocesses to tackle
  possible errors before they occur.

- Establish a time frame or a standard execution time.
- Distinguish between processes which are visible to the client and those which are not. Manage any implications arising from this.
- Analyse profitability.

3. Use of the tool

Originally Shostack offered the concept of blueprinting alongside molecular modelling (see further on) and suggested that academics develop and test both for more generic use by business. Later writers on the subject have neglected the former and not substantially developed the use of blueprinting in service design. This may be because the popularity of 'O&M' waned somewhat in the 1980s, although the concept of process mapping has received attention because of the emphasis in senior management circles on the concept of 'process re-engineering'.

Yet the process that clients experience is important to both the delivery of good service and to the experience of the client. As explored in this book, it can create opportunities for new services and for new market strategies. Blueprinting is a practical and straightforward method to use in designing these aspects of a service.

The Boston matrix

Application: analysis of business portfolios

	High — Relative market share	Low
High Market growth	**'Star'** • Defend leadership • Accept moderate short-term profit and negative cash flow • Consider geographic expansion • Consider line expansion • Aggressive marketing posture • Price for market share	**'Question mark'** • Invest heavily in selective businesses • As for 'rising star'
Low	**'Cash cow'** • Maintain market position • Cut less successful lines • Differentiate to maintain share of key segments • Limit discretionary marketing expenditure	**'Dog'** • Prune aggressively • Maximise cash flow • Minimise marketing expenditure • Maintain or raise prices at the expense of volume

Figure T.6 *The Boston matrix.*
Source: Boston Consulting Group (1968). Reproduced by permission of The Boston Consulting Group.

1. The tool

One of the best known portfolio management tools is the Boston growth share matrix (Figure T.6), which was developed by the Boston Consulting Group based on the concept of the 'experience curve'. The consultancy demonstrated that, over time, companies specialising in an area of expertise became more effective in their market, reducing costs and gaining competitive advantage. A company might be at various points on the experience curve, depending on its maturity and the accumulated investment in its prime area of focus. The Boston matrix, which plots relative market share against relative growth, was an attempt to give corporate strategic planners a way of evaluating different business units in different markets.

2. How to construct it

First, the annual growth rate of each business unit in each market is calculated. This is plotted on the matrix, depending on whether its growth is high or low. (Note: the horizontal axis of the matrix is not positioned at zero on the vertical axis but at 10%.) Second, the relative market share of each unit is calculated and plotted on the matrix. The turnover of each unit is then represented by appropriately sized circles.

The portfolio of business units is then categorised by the matrix into four groups:

- The **question marks** (otherwise called 'problem children' or 'wild cats') have low market share in high growth markets. A business which has just started operations would be a 'question mark' because the ability of the management team to improve on its competence would be unproven. These are businesses with long-term potential which may have been recently launched with services that are being bought, primarily, by buyers who are willing to experiment. They need large amounts of cash if they are to be developed to their full potential because the company has to keep adding equipment and personnel to keep up with the fast growing market.
- The **rising star** is a company that has established itself in the market and is beginning to thrive. It is a leader, with high share in a high growth market. It requires significant investment in order to maintain and grow market share. It does not necessarily produce a positive cash flow but stars are usually profitable and can become 'cash cows'.
- The **cash cows** are companies that are well established and profitable. They have high share in low growth markets. They are producing profit

but are unlikely to achieve much incremental improvement. They are generally cash positive and can be used to fund other initiatives.

- The final group are known as **dogs**. They have low share in low growth markets. These are companies in decline and worthy of withdrawal. They have weak market share in low growth markets and tend to be loss-makers, providing small amounts of cash, if any.

3. Use of the tool

The matrix can be used to determine strategy for major firms. A multi-business company needs a balanced portfolio of businesses or strategic business units (SBUs) which use cash from the cash cows to invest in other development issues. It is thought that an unbalanced portfolio of businesses can be classified into four areas:

- Too many losers, causing poor cash flow.
- Too many question marks, requiring too much investment.
- Too many profit producers.
- Too many developing winners.

The matrix is used to formulate different business strategies and corporate requirements for each business unit according to its position on the matrix. Objectives, profit targets, investment constraints and even management style are likely to be different according to their position. Strategies set by the leadership are likely to include:

- **Build:** this means increasing the market share using cash, resources, marketing programmes and management attention.
- **Hold:** this means maintaining the market share and is appropriate for strong cash cows if they are to continue to yield cash.
- **Harvest:** this means using resources to get as much cash from a business unit as is possible regardless of long-term effect. It is appropriate for weakening cash cows whose future is uncertain or dim.
- **Divest:** this means selling or liquidating the business, and is appropriate for dogs and question marks that are acting as a drag on company resources.

Due to inadequate teaching and lack of understanding, some companies have tried to use this conceptual framework to understand the positioning of their individual products or services rather than business units. Managers can be heard to talk of their offers as either being a 'cash cow' or a 'dog'. This misuse of the concept is dangerous because it muddles two different concepts (the experience curve of a business and the product lifecycle).

More worrying for professional services firms, though, is the fact that the tool is based on the two axes of growth and market share. It is an assumption of the matrix that growth and share are the two key success criteria of a business. However, that is not always the case in the professional services industry. Chapter 9 shows, for example, that high share would eventually be countereffective for the executive search suppliers. Also, some firms pursue a strategy of margin maximisation rather than growth. This tool is unlikely to be helpful to such firms.

Contact audit

Application: client service and communication

Type	Frequency	Typical reasons	Average quality	Outcomes
Letters				
Invoices				
Brochures, etc.				
Mailings				
Telephone reception				
Website and email				
Account meetings				
Project management				
Receptions				
Client service staff				
Buildings, security guards, etc.				
Advertising (TV, Press)				
Hospitality events				
Reports				

Figure T.7 *Contact audit.*

1. The tool

This practical method, shown in Figure T.7, evolved within the UK's direct marketing industry and puts emphasis on the effect of other interactions of the firm than advertising on the opinion of buyers. The marketing profession had previously limited itself largely to 'above the line' marketing techniques. The approach of direct marketing is to identify other

communications media (such as mail, email, interaction with staff) as mechanisms by which the same message can be reinforced. Before the evolution
of the concepts of loyalty, service and integrated communications, it encouraged the thoughtful professional to think beyond the pushing of messages.

2. Constructing the tool

The firm should first list all interfaces with the client. These range from
client service staff contacts through to written materials and attendance at
events. This alone can help leaders to think about the effect of some surprising items. For instance, clients who visit a scruffy office, are kept waiting
by reception staff or who have to negotiate difficult security staff can have
their confidence in the professional's expertise undermined, even if some of
these people are clearly employed by contractors.

The tool then causes the firm to consider the frequency with which
clients use a particular interface and the reason why. If the reason is very
important or emotionally distressing to them, then the impression it forms
is likely to be very influential. Client service issues are likely to arise if the
supplier neglects this. Finally, it leads to consideration of the quality that
clients experience and the outcomes they receive. These are best completed
in discussion with a sample of them (although internal judgement is also
effective).

3. Use of the tool

This tool is a simple planning mechanism which identifies improvement
areas in the client service interface. It emphasises all aspects of the interface with the firm and prompts professionals to think beyond technical
delivery alone.

Cultural web

Application: change management

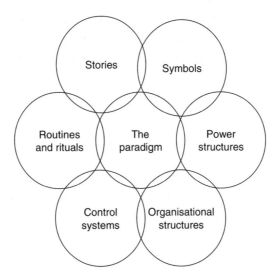

Figure T.8 *Mapping organisational culture using the cultural web.*
Source: Johnson and Scholes (2004). Exploring Corporate Strategy Text and Cases 7 Edn,
Johnson and Scholes. Copyright © 2004 with permission from Pearson Education Limited.

1. The tool

The 'cultural web' devised by Gerry Johnson and Kevan Scholes (Johnson
and Scholes, 2004), shown in Figure T.8, identifies the elements of an organ-

isation which need to be taken into account when planning major strategic change. They are:

- The **paradigm:** the way the organisation views the world. This may have a number of facets such as the sector or segment it concentrates on, its products or its competitors.
- **Organisational structure:** the way people interrelate within the firm.
- **Power structures.** This acknowledges the authority that people have in the organisation and how they use it. It covers both formal and informal power.
- **Control systems** are built into the structure of the firm to ensure that objectives are met. They might be processes, systems or measures.
- **Routines and rituals** may not be overtly described by the firm or part of its acknowledged policies, but they can be very powerful nonetheless. Very often they are the real functions of the organisation.
- **Symbols** are physical evidence of past victories, failures, moments of history or power. They are very influential and can cause deep emotions to be stirred.
- **Stories** circulate in an organisation and effect behaviour.

2. Constructing the tool

The tool is best configured using internal interviews. Employees can either be shown the tool and asked to contribute or interviewed on a range of subjects to reveal the components of the web.

3. Use of the tool

The tool can be used to plan major change programmes, internal communication campaigns and internal marketing. The components of the web indicate the full range of activities that need to be considered if change or communications are to be effective.

Directional policy matrix

Application: business portfolio tool

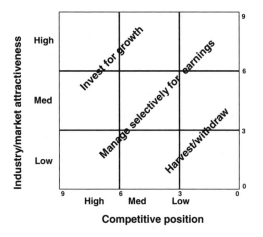

Figure T.9 *The directional policy matrix.*

1. The tool

Another well-known product portfolio technique is the directional policy matrix (Figure T.9), developed by McKinsey for its client General Electric (GE) in the 1970s soon after the Boston matrix and as a result of that tool's inadequacies. It was typical of several methods of 'multifactor portfolio models' which were developed at the time.

Table T.1 *Factors of market attractiveness and business strength used in the original GE matrix.*

Market attractiveness	Business strength
Size	Size
Growth rates	Growth rate
Competitive intensity	Market share
Profitability	Profitability
Technology impacts	Margins
Social impacts	Technology position
Environmental impacts	Strengths and weaknesses
Legal impacts	Image
Human impacts	Environmental impact
	Management

This is a way of categorising businesses against markets and is more flex-ible than the Boston matrix because it uses criteria created by the manage-ment team themselves. As such it is more relevant to the individual strategic position of the company in its market place. The grid plots 'market attrac-tiveness' against 'business strength' and allows management to prioritise resources accordingly.

The original GE matrix used the factors of market attractiveness and busi-ness position which are shown in Table T.1.

GE used these key factors because it believed that, taken together, they had the most influence on return on investment. However, this list should be modified for each company according to its own particular circumstances.

2. Constructing the matrix

There are clear steps in compiling the matrix. They are:

(i) Identify the strategic business units (SBU).
(ii) Determine the factors contributing to market attractiveness.
(iii) Determine factors contributing to business position.
(iv) Rank and rate the market attractiveness and business position features.
(v) Rank each SBU.
(vi) Plot the SBUs on the matrix.
(vii) Represent the total size of the market and the businesses' share by a pie chart at the appropriate plot on the matrix.

Steps (iv) and (v) involve numerically rating the relative importance of each feature. Multiplying these together and totalling them for each business unit gives a composite score which enables the matrix to be compiled. The total size of each market the firm's businesses operate in and their share of it can be represented by a pie chart centred on each plot. As with the growth/share matrix, the visual presentation enables complex information to be presented in an easily understood form.

3. Use of the tool

Strategy can be deduced from the matrix as follows: where a business unit scores high or medium on business strength or market attractiveness, the firm should maintain or grow investment. Whereas those which score low/low or low/medium should have investment reduced. If possible, cash should be harvested from them. Units scoring high/low or medium/medium should be examined to see if selective investment should be made to increase earnings.

There has been some critical evaluation of this matrix. Many people consider the fact that it uses several dimensions to assess business units instead of two, and because it is based on return on investment (ROI) rather than cash flow, it is a substantial improvement on the Boston matrix. However, it is criticised because:

- It offers only broad strategy guidelines with no indication as to precisely what needs to be done to achieve strategy.
- There is no indication of how to weight the scoring of market attractiveness and business strengths. As such it is highly subjective.
- Evaluation of the scoring is also subjective.
- The technique is more complex than the Boston matrix and requires much more extensive data gathering.
- The approach does not take account of interrelationships between business units.
- It is not supported by empirical research or evidence. For instance there does not seem to be evidence that market attractiveness and business position are related to ROI.
- It pays little attention to business environment.

Nevertheless, it is really powerful as a tool to reach consensus among a group of partners or fellow professionals. The definition of business units, the agreement of common criteria and, particularly, the joint scoring exercise stimulate debate which is very valuable. Experience suggests that it is therefore a tool which is very relevant to professional services firms.

Experience curves

Application: new service development, competitive strategy

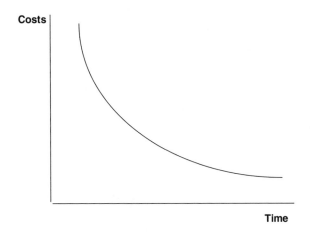

Figure T.10 *The experience curve.*
Source: Boston Consulting Group (1968). Reproduced by permission of The Boston Consulting Group.

1. The tool

This concept, pioneered particularly by the Boston Consulting Group during the 1960s, suggests that unit costs of a firm fall with experience of operating in an industry and with a company's cumulative volume of production (Figure T.10). The consultancy invested substantial time over many industries (including service industries) and used 'the scientific method' to validate the concept. Although appearing deceptively simple, and intuitively right, the concept can be used to set exhilarating strategic objectives.

Costs decline due to a combination of: economies of scale, a learning curve for labour and the substitution of technology for labour. The cost decline gives competitive advantage because new competitors can face higher costs if not entering with a major innovative advantage. Some have argued that the advantage is so great that established leaders should drive to gain further advantage through actions such as price cutting.

2. Constructing the tool

Plot the firm's prices or costs against unit volume, projecting back in time as far as is sensible. The resultant curve should reveal the accumulated gains by the firm. In professional services markets it is also normally possible to obtain estimates of number of employees in competitor firms, so a comparison with competitor gains should be possible.

(Note: for the analytically minded, the Boston Consulting team recommended using double logarithmic scales because they show percentage gain as a constant distance. 'A straight line . . . means, then, that a given percentage change in one factor results in a corresponding percentage change in the other . . . reflecting the relationship between experience and costs and experience and prices' (Boston Consulting Group, 1968).)

3. Use of the tool

The tool can be used to identify cost gains and advantages compared to competitors. As a result, it can become a benchmark by which the firm can set strategy for business units to improve costs. It can also be used to predict and set prices by giving a directional indication of industry costs and likely competitive responses.

The tool can also be used to plan and sell outsourcing concepts. As illustrated in Figure T.11, a firm whose business is focused on a particular function is likely to be further down the experience curve than a client's in-house team. If the in-house operations are passed to the supplier, the client gains advantage of the supplier's 'experience'.

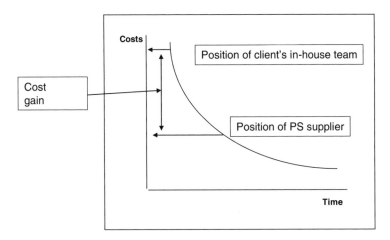

Figure T.11 *The experience curve and outsourcing.*

When, in 1990, the UK government's audit office first reviewed public sector outsourcing deals initiated by the Thatcher government in the 1980s, it found gains of up to 20%. This sparked the outsourcing trend in much of Europe. Note, though, that over time further dramatic gains are unlikely and continuing success depends on the nature of the relationship between the two parties. If the relationship breaks down, the client loses the supplier's experience and begins to build cost back into its business.

Features analysis

Application: service design

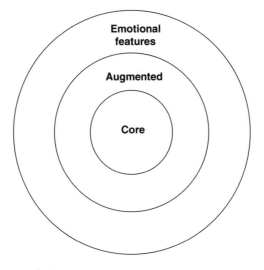

Figure T.12 *Features analysis.*

Features analysis is a concept used in product design to plan the content of the offer proactively. It is a development of leading marketing thinker Phillip Kotler's theory that products and services are propositions augmented by marketing concepts such as brand and design.

As shown in Figure T.12, it says that each product offer comprises three sets of features. They are:

- **The core feature:** this is the hub of the offer and is the prime benefit to buyers. In the case of a briefcase it will be to 'carry documents'; in the case of a car it will be 'personal transportation'. Experience shows this to be one of the most difficult aspects of product and service design. Service designers find it inordinately difficult to settle on the core proposition.
- **Augmented features:** these are the physical components of the product which the product manager chooses to use to represent the core feature. In the case of a briefcase, it would include the choice of leather, latches, nature of stitching, internal construction, etc. In the case of a car it would include the engine, the bodywork, the colour and the physical layout of the car. This is very much the design and assembly of physical components based on identified customer need.
- **Emotional features:** these are designed to appeal to the buyers' underlying, often unknown and unarticulated, emotional requirements. These are often the most influential aspects of the appeal of the proposition to the buyer. They particularly affect perceptions of value. Without them many offers become commodities.

  Although these are actually offered through the physical (augmented) features, the emotional ring of the planning tool is there to remind designers to plan their presence proactively. They are particularly tied to the firm's brand values. For example, the emotional promise of a briefcase that is labelled 'Gucci' will give a different message, for example, than one which is labelled 'Woolworths'.

  Incidentally, the importance of emotion in the planning of a business-to-business proposition is just as critical as it is in consumer propositions. Early writers and teachers of marketing had suggested that business-to-business marketing is more 'rational' than consumer marketing because formal buying processes exist. This is nonsense. Business buyers are human beings who experience emotions at work. The degree of risk, personal enhancement or political effort in a purchase, particularly a service purchase, can be decisive.

It is the proactive management of this mix of features that allows managers to design increasingly sophisticated versions of their offer in the light of feedback from markets. This allows evolution of real choice and the supplier to create profit through the development of differentiated offers.

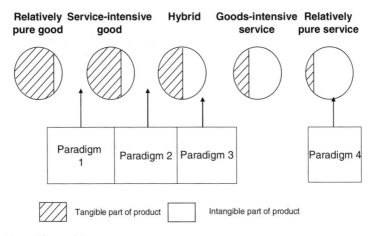

Figure T.13 *The goods/services spectrum.*
Source: Berry and Parasuraman (1991) and adapted by Young (2005)

In service businesses, this technique needs to be adjusted to take on board the observation by Lynn Shostack that propositions from companies are neither all product nor all service. Her goods/services spectrum of offers, adapted by Leonard Berry (Berry and Parasuraman, 1991) and further adapted by the author, is shown in Figure T.13. It can be used as the basis for the following four models.

The first model, as shown in Figure T.14, represents a proposition where service is primarily an emotional reassurance to a product offer. The core proposition is a product that has been augmented by physical features. However, the supplier has accepted, generally because it is based on new technology, that faults will occur in their product. Service has to be provided as an emotional reassurance to the purchaser of the enduring provision of those benefits. Service is therefore an emotional feature of the product. This has been in evidence with many product offers over the years, from washing machines and cars through to computers and elevators.

The second model, in Figure T.15, represents an evolution in a market where suppliers begin to build service into the product concept. It occurred, for example, in the computer industry during the latter half of the twentieth century. Suppliers began to provide preventive maintenance through a monitored service offer involving people, procedures and technology. It was sold as part of the product offer so that computers failed less due to self-diagnostic technology and preventive maintenance. (This was an entirely

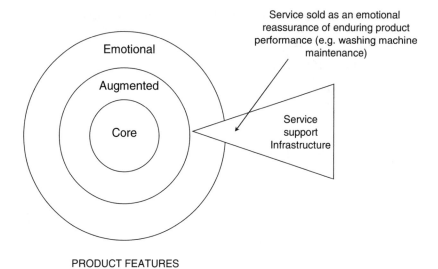

PRODUCT FEATURES

Figure T.14 *Models of service 1: high product content.*

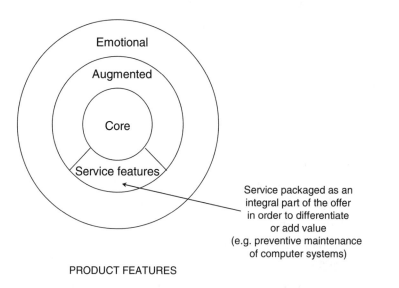

PRODUCT FEATURES

Figure T.15 *Models of service 2: service used to differentiate a product.*

different proposition to the previous maintenance contracts which promised 'Don't worry, if it goes wrong we'll repair it quickly'.) In this model, service has become an augmented component of the product offer.

The third model, in Figure T.16, represents a position where people are buying a mix of service and product. It is common in industries which offer

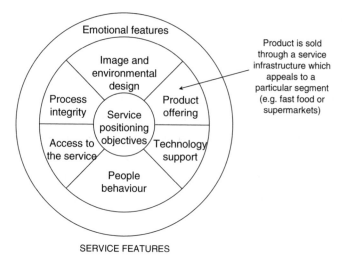

SERVICE FEATURES

Figure T.16 *Models of service 3: low margin product sold through a service environment.*

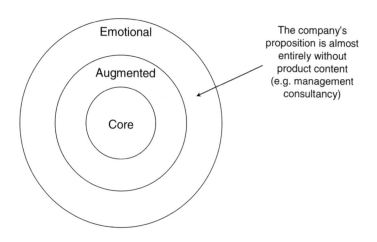

FEATURES OF A SERVICE OFFER

Figure T.17 *Models of service 4: service only or 'added value' offering.*

a high volume, low margin product. The fast food industry, for example, uses service to sell a cheap product. The brand, environmental design, product range, technology support, people behaviour, method of accessing the service and the process through which the service is provided are all integrated into a holistic experience which people buy. This, the core service of fast food retailers, is a concept which has evolved over a long period of time.

Finally, Figure T.17 represents a service offer which applies to many professional services firms. It has almost no physical or product content. An example would be management consultancy where any physical components (e.g. slides or bound reports) are merely an emotional reassurance to the buyer that good quality and high value exist in the offer. The tangible elements are a reassurance of the intangible benefit.

If a service designer chooses to use features analysis, it is essential to use the correct design model. It may be, for example, that market conditions have changed and a service which was once associated with a product offer (model one) can be positioned as an entity which has value in its own right (model four). In this case, a different features mix must be used.

Gap model

Application: diagnosis of client service issues, development of service strategy

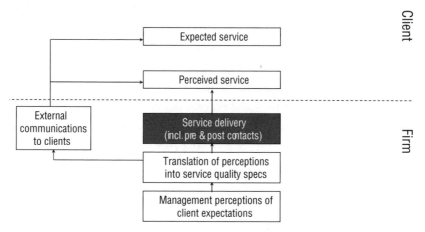

Figure T.18 *Gap model – service delivery process.*
Source: Zeithaml *et al.* (2000)

1. The tool

This model was designed and proposed by a group of academics who specialise in service marketing studies. It acknowledges that:

- Buyers find service quality more difficult to evaluate than product quality. They have few tangible clues as to quality so must rely on other clues.
- Quality is a comparison between expectation and actual performance. Satisfaction depends on the degree to which the two match or not.
- Quality evaluation by buyers depends on outcomes and processes. Quality can be influenced by technical outcomes and functional or client service outcomes. It can also be influenced by physical aspects of the service and by company image as much as by the interaction with client service staff.

The original investigation to substantiate the model was conducted in financial and product repair services. It has, however, been widely tested and developed since.

The model focuses upon five 'gaps':

- **The management perception gap:** this is any difference between management's views and those of clients or the market in general.
- **The quality specification gap:** this exists when quality standards, strategy or plans do not reflect management objectives or views.
- **The service delivery gap:** this exists if there is a difference between quality strategy or plans and the firm's delivery to clients.
- **The market communications gap:** this tracks any difference between marketing communications and service delivery.
- **The perceived service gap:** this exists if there is a difference between the service delivery perceived or experienced by clients and their expectations.

2. Constructing the tool

The representation of the tool in Figure T.18 is used as a format for analysis, representing as it does major parts of the firm. Research and data collection needs to be undertaken at the point of each gap to compare and contrast opinion or experience.

3. Using the tool

In business the tool is best used as a diagnostic for the improvement of service strategy. Its analysis brings into sharp relief the differences between various perceptions and experiences. It allows the leadership to construct very specific improvement programmes in all relevant areas of the business.

Hofstede's cultural dimensions for management and planning

Application: international marketing

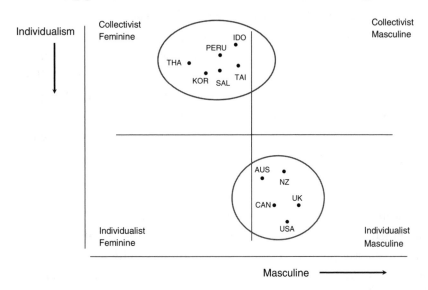

Figure T.19 *Individualism × masculinity/femininity.*
Source: Hofstede (1980)

1. The tool

In the 1980s Geert Hofstede researched, developed and published a number of dimensions of cultural difference. He grouped, tested and demonstrated the effect of these dimensions on management practice. They can be used to guide international strategy and planning.

The dimensions are:

- **Individualism versus collectivism:** some societies are loosely knit, where individuals are supposed to take care of themselves and their immediate families. Work, career, economic provision and progress are centred around the individual. Others are more collective. Individuals can expect their relatives, clan or gang to look after them in exchange for unquestioning loyalty.
- **Power distance:** this is the extent to which members of a society accept that power in its institutions is distributed unequally. This attitude affects the behaviour of those with and without power. Large power distance cultures accept hierarchical order in which everyone has a place, while small power distance cultures strive for equalisation. This issue affects how societies handle inequalities when they occur.
- **Uncertainty avoidance:** this is the degree to which members of a society feel uncomfortable with risk, ambiguity and uncertainty. Uncertainty avoidance cultures maintain rigid codes of belief and behaviour. They are intolerant towards deviants. Weak uncertainty cultures are the opposite.
- **Masculinity versus femininity:** in Hofstede's view masculine cultures prefer achievement, heroism, and material success, whereas feminine cultures stand for relationships, modesty, caring for the weak and quality of life.

This work shows how different cultures cluster and are similar under different dimensions. Figure T.19 represents just one set of pairings (individualism/collectivism with masculinity/femininity). This clearly shows the clustering of the Anglo Saxon-influenced cultures of the US, UK, New Zealand and Canada. A proposition built on the assumptions of individualistic masculinity (like high end executive search) is likely to succeed in this group.

2. Constructing the model

The first step is to determine the dimensions that have the most profound association with the product service or strategy. Then group the firm's existing international operations and any target countries using the clustering on the relevant dimensions. Adjust the programmes to fit key clusters.

3. Use of the model

The model can be used as an aid to almost any international marketing function. It can help formulate the growth and acquisition strategy. It readily reveals compatible cultures that will be a low risk target. It also shows how communications and product or services need to adapted to penetrate different cultures.

Industry maturity curve

Application: strategic insight into market development

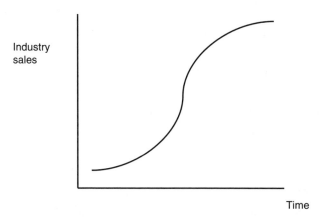

Figure T.20 *The phenomenon of industry maturity.*

1. The concept

The industry maturity curve is often mistakenly referred to as the 'product lifecycle concept'. Yet the phenomenon occurs in the sales volume of product groups over time, not individual products. There must be multiple suppliers and multiple buyers in markets that develop over time for it to be observed. (Individual products rarely go through the sales history repre-sented above. Most die soon after launch.)

The concept draws on an analogy between biological lifecycles and the sales growth of successful product groups by suggesting that they are born, introduced to the market, grow in sales, mature (sales growth stops) and then decline (sales fall). In fact, it represents an iterative learning process between the buyers and suppliers in a market. The cycle is represented by the well-known diagram in Figure T.20.

At 'birth' – the first introduction of the proposition to the world – a new product concept sells poorly. Buyers are unaware of its existence, suspicious of the new idea, or experience problems when ordering (with production capacity, effective distribution or product quality). 'Bold' or 'innovative' people buy the new product during this stage as a substitute for an existing product or to meet a newly identified need. Profits may well be low or non-existent because of the high cost of sale.

In phase two, sales growth develops as a consequence of 'word-of-mouth' communication. Early buyers pass on the good experience of the product to others or repurchase it. Producers and distributors (whether new to the market or well established) recognise the opportunity and switch over to produce their own version. The market broadens through policies of product differentiation and market segmentation. Profit margins peak as experience reduces unit costs and promotional expenditure is spread over a larger sales volume.

Maturity occurs because all markets are ultimately finite (in time, volume and geography), and the market becomes saturated. Sales growth becomes more or less flat as sales settle down to a level which reflects the regular volume of new buyers entering the market plus repurchase rates. Profits decline because of the number of competitive offerings, cost reductions become more difficult and smaller and/or specialist competitors enter the market.

Decline occurs as customers switch to new offers which offer advantages or benefits not present in the existing product. Producers therefore initiate a new curve, bringing to an end that of the product group to be displaced. Declining sales are accompanied by falling profit margins as too many competitors fight for the remaining market. Price cutting is prevalent and marginal competitors move out of the market.

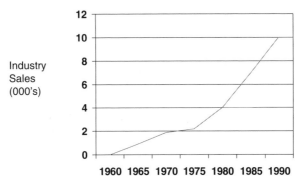

Figure T.21 *Case study: growth of executive search in the UK.*
Source: Young (1996)

This is a basic description of the industry maturity concept that has been tested, examined, criticised and developed over the past four decades. It was first observed by an economist and then brought to prominence by leading marketing writers. The history of its development gives clues to its usefulness today, especially in service markets.

2. Constructing the curve

Industry sales figures are often difficult to obtain for professional services markets. It is often easier to obtain government or industry figures on the number of firms or professionals operating in a particular market. By making a judgement about average industry project size and case load, the volume of sales of a type of professional services project can be estimated. Backdating this analysis will show the category's sales curve. The diagram in Figure T.21 shows an actual version for the UK executive search market.

3. Use of the concept

As the phenomenon occurs when there are independent variables (i.e. groups of suppliers and buyers), and rarely applies to individual products, it can be used to create marketing strategy. Many have found that the concept can be used to form a judgement about movements in the category's sales growth curve. They can then develop marketing strategies appropriate to each stage in the lifecycle.

Table T.2 *Strategic implications of different phases of industry maturity.*

	Introduction	Growth	Maturity	Decline
Characteristics				
Sales	Low	Fast growth	Slow growth	Decline
Profits	Negligible	Peak levels	Declining	Low or zero
Cash flow	Negative	Moderate	High	Low
Customers	Innovative	Mass market	Mass market	Laggards
Competitors	Few	Growing	Many rivals	Declining
Responses				
Strategic focus	Expand market	Penetration	Defend share	Efficiency
Marketing spend	High	Declining	Falling	Low
Marketing emphasis	Product awareness	Brand preference	Brand loyalty	Selective
Distribution	Patchy	Intensive	Intensity	Selective
Price	High	Lower	Lowest	Rising
Product	Basic	Improved	Differentiated	Rationalised

Source: Doyle (1976)

The concept is also useful in indicating the maturity of a market (i.e. the relationship of the group of customers to the group of suppliers, and the level of maturity of the understanding of the concept). An individual product being offered into that market place can then be adjusted in the light and understanding of that relationship. The likely strategies in each phase are summarised in Table T.2.

Professional services firms can thus use this concept to understand the position of their firm and service in the light of a total market's evolution. Business strategy for their practice should be developed based on this.

Marketing mix

Application: planning and influence

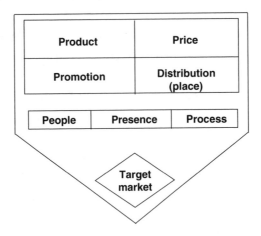

Figure T.22 *The marketing mix for services.*

1. The tool

This concept focuses on the aspects of marketing which need to be coordinated in order to influence the buyers (Figure T.22). They are the 'four Ps' of marketing:

- The **product**, or the offer to clients.
- The **price** at which the product is offered.

- The **promotion** of the product to the target buyers.
- The **placing** of the product in the market through sales and distribution channels.

Classic marketing training emphasises that all these elements need to be planned in order to achieve success. However, there are two other ingredients. The first is a clear knowledge of the target market. Suppliers need to know, in detail, the attributes and benefits that the buyers will value. The second is the 'mix' of components that will most appeal to the buyers. These need to be planned and balanced carefully.

In reality, few marketers have direct line responsibility for all the components of the mix. They therefore need to gain influence over these other areas in order to achieve their objectives and to create value for their employers. Experience suggests that they will fail to have impact if they are restricted to just short-term tactical aspects of one or two aspects of the mix.

The mix for a service business is different. First, the offer is not a tangible product but a proposition which is likely to be a mix of intangibles and tangibles. This changes marketing dramatically. However, it is generally accepted that there are three further aspects of the marketing mix for services, three extra 'Ps'. They are:

- The **people** who deliver the service because the buyer often cannot separate them from the value they buy.
- The **physical evidence**, or tangible aspects of the offer designed to help deliver perceived value to the buyer.
- The **process** through which the buyer moves while using or buying the service.

Again, all aspects of the mix need to be designed to match the aspirations of the intended buyers. There is, of course, complexity behind this concept. Each 'P' has many detailed aspects. For example, this book has complete chapters dedicated to the 'P' of promotion and that of service 'proposition'.

2. Constructing the tool

In any planning situation simply list the elements of the mix and ensure that they have been considered for the particular target market.

3. Use of the tool

The marketing mix is most often used in management dialogue or communications. It can act as an informal checklist for those involved to ensure that all aspects of a proposition have been properly considered. However, it can also be used in detailed marketing planning. Once strategy has been decided, a full campaign which comprises all elements of the mix should be created for each target market.

Molecular modelling

Application: service design

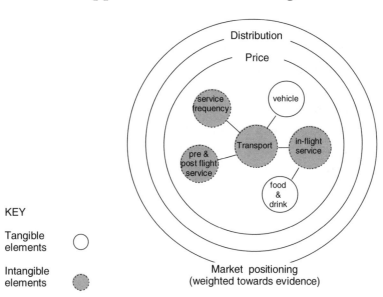

Figure T.23 *Molecular modelling: airlines.*
Source: Shostack (1977). Reproduced from the Journal of Marketing by permission of the American Marketing Association.

1. The tool

This is a method of planning the detailed components of product or service offers. It was suggested as a technique, based on actual experience, by Shostack (Shostack, 1977).

This technique allows planners to create a picture of the total proposition, whether this is service or product dominant. It reflects the fact that propositions might have different degrees of physical or service components without diminishing the importance of either. It also allows marketers to adjust their technique according to the degree of service content in the total offer.

The method breaks down the offer into 'tangible' and 'intangible' elements. Tangible elements are represented by a firm circle whereas intangible elements are represented by dotted lines. The outer rings stand for various aspects of marketing such as price, distribution and market positioning. Lines interconnecting the various elements show the interrelationship of process in delivering the service. The classic model of the technique (for airlines) is reproduced in Figure T.23.

The benefit of this technique is that it acknowledges that there are tangible and intangible elements to the offer. It allows the service designer to vary components to match the requirements of different markets to which different elements are important and to integrate service components into a product. For companies in transition from product to service dominant propositions, it helps product champions to establish service managers for their proposition because the interrelationship of the service offer to core product can be clearly identified.

2. Constructing a molecular model

Molecular modelling is carried out in the following way:

- Identify the 'nucleus' of the proposition. (In the case of cars it is personal transportation.)
- Identify physical and intangible elements, linking them appropriately.
- Link the elements.
- Ring the total entity and define it by a set value.
- Circumscribe it by its distribution method, so that its relationship to the market is clarified.
- Describe its brand positioning or 'face'.

3. Use of the tool

Molecular modelling has suffered from a lack of recognition rather than being an impractical or irrelevant method. Managers responsible for the creation of new services might start to use the technique with a service which is well known in their company. By breaking it down into its different components they may identify new elements of the offer which need to be designed and also ways of adjusting the offer to make it more relevant to new markets or to new segments. Having experimented with the technique, and tested it, they are likely to find it a practical method for the detailed design of service offers.

Perceptual maps

Application: positioning, competitive strategy

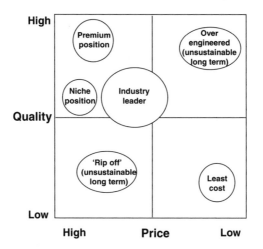

Figure T.24 *Competitive positioning – the perceptual map.*
Source: Lambin (2000), adapted by Young (2005)

1. The tool

Perceptual maps are used by brand managers in many different businesses to set strategy and to gain insight. There are two axes which, for many companies, are a derivative of critical issues that are success factors in the market. These are normally issues which are uppermost in the minds of most buyers. By understanding these and ranking the buyers' views of all the significant offers, strategists can deduce and set direction for their offer.

The resultant diagram shown in Figure T.24 is a 'perceptual' map of buyers' views because it concentrates on buyers' views of the issues that are important to them and the way suppliers respond. These views may not be technically correct or factually accurate, because they are based on buyer perception. It may be that there are offers which provide excellent technical performance (one version of quality) but are not perceived to be the leading offer or the best quality offer by the majority of the market. (This insight in itself shows suppliers that they need to change that perception.)

Figure T.24 is a generic model which uses two axes: quality and price. Together they form buyers' views of value (i.e. value = price × quality). The market leader normally takes centre stage. It has the offer by which all are judged. It sets the price/quality expectations and has the power to change the whole market. The premium position (normally a heritage brand) is taken by a features-rich offer at a high price, while the least-cost supplier strips out all that is possible to achieve low price. Various niche providers set themselves against the market leader and survive by providing a different offer.

There are two unsustainable positions. The 'rip-off' has low quality at high price. It normally exists because of some distortion or recent trauma in the market. However, it cannot keep this position in the long term because buyers will compare offers and desert to other suppliers with an offer nearer to their values. The 'overengineered' supplier might be a naive new entrant or a recently privatised or demonopolised supplier. Again, it must move in the long term.

2. Constructing the model

The tool is best constructed using detailed conjoint research among representatives of all buyers in the market. Contrary to popular belief, they will not all want the cheapest offer. They will want a mix of features and price which represents value to them. Some seek a features-rich offer with a high price and some a basic offer at a low price.

The likely output of this research, reflecting buyers' needs and requirements, is likely to be near to the diagram in Figure T.25. The buyers' ideal purchases will be scattered around a line (the line on which suppliers can

Figure T.25 *Clients seeking different value propositions.*

achieve long-term position). In a market which is not distorted by monopoly or regulation, most buyers cluster around the middle, a position that the market leader can dominate.

The research will also reveal buyers' perceptions of where all suppliers (including the firm doing the work) are positioned.

3. Use of the tool

The prime use of the tool is to work out where the target buyers' values lie and to move the firm's offer towards them. 'Positioning' the firm in this way is a guide for new product and service development (NPD and NSD) strategies, as well as a basis of communication and marketing programmes. It can be used to create both corporate and competitive strategy, while the leadership will find it helps them reach consensus on the position that they want the firm to take in the market. It is thus a very powerful tool to guide the debate about strategy among leadership teams.

The tool can also act as an internal communication aid. First, it is a very simple and clear summary of the market and the firm's ambitions, which can be used effectively in team meetings. Second, it can be employed as a diagnostic tool to develop internal communications programmes. By using it as a basis for internal research of employee opinion, it can be contrasted against client views. Training and communications programmes can then be designed to address any gaps.

Porter's competitive forces

Application: competitive analysis, market analysis, strategy development

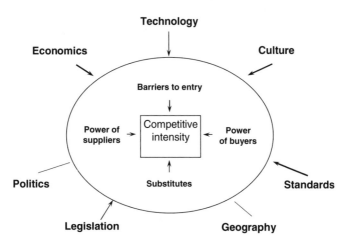

Figure T.26 *Porter's perspective.*
Source: Porter (1979). Reprinted by permission of *Harvard Business Review*. From 'How competitive forces shape strategy' by M. Porter, March 1979. Copyright © 1979 by the Harvard Business School Publishing Corporation; all rights reserved.

1. The tool

Among Michael Porter's impressive and prodigious work on competitive strategy has been the development of a powerful conceptual framework which works well as part of the market analysis and strategy development process. His 'five forces' of competition seen in Figure T.26 are a useful checklist for strategists and marketers to work through when analysing a market. They are:

- **The power of buyers:** buyers can influence a market by forcing down prices, by demanding higher service and quality or by playing competitors off against each other. Porter suggested that there are a number of circumstances when a buyer group is powerful, including: if they are concentrated, if buying commodities, or components, if driven to get price cuts or if the purchase is unimportant to them.
- **The power of suppliers:** suppliers can exercise power by raising prices or reducing the quality of the offer. They can squeeze profitability out of the industry. They are powerful if they are dominated by a few, have unique offers, are not obliged to compete, threaten forward integration or are not part of an important industry to the buyers.
- **The threat of new entrants:** these bring new capacity, the desire for market share and resources. The seriousness of the threat depends on barriers to entry which have six sources (economies of scale, product differentiation, capital requirements, cost advantages, access to distribution and government policy).
- **The threat of substitute offers:** these affect the profit of an industry by placing a ceiling on what it can charge through offering an alternative price/feature option.

2. Constructing the tool

The concept can simply be used as a checklist to prompt planners to cover relevant issues during market analysis and strategy development. However, it is most powerful when good analysis is put behind the thinking so that judgements can be made with the benefit of real data. Summaries of industry reports and original research can be put into the model and used as criteria by which to develop competitive responses or critical success factors.

3. Use of the tool

The tool can help guide debate and is also effective as a communications device. Its clarity summarises graphically and quickly the competitive landscape and can be used as part of the rationale for competitive programmes. It is best used, though, as a background planning tool in the market planning process.

Research

Application: client, competitor or market insight

When you and your company are selecting a professional services consultant or solution provider, how important is it that this vendor ___?

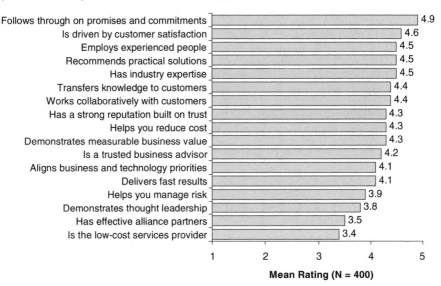

Mean Rating (N = 400)

Figure T.27 *Importance ratings of IT professional services firms' attributes.*
Source: ITSMA (2004)

1. The tool

Field research is familiar to many business leaders and client service professionals. They may have seen the results of research presented at internal meetings or read research reports while training or during client work. Some will have been involved in research projects designed to catch clients' attention when published or they may have commissioned it. Unfortunately, familiarity can breed contempt, making the processes, the techniques and the outcomes seem deceptively simple. As a result, there are many unconvincing or poor research reports resulting from poor specification or poor use of the research industry.

Yet, undertaken properly, field research yields insights into client needs, client views (which can be different to needs), competitor performance and market trends. It can reveal the different elements of a professional service which clients value and how they combine with different price points to form packages that they will buy.

Moreover, it can reveal how these vary between different client groups, creating opportunities through variation of the offer in different market segments. It can also save money by stopping new service ideas, marketing programmes or thought leadership initiatives which the market will reject. Yet to do all this it has to be properly specified and managed. It needs a brief and a managerial process (detailed in Chapter 2) if it is going to produce results. This needs to ensure that the sample frame, the approach, the technique and the questionnaires are appropriate.

2. Constructing research projects

There are two main types of research. The first is the qualitative or 'in-depth' approach. This involves spending time with a relatively small number of clients and seeking deep answers to questions. It gives colour to views and can reveal underlying feelings and motivations that can be enormously valuable. Quantitative research, on the other hand, involves a wider number of contacts, normally to investigate trends. Both have their strengths and their weaknesses.

Methods used to collect data vary enormously. They range from face-to-face interviews and observed discussion groups to telephone, postal or internet surveys. All are used in the professional services industry.

There are several different research techniques:

- **Conjoint research:** this uses questions (either in face-to-face meetings with clients or via mail or telephone) designed to trade off different pairs of values or ideas. Interviewees are forced to choose. It mimics the thought processes of clients when considering purchase and yields the type of detailed output illustrated in Figure T.27. It can provide powerful insight into new service needs and adjustments needed to client service.
- **Observational research:** as the name suggests, this involves a researcher observing behaviour of clients. It can give real insight into behaviours which reflect client views of service quality and future service needs. For example, two academics from Manchester School of Management (Karantinou and Hogg, 2001) used observation to understand the dynamics between consultants and clients when working on a project. They discovered 'scepticism, reservations, and the fear of a hidden agenda' as well as 'How and why hostility develops . . . how it could be reduced.'
- **Explorative research:** this is normally used in developing a new proposition or identifying a new client segment. This technique follows issues until a trend suggests that they are likely to be substantive. The work can be iterative, involving checking back and adjusting the idea as interviewees respond.
- **Concept testing:** this involves testing ideas for new propositions or approaches with clients before launch. Clients are shown an idea or marketing programme and asked to comment on it in a structured way.

3. Use of the tool

Field research ought to carry an arrogance warning. Managers and leaders in all sectors of industry can be very dismissive of it. Many have been heard to remark that there is little that field research can tell them about their buyers. Yet they are almost always wrong. In fact, some very senior business leaders have been chastened by the direct comments they have heard their buyers make when sitting behind two-way mirrors watching focus groups.

Research needs to be used properly. It should fill a gap in knowledge. It is sensible to start by conducting an exhaustive desk review to see if libraries, professional societies or academic institutions have conducted research or provided commentary on the subject in question. Many people in large companies which lack a structured research library find, after a brief search, that their own company has conducted research near to the subject in question on previous occasions.

When this preliminary work has been completed, the gap in knowledge ought to be clearly defined in a brief to a specialist research agency. This should specify the purpose of the research. It might be to test a new service idea, to test segmentation dimensions, to understand a new concept or to identify client needs. The exercise will be confused if there are too many objectives. In particular, the information yield that is expected must be made clear to the supplier.

Once results come through, careful interpretation is needed. It is important to understand not only the statistically valid representation of results but also their meaning. Human beings often do not know what they want and, sometimes, why they behave in a particular way. They will say they want cheapness yet spend outrageous sums on a consultancy project from a branded supplier.

There numerous examples of mistakes due to poor interpretation. In the late 1980s, for example, one American telecoms supplier commissioned a leading consultancy firm to judge the ultimate size of the worldwide mobile phone market. The consultancy, which was not a specialist research firm, interviewed people in various parts of the world and estimated the size of the mobile phone market to 'never exceed a million handsets'. They did not understand just how powerfully this technology would meet people's social need for quick and immediate personal communications.

Research therefore needs careful commissioning, good execution and enlightened interpretation. Yet the expense and effort is more than worthwhile. It can lead to profitable new insights that build strong future revenue streams and it can help prevent mistakes.

SWOT analysis

Application: strategy development

Strengths	Weaknesses
Opportunities	Threats

Figure T.28 *SWOT analysis.*

1. The tool

Probably the best known of the strategy tools, the matrix in Figure T.28 helps structure discussion by summarising a firm's strategic position into: strengths, weaknesses, opportunities and threats (SWOT).

2. Constructing the matrix

A SWOT analysis can easily be created during discussion among a management team. Valuable insight and debate can emerge from its succinct summary of the firm.

However, it can also be constructed using detailed analysis. The market analysis techniques outlined in Chapter 2 can be summarised into it. Competitive analysis will reveal 'threats', for example, and client research will give insight into 'opportunities'. On the other hand, an environmental analysis which reviews 'PEST' (political, economics, society, technical) factors can contribute to both of these.

Those wishing to take a thorough, analytical approach can use the 'TOWS' method. Here, each opportunity and each threat are numbered consecutively. Then, one at a time, each individual opportunity is compared with the list of the firm's strengths, and each threat with the list of weaknesses, in a systematic search for strategic options. As the strengths and weaknesses arise from debate about the firm's competencies, the strategist is, in fact, checking these against market developments through this process.

3. Use of the tool

The tool is best used in the strategy development process to summarise analysis. It allows senior people to focus their debate and decision-making.

References

Aaker, David, *Brand Leadership*, Free Press, 2000.

Ambler, Tim, *Marketing and the Bottom Line*, FT Prentice Hall, 2003 (2nd edition).

Ansoff, Igor, 'Strategies for Diversification', *Harvard Business Review*, Sept/Oct, 1957.

Baddeley, Simon and James, Kim, 'Management Education and Development', Institute of Local Government Studies, University of Birmingham, Vol. 18, Part 1, 1987.

Bateson, John E.G. and Hoffman, Douglas K., *Managing Services Marketing*, Thomson Learning, 1999.

Berry, Leonard, *On Great Service*, Free Press, 1995.

Berry, Leonard and Parasuraman, A., *Marketing Services: Competing Through Quality*, Free Press, 1991.

Boston Consulting Group, 'Perspectives on Experience', 1968.

Bullmore, Jeremy, 'Posh Spice and Persil', British Brands Group lecture, December 2001.

de Brentani, Ulrike, 'Success Factors in Developing New Business Services', *European Journal of Marketing*, Vol. 25, No. 2, 1991.

Denvir, Paul, Ferguson, Cliff and Walker, Kevin, *Creating New Clients: Marketing and Selling Professional Services*, Thomson Learning, 1998.

Doyle, Peter, 'The Realities of the Product Life Cycle', *Quarterly Review of Marketing*, 1976.

Fifield, Paul, *Marketing Strategy: How to Prepare It – How to Implement It*, Butterworth-Heinemann, 1992, 1998 (2nd edition).

Gronroos, Christian, *Service Management and Marketing*, John Wiley & Sons Ltd, 2003.

Gummerson, Evert, *Total Relationship Marketing*, Butterworth-Heineman, 2002.

Hakansson, H. and Snehota, I., *Developing Relationships in Business Networks*, International Thompson Business Press, 1995.

Haley, R.I., 'Benefit Segmentation: A Decision-oriented Tool', *Journal of Marketing*, July 1968, pp. 30–35.

Halliday, Sue, 'How Placed Trust Works in a Service Encounter', *Journal of Service Marketing*, Vol. 18, No. 1, 2004.

Harte, H.G. and Dale, B.G., 'Improving Quality in Professional Service Organizations: A Review of the Key Issues', *Managing Service Quality*, Vol. 5, No. 3 1995, pp. 34–44.

Hofstede, Gert, *Culture's Consequences: International Differences in Work Related Values*, Sage Publications, 1980.

Information Technology Services Marketing Association, 2004 Brand Tracking Study, Competing for Position in Professional Services and Solutions, Boston, March 2004.

Joachimsthaler, E. and Aaker, D.A., 'Building Brands without Mass Media', *Harvard Business Review*, Jan–Feb 1997.

Johnson, Gerry and Scholes, Kevan, *Exploring Corporate Strategy: Text and Cases*, FT Prentice Hall, 2004.

Johnston, R. and Clark, G., *Service Operations Management*, Prentice Hall, 2001.

Karatinou, K. and Hogg, M.K., 'Exploring Relationship Management in Professional Services: A Study of Management Consultancy', *Journal of Marketing Management*, No. 17, 2001.

Klein, Naomi, *No Logo: Taking Aim at the Brand Bullies*, Picador, 2000.

Kotler, Philip and Armstrong, Gary, *Principles of Marketing Management*, Prentice Hall, 2003 (10th edition).

Kotler, Philip, Hayes, Thomas and Bloom, Paul N., *Marketing Professional Services*, Prentice Hall Press, 2000 (2nd edition).

Kumar, Nirmalya, *Marketing Strategy: Understanding the CEO's Agenda for Driving Growth and Innovation*, Harvard Business School Press, 2004.

Kurtzman, Joel, Yago, Glenn and Phumiwasana, Triphon, *The Global Costs of Opacity*, MIT Sloan Management Review, Fall 2004.

Lambin, Jean-Jacques, *Market-driven Management: Strategic and Operational Marketing*, Palgrave Macmillan, 2000.

Levitt, Theodore, 'The Industrialization of Services', *Harvard Business Review*, January 1976.

Levitt, Theodore, 'The Globalization of Markets', *Harvard Business Review*, May 1983.

Levitt, Theodore, 'Marketing Myopia', *Harvard Business Review*, 1960, republished July 2004.

McDonald, Malcolm, *Marketing Plans*, Butterworth-Heinemann, 2002.

Maister, David, *Managing the Professional Service Firm*, Free Press, 1993.

Maister, David H., Green, Charles H. and Galford, Robert M., *The Trusted Advisor*, Free Press, 2001.

Peters, Thomas and Waterman, Robert H., *In Search of Excellence: Lesson from America's Best Companies*, Warner Books (re-issue), 1988.

Piercy, Nigel, *Market-led Strategic Change: Transforming the Process of Going to Market*, Butterworth-Heinemann, 2001.

Porter, Michael E., 'How Competitive Forces Shape Strategy', *Harvard Business Review*, March 1979.

Porter, Michael, *Competitive Strategy*, Free Press, 1980.

Purchase, Sharon and Ward, Antony, 'ARR Model: Cross-cultural Developments', *Industrial Marketing Review*, Vol. 20, No. 2, 2003.

Ringland, Gill, *Scenario Planning: Managing for the Future*, John Wiley & Sons, 1997.

Rust, Roland T., Zahorik, Anthony J. and Keiningham, Timothy L., *Service Marketing*, HarperCollins, 1996.

Scott, Mark C., *The Intellect Industry*, John Wiley & Sons, 1998.

Shamir, Boas, 'Service and Servility; Role Conflict in Subordinate Service Roles', *Human Resources*, Vol. 33, No. 10, 1980.

Shostack, G. Lynn, 'Breaking Free from Product Marketing', *Journal of Marketing*, April 1977.

Shostack, G. Lynn, 'How to Design a Service', *European Journal of Marketing*, Vol. 16, No. 1, 1982.

Sieff, Marcus, *Don't Ask the Price*, Ulverscroft Large Print Edition, 1988.

Strong, E.K., *The Psychology of Selling*, McGraw-Hill, 1925, p. 9.

Sun-Tzu, Sun Pin, Sawyer, Ralph D. and Sawyer, Mei-Chin Lee, *The Complete Art of War (History and Warfare)*, HarperCollins, 1996.

Venetis, K.A., 'Professional Service Quality and Relationship Commitment; a Preliminary Study on the Physician–Patient Relationship', EMA conference paper, May 1996.

Wilson, M.S., Gilligan, Colin and Pearson, David J., *Strategic Marketing Management: Planning, Implementation and Control*, Butterworth-Heinemann, 1992.

Young, L., *Making Profits from New Service Development*, FT Pearson, 1996.

Young, L. and Stone, M. *Competitive Customer Care*, Croner, 1994.

Zeithaml, Valarie, Berry, Leonard and Parasuraman, A., 'The Nature and Determinants of Customer Expectations of Service,' *Journal of the Academy of Marketing Science*, Winter 1993, pp. 1–12.

Zeithaml, Valarie, Bitner, Mary Jo and Gremler, Dwayne D., *Services Marketing*, McGraw-Hill/Irwin, 2000.

Zeithaml, Valarie, Parasuraman, A. and Berry, Leonard L, 'A Conceptual Model of Service Quality', *Journal of Marketing*, American Marketing Association, Vol. 49, 1985.

Zeithaml, Valarie, Parasuraman, A. and Berry, Leonard L., *Delivering Quality Service: Balancing Customer Perceptions and Expectations*, Free Press, 1990.

Index

Index compiled by Annette Musker

DATE DUE
